THE MONOLOGUE WORKSHOP

*From Search to Discovery
In Audition and Performance*

THE APPLAUSE ACTING SERIES

THE MONOLOGUE WORKSHOP

From Search to Discovery
In Audition and Performance

by Jack Poggi

APPLAUSE
THEATRE BOOK PUBLISHERS

THE MONOLOGUE WORKSHOP
From Search to Discovery in Audition and Performance

Copyright © 1990 by Applause Theatre Book Publishers

Library of Congress Cataloging-in-Publication Data

Poggi, Jack, 1928-
      The monologue workshop / by Jack Poggi.
         p.   cm. --(The Applause acting series)
      Includes bibliographical references
      ISBN 1-55785-031-2 :
      1. Acting 2.Monologue. I.Title. II. Series.
PN2061.P59 1990
792'.028--dc20   89-18084
                                    CIP

British Library Cataloging-in-Publication Data
A catalogue record for this book is available from the British Library

APPLAUSE BOOKS
211 West 71st Street	406 Vale Road
New York, NY 10023	Tonbridge KENT TN9 1XR
Phone: 212-595-4735	Phone: 0732 357755
Fax: 212-721-2856	Fax: 0732770219

Fifth Applause Printing, 1997

Printed in Canada

To My Fellow Actors

With Thanks for the Pleasure of Your Company

Acknowledgments

Parts of this book were first published as a series of articles in *Back Stage* under the title "The Monologue Shop." I want to thank Sherry Eaker, Theater Editor of *Back Stage*, for her recognition and support of my work. I am grateful also to Glenn Young, my editor and publisher, for his unwavering enthusiasm for this book and his dogged insistence that it could be made better, and to Jeanlee M. Poggi for her thoughtful comments on earlier drafts.

My thanks to John Nassivera, Jill Charles, and Gene Sirotof for their hospitality at the Dorset Colony House in Vermont, where several chapters of this book were completed in idyllic surroundings.

The exercises described here were developed in collaboration with the hundreds of actors who have participated in my monologue workshops or come to me for private coaching. Much of what I have to say about developing clear and specific goals as a performer derives from my participation in workshops and career counselling sessions with Jay Perry, David Rosen, Henry House, and the staff of Actors' Information Project in New York.

My greatest debt is to Mira Rostova, my mentor for many years. She taught me how to look at a text closely, see exactly what the character is communicating from moment to moment, and understand how all the moments are connected. She illuminated so many texts so clearly for me that, whenever I look at a monologue or scene, I feel as if she is at my side still, pointing out possibilities I might otherwise have missed.

CONTENTS

APPENDIX:
USEFUL LISTS

FOR ACTORS WHO HATE MONOLOGUES

It happens often enough: you read a notice in the trade papers or get a call from an agent or casting director, and you find that in a few days you are expected to do a three-minute monologue, or perhaps two contrasting monologues, for an audition. If your heart doesn't exactly leap with joy at the prospect, if a vague sense of dread and loathing begins to gnaw at your innards, you're probably like a lot of other actors I know. When I ask actors what prompted them to sign up for my monologue workshops, they usually tell me, "I just can't seem to find a monologue that is right for me!" or "I have no idea how to go about working on a monologue on my own!" or "I just can't stand being up there all by myself!" One actor said it all in one simple, heartfelt cry of anguish: "*I hate monologues!!!*"

Unfortunately for those who feel that way, monologues are more and more in demand these days. Heads of professional training programs usually require them for admission. An agent is likely to call you into the office and ask to see some monologues before agreeing to represent you. If you have not been submitted by an agent for a role, your only chance to be considered for it may be to do a monologue for the casting director at an open call or an "Eligible Performer Audition" (open to those with a certain amount of professional experience as defined by Actors Equity Association) in competition with hundreds of other actors, only a handful of whom may be called back to read from the script. You will also be asked to do monologues at general auditions for a company's season and at audition workshops set up by schools and independent networking organizations to give actors a chance to meet agents and casting directors. You will need to have a repertoire of good monologues at your command from the time you begin your career until that happy day when you are signed exclusively with a powerful agent and your work is well known to the hundreds of casting directors in the business.

• • •

At the same time that the monologue has become a necessary first step in the audition process, it has also become more and more popular as an art form in itself. Following the example set some years ago by Ruth Draper, Emlyn Williams, and Hal Holbrook, and more recently by Lily Tomlin, Eric Bogosian, and Spalding Gray, actors in increasing numbers are venturing onto the stage alone. Unlike the poor actor suffering through an audition, these performers enjoy working alone, and not just for three minutes, but for a whole evening. Do you imagine that Tomlin, for example, wakes up in the morning and thinks, "Oh my God, I've got to do a monologue tonight! I'll be out there all by myself for two whole hours! How will I ever get through it?"

Obviously the Tomlins and Bogosians and Grays love what they do or they wouldn't do it. What makes them go out there is a passion to share with others some material they love. If you could approach an audition with a similar goal in mind, you might lighten your burden considerably. Instead of resenting an audition as something you "have" to do, instead of feeling that you are being judged, you can look on the occasion as a chance to do your own three-minute solo performance for an audience of one or two people. God knows you have few enough opportunities to perform in this crazy business, you might as well enjoy those you have. Yes, even auditions.

The key is to find material you really *want* to perform. Instead of being intimidated by the task of finding material, think of a monologue audition as an opportunity to discover or create for yourself the role of your dreams. How many times have you read or seen a play and felt, "God, I'd love to do that part!" Now you can choose to do any role that has ever been written in the entire history of the theater. You can adapt the work of a favorite writer, as Hal Holbrook did with Mark Twain and Emlyn Williams with Dickens. Or you can write your own material, as Bogosian and Gray do, or you can get somebody to write something especially for you, as Tomlin does.

In Part One of this book I'll offer some suggestions for finding or developing your own monologue material. What you will *not* find here, however, is a monologue that is ready-made for you. First of all, I don't know you, and even if I did, even if I were able to find a piece that is just right for you, the fact that it is published in this book would make a lot of other actors want to do it too, and pretty soon it would become one of those old warhorses that are so familiar to agents and casting directors that they cringe at the mere announcement of the title: "Oh no, not that one again!"

Instead, I plan to show you how to get to new material before a lot of other actors start using it. I'll show you how to dig out older material that has been neglected, how to adapt material from nondramatic sources (novels, short stories, letters, diaries, autobiographies, essays, even newspaper columns) and how to write your own material if you choose, so that eventually you can come up with a piece that nobody else ever does.

As an actor in one of my workshops put it, I'm not going to serve you broiled fish on a platter, I'm going to provide you with tackle, take you to where the best waters are, and show you how to fish.

• • •

In addition to the difficulty of finding monologues, there are also special difficulties in acting them. Even when you are working on a monologue in the context of a play, getting reactions from a partner and feedback from a director, it may be hard to manage. Just knowing that you have another page and a half to go before another actor can come to your rescue may make you rush or get caught up in *how* to say all those words rather than in what you want to convey with them. It's worse still when you are preparing for an audition, sitting alone in a room with a piece of paper in your hands. What do you do now?

Part Two of this book describes a systematic, step-by-step

process for rehearsing a monologue for an audition, acting class, or public performance. Several of the steps encourage you to improvise on the content of the monologue or on a parallel theme and then go back and forth between improvisation and the text until you find yourself speaking the text *as if* you are improvising. Other steps are designed to help you break a monologue down into manageable chunks and to understand exactly what you are doing in each part and how all the parts are connected. Once you have a firm grasp of the underlying structure of a monologue, you may find it easier to embark on the speech pretty much as you would in life, with a sense of where you're headed but a feeling that you're making up the words as you go along. Finally, some steps are meant to help you cope with the special problems of working alone and getting started out of context.

Although the rehearsal process is described in a systematic fashion, you don't have to work along doggedly, step by step. Most art is created by a combination of system and accident, and the breakthroughs usually seem to come by accident. Use the steps to get you started, but if you find yourself moving in a direction I had not suggested, *go* that way, follow your instincts. If you get stuck, go back to one of the steps. Or try something else—anything that comes to mind. You may end a rehearsal feeling that you've accomplished absolutely nothing and that you are stuck forever in the same dreary landscape. Don't be surprised, however, if some time later, when you are thinking of something else, or not thinking at all, a whole new way of moving ahead in the work suddenly pops into your head.

• • •

Besides the difficulties of finding material and working on it, actors often give a third reason for dreading monologues: the feeling that they must "prove themselves" to casting people. They tend to approach an audition with all the trepidations of a sinner at the Last Judgment. And yet these same actors may feel perfectly comfortable performing for an audience in the theater. Or they may feel fine auditioning with a song rather than a monologue, or with a cold reading.

In Part Three of this book I'll suggest ways of coping with anxiety and self-doubt in *any* performing situation. I'll help you discover exactly what you want to do in your acting career and show you how to develop networks and support systems to keep you moving towards your goals. I'll take you through a typical audition with a monologue, trying to answer the questions that actors commonly have about the process. Finally, I'll suggest some ways you can prepare yourself psychologically, so that every performance can be, if not a "peak" experience, at least a satisfying one.

I can't guarantee that you will learn to love monologues, but I do hope you will find some satisfaction in mastering the skills that are necessary to present a monologue effectively. Beyond that, I hope that you will come to see the monologue not just as something to be gotten through, but as a fascinating form of human expression. You may find that the exercises you learn in this book will help you not just when you're auditioning, but every time you embark on a long speech, maybe even when you embark on a whole scene or play. Some of you may be prompted to embark on what might be called the ultimate monologue: your own one-person show. You may be surprised to find that, with a little work, the experience of being alone on stage can be transformed from a terror into a joy.

Part One:

THE SEARCH FOR YOUR IDEAL MONOLOGUE

1

"Am I Worthy?"
vs.
"What Do I Have to Offer?"

Let's face it: doing a monologue for an audition is an unnatural act. An actress I coach called it a "perversion," and I don't think she was far from the truth. Instead of an audience who have presumably come to enjoy themselves, we are faced with a single auditor, or perhaps two or three, who stare at us intently, as if passing judgement on our ultimate worth. Instead of engaging with a partner in an interplay of thought and feeling, we are out there all alone, on display. Instead of being in a familiar environment, surrounded by objects that lend reality to our stage fictions, we are in an alien space, bathed in a harsh light that illuminates the whole room but seems to glow with special intensity on our staring auditors.

How on earth do we begin? And *where* do we begin? Unfortunately we usually have to begin somewhere in the middle. Many monologues are the culminating expression of thoughts and feelings that have been building up in the character for some time. If we were doing the whole play we would already have undergone all the experiences that lead us to the bursting point, where only the monologue will satisfy our need for expression. But in an audition we have to plunge right in. It's a bit like asking a pianist to start near the top of a crescendo—and without a warm-up!

No wonder many actors, and I count myself among them, are appalled to think that under these circumstances we are expected to do work good enough to make people want to hire us. And yet what are we to do? I suppose we could try to reform the theatrical profession. Or we could give it up and do something sensible with our lives. Or, finally, we could learn to cope.

• • •

I want to begin by suggesting some strategies for coping with what seems to me the fundamental problem in all auditions, not just monologue auditions, and sometimes in public performances, too: the fear of being found unworthy.

A few years ago I began auditioning again after twenty years of teaching acting in a college. I found the process excruciating: I would shake uncontrollably, I couldn't stop listening to myself, I rushed, I made all the mistakes I'd spent most of my adult life teaching others to avoid. And I'd come away imagining my auditors were saying, "Who is *he*? What right does he have to call himself an actor?" And this torture went on for more than a year!

Only gradually did I come to understand the source of the tension: I was trying to prove that I was good enough to get back into the business. I wasn't always conscious of that need, but it was there, subliminally, the whole time. I was setting up my auditors as my judges. *They* were supposed to decide whether I was talented enough to compete with all those other men my age who had been busy acting, accumulating all those Broadway and regional theater and major film credits on their resumes, while I was teaching. If I got the part, that meant I was worthy to be admitted to this elite company. If I didn't, then it's "back to the classroom with him!"

Once I examined the assumption I was making, I saw the absurdity of it. Why should I hand over to anybody else the power of deciding who and what I am? I came back to acting because I love it. I wanted to investigate once more, at first hand, a process that has always fascinated me and to pass on what I found to others. If that's what I want to do, I can just do it, worthy or not. I'm not saying it's easy to avoid turning an audition into a test of worth. I still don't find it easy. That's because a part of me remains convinced that I am so talented that if I really audition well, if I show them what I can do when I am at my best, they will *have* to give me the part. But this assumption is not only unrealistic, it's downright arrogant. Am I really that much better than all those other guys? There's no more reason to assume that than to assume I'm completely unworthy of being in their company. In fact, one assumption feeds the other: the more exalted my secret opinion of my worth, the more frightened I become of falling short of it. And even if I were a genius, if I were, say, Charlie Chaplin, the role might be one that even Chaplin would not be right for. Or if he *were* right for it, the auditors might *still* be looking for somebody else.

• • •

Does any of this sound familiar? When you go into an audition do you ever have some secret expectation that your auditors will be so overwhelmed that they will hire you on the spot, or some not-so-secret fear that they will look at each other sideways and roll their eyes and shake their heads? Of course it's always encouraging when people praise our work and disappointing when they seem bored or disinterested, but many actors take responses of both kinds to signify more than they really mean. Words of praise usually mean only that your auditors liked your work and perhaps liked you as a person and might want to work with you. They do not mean that you are certain to win an Academy Award. A curt dismissal may mean that your auditors didn't like your work or possibly didn't like you; but it can also mean that they were tired or irritable or that the role was already cast or that they felt you were not what they wanted as soon as you walked through the door. Even if it means they did not like you or your work, what does *that* mean? Do *you* always like your own work? Do you like the work of every actor who has ever been successful in the business? Would you want to work with everybody you audition for?

If you go into auditions determined to resolve, once and forever, that tormenting question, "Am I worthy?", you are setting yourself up for unending agony and frustration. No amount of effort on your part can insure that your auditors will like you or call you back or cast you. These are goals that are simply not in your power to attain. If you assume that they are, then whenever you don't achieve them, you will, quite logically, begin to blame yourself. After all, you set out to do something and did not succeed. Therefore you are a "failure." And the great paradox here is that the more determined you are to prove something to your auditors or to yourself, the more you will prevent yourself from acting naturally and spontaneously, and so the less likely you are to win the very success that you crave.

• • •

An audition does not *have* to be a test of worth. It can simply be an opportunity to perform before a small audience who may be in a position to help you reach a larger audience. Try asking yourself what you have to offer to both audiences. What do you love about acting? What can you bring to the stage that is special? What kinds of characters do you love to play? Which medium—stage, film, television—do you see yourself working best in? What kind of writing attracts you? Do you have anything to say with your acting? Is there anything you can bring to an audience that will make their lives more enjoyable or meaningful? What *kind* of audience do you want to reach? Answers to some of these questions may be slow in coming, but the clearer you can be about what you have to offer, the easier it will be for you to put together a repertoire of monologues as a kind of sample case. You can display your wares to people and realize that if they're not in the market that day for what you have in stock, that doesn't mean that your product is worthless.

Rather than going into an audition feeling helpless, dependent on other people to assure you of your worth, walk in saying, in effect, "OK, here is what I do: I play these kinds of characters, I amuse people in this particular way, I touch them in that way. Here's what I do well—not necessarily better than everybody else, but in a different way, my own way. My work is hand-made, unique, nothing else quite like it. Let me show you what I can do." Like the clowns riding the elephants into town in that ancient tradition that still survives one day each spring at 2:00 a.m. at the mouth of the Midtown Tunnel in Manhattan, give the folks a little sample of what you have to offer, just enough to make them plunk down their money to see what is going on under the big tent.

Those who have discovered their particular calling in life seldom make a great fuss over who they are. "I'm just a song and dance man," Gene Kelly remarked once at the end of a television documentary on his life and career. I love that: JUST!!! A man who moved with such extraordinary power and grace! And Kelly was not just being modest; he seemed genuinely to believe that he might have been a worthier person if he had been able to play Hamlet. Noel Coward in "If Love Were All" (a song that is a kind of personal credo) also makes light of what he did so well: "The most I had is just a talent to amuse." Chekhov liked to refer to his medical practice as his "wife" and the theater as his "mistress." Astrov in his *Uncle Vanya* is a doctor who spends a good deal of time at what he calls his "hobby": planting trees and campaigning to save forests from the ax. When asked if his preoccupation with what we would now call an environmental issue doesn't interfere with his "real work," he replies, "Only God knows what a man's real work is."

Try asking God (or your "inner voice" if you prefer) what you are meant to do at this point in your life, and if you are lucky enough to get an answer, just do whatever you're told. Never mind whether it promises to enhance your status in the world.

• • •

There's a certain hot-dog vendor in the Chelsea district of Manhattan who lays out each perfectly cooked frankfurter on a warm bun, places on it just the right amount of ketchup, mustard, or onion to meet your particular taste, wraps it neatly in a napkin, and hands it to you with a flourish and a look that seems to say, "Here, see what you think of *that!*" Now that man has a mission in life.

The problem with actors is that we tend to confuse ourselves with the hot dog. That's only natural, since we use our own bodies and voices, our own personalities even, in our work. We ourselves are the ingredients of our own product. But that doesn't mean we *are* the product: we make it, out of the best materials at hand, working with the best collaborators we can find, and we offer it to the public as something that might be useful or entertaining. Sometimes people like our product and sometimes they don't, but we would be foolish to imagine that our identity and worth are established once and forever by the reception given to a particular performance.

We may envy other actors who seem to have been provided by nature with more promising ingredients. Not everybody has an attractive physique, a resonant voice, and handsome features. And yet it's possible to be successful without them. I imagine that Dustin Hoffman, Linda Hunt, and Kathy Bates, for example, must have been told at one time that they were poorly endowed for careers in the theater, but they are absolutely compelling on stage! Their own unique energy flows freely and spontaneously. They share the one irreplaceable quality that distinguishes the work of first-rate actors everywhere: vitality.

Rather than agonizing over whether you are "good enough," make it your purpose in life to develop your own special gifts in a way that enlivens both yourself and others. Work to dissolve the blocks that keep you from expressing yourself freely. Develop ease and grace, or the ability to do a task with no unnecessary effort, like a great shortstop or sushi chef. Develop spontaneity, learn to stay in the moment and follow the promptings of your intuition. Develop your sense of humor and your capacity for understanding and empathy.

• • •

Your search for monologue material is only part of a much larger search. You need to keep looking for what is most alive in you, trying on different roles, and getting feedback from others. Eventually you will develop not only a repertoire of monologues that serves you well at auditions, but also a sense of what you have to offer as an actor to an audience and as a human being to your family, lovers, friends, and neighbors. You may not rid yourself entirely of the habit of questioning your own worth, but if you can get caught up in doing something you value and want to share with others, the question will be of little importance.

2

Identifying Your Ideal Role

Imagine that a writer has offered to write a role especially for you. Not just any writer, but your favorite one—and the role may be in a play or film or television show. You need only describe to the writer exactly what you want. Sit back, relax, close your eyes, and begin to imagine yourself in your ideal role. What personal qualities would emerge in your character? What kinds of situations would you get caught up in? How would you relate to others? Picture yourself physically. See yourself at a certain age, dressed a particular way, coming from a particular background, engaged in a certain occupation. Explore your character's ambitions, dilemmas, self-doubts, strengths, insecurities, romantic propensities. Keep entertaining whatever possibilities come to mind until you are fairly clear about what you want. Then take paper and pencil and jot down your "order."

My ideal role at this point in my life, for example, would be a man in his early sixties with a tremendous appetite for life, brimming with vitality, very witty and funny and charming, and yet with something missing in his life, maybe he's haunted by some lost opportunity of his youth. He is warm and compassionate, loves to take care of others, but is still something of a loner. He's a professional of some kind, could be a doctor or lawyer maybe, and he's either not quite made it or has made it and isn't very happy about it.

What I've described is a kind of idealized (and perhaps

slightly romanticized) self-image. It's not at all a realistic self-portrait. I've left out all my pettiness and irritability, for example, though I could use those qualities in another role. The main difference is that my onstage persona would have ten times more energy than I am ordinarily able to bring to my workaday world—he would glow with a greater intensity. He would be more open and unguarded. And he would certainly be more articulate. In fact, he would speak absolutely brilliantly.

It's possible to imagine more than one ideal role. I can also see myself, for example, as a real down-and-out bum, a derelict, filthy, unshaven, reeking of cheap booze, who loves to tell stories and doesn't seem to care if he bores people. And he would be filled with guilt and self-loathing. Actually I played a role like this once (Marmeladov in Dosteovsky's *Crime and Punishment*), and it's an even further cry from my "real self," whatever that is. I don't feel that I am like that man in any way, and of course I don't want to be like him, and yet I would love to play him, perhaps because he's the opposite of my idealized self-image. It might be rather satisfying to flaunt before the public the most loathsome and repellent qualities imaginable.

• • •

Now get a sense of what roles you might do best from someone else's point of view. Get together with a few other actors, perhaps informally over a cup of coffee after a class or rehearsal. Taking turns, each actor listens while the others throw out suggestions for the various character traits this actor might conceivably convey. For example, "I see you as sultry and exotic" or "You could do a Wall Street executive." The suggestions do not have to be consistent with each other or accepted by everybody in the group. Just keep generating ideas, without discussion or argument, until you have accumulated about a dozen. One actor should volunteer to take notes and give them later to the actor under considera-tion. When it's your turn, try to just listen, without comment.

Remember that what the others are describing is not what they think you really *are*, but what they sense you might be capable of *playing*. Some actors, for example, readily project a "menacing" quality, although they may in fact be the kindest of souls. Others may appear quite "sexy," though that is no guarantee of how they are in bed. So don't take it personally if someone sees you as a potential "petty tyrant" or "country bumpkin." Instead think whether you might get some satisfaction out of playing such a person.

Oddly enough, you don't have to know each other very well for this exercise to work, but you do have to feel comfortable with each other and be able to take the whole thing in a playful spirit. In my weekend monologue workshops I ask actors who have never met before to do this exercise over lunch together on the first day. I am often surprised at how keenly aware strangers can be of each others' latent capacities.

Try the same exercise at a later date, dressed and groomed completely differently. Play around with different ways of presenting yourself, and notice how other people react. As you grow as a person, as you become more flexible, spontaneous, and trusting, others will see more and more potential roles for you. An actress I know seems so innately "funny" that people laugh at almost anything she does, even if she just stands on stage. It's a great gift, but one day she decided that she didn't *have* to be funny all the time, and she suddenly revealed a vulnerability that astonished and touched even those who thought they knew her well.

• • •

Next, make a list of two or three of your favorite actors. If you would love to do the kinds of roles that Glenn Close does, for example, or Glenda Jackson or Marlon Brando or Eddie Murphy (or if others describe you as the same "type"), what is it about that actor that appeals to you? Is it only their technical skill that you admire? Or do they "mirror" some trait in yourself (perhaps sensuality, or a dry wit, or a certain wildness) that you value and want to foster? Use the actor as a model to develop a certain aspect of your personality, but find your own particular way of expressing yourself. Remember that no matter how much you actually *are* like your favorite actor or would *like* to be, you are not quite like anybody else who has ever trod the boards. Perhaps somewhere there is a role so uniquely suited to your special gifts that nobody else could ever quite do it justice.

Maybe your ideal role hasn't been written yet. I wonder, for example, if Kevin Kline would have become the particular kind of actor he is if Michael Weller had not written *Loose Ends*. The role of Paul in that play gave Kline the opportunity to play with that superintelligent, ironic, and very private sense of amusement that has been a kind of signature in everything he has done since, including Hamlet. It also works the other way around: Weller's play would have been very different without Kline. Just as actors look for ideal roles, so writers look for ideal actors, and once in a while the two come together.

• • •

Now compare your description of your ideal role with your notes on how others see you and your list of favorite actors. The more clearly you can come to see exactly what you want to play, the easier it will be for you to find or create material for yourself. Again and again I find that when actors ask me to suggest "a monologue" for them, my mind goes blank, but when they ask for a particular kind of material, all kinds of suggestions come to mind. Moreover, when actors become clear about what they want and learn how to do their own research, they frequently surprise and delight me by coming back with a piece that I have never heard before.

If you told me, for example, that you wanted a "comic" monologue, I would ask you to consider what it is you do, say at a party, that makes people laugh. Are you funny intentionally or unintentionally? If intentionally, do you use sarcasm a lot, or is your sense of humor more gentle? What do you joke *about*—your hometown, family, job, personal difficulties? If you are funny unintentionally, you are probably being very naive and earnest about matters that others do not take so seriously. Or you may be letting loose the "child" in you. Next time you find yourself being very playful, maybe even a bit silly, remind yourself to look for a monologue that allows you to behave exactly that way on stage.

If you are looking for a serious piece, what do you tend to get serious about? For example, an actress told me that she was terribly upset by injustice of any kind—personal, social, or political. I suggested that she look at some plays about the current repression in South Africa, and she came back with several striking pieces, some of which were new to me. Another actor told me he wanted a monologue in which a son confronts a parent with feelings of having been hurt and neglected. I suggested a few of the classic plays on the conflict between generations (*The Glass Menagerie, Long Day's Journey Into Night*, and *Look Homeward Angel* among them), and he turned up a surprising amount of material.

You might be afraid that by asking for something too specific you will limit your possibilities. Actually you are likely to increase them. That's true of any kind of search. If you have a vague idea that you want a "relationship," you won't know where to begin to look, but if you picture yourself connecting with a particular kind of person in a particular way, that person may turn up in the most unexpected places. If you want an apartment, imagine one with a certain floor plan in a specific neighborhood at an acceptable rent and "move in" in your mind. You may need to modify your vision as you encounter reality, but with a concrete picture in mind you will be able to spread the word among your friends and coworkers, you can put notices on neighborhood bulletin boards, you can ring superintendents' doorbells.

• • •

Just imagining that you already have what you are looking

for may in itself release those energies that will get you doing what you need to do in order to find it. You may still need some help learning where to look and how to organize your search. The rest of this chapter will suggest some things you can do to get started on a systematic, ongoing search for material that you would enjoy playing.

What you need to look for first is not a particular monologue but rather a particular playwright who deals with issues that matter to you and characters you can relate to in language that you would love to speak. If you then go on to read everything that writer ever wrote, you are likely to turn up an abundance of material, not only monologues, but also complete roles that you will want to find a way to play some day.

Perhaps you already know some playwrights whose work excites you personally, animates you, makes you want to get out on stage and act. Take a pencil and paper and jot down their names. Don't just put down playwrights you think you are supposed to like because of their literary reputation. Go instead by your own gut reaction. It's not always easy to define what stirs you, but it is easy to recognize it. When Emily Dickinson was asked for her definition of poetry, she replied, "If I read a book and it makes my whole body so cold no fire can ever warm me, I know that is poetry. If I feel physically as if the top of my head were taken off, I know that is poetry. These are the only ways I know it. Is there any other way?"

Let's say that you list Chekhov, Tennessee Williams, and Sam Shepard. You may think that you have already exhausted these resources, but on your own bookshelf you might find, for example, an anthology of plays by Williams that includes one or two you've never read. Or just in skimming through a play of his you read years ago, you may become fascinated with a role that you'd hardly noticed the first time around, possibly because you weren't ready for it then. If you go to a bookstore or library you will probably find other plays of Williams that you don't know. Pick out some and start reading. When you've read or reread or at least skimmed through everything Williams wrote, start in on Chekhov and Shepard.

Perhaps you're new to the theater and don't know any playwrights. Or maybe you've just accepted whatever roles were assigned to you and are not used to seeking out material on your own. If so, start by sampling some of the writers I have listed as belonging to "the standard repertoire" (List A, p. 277) at the back of this book. If you find yourself strongly drawn to the work of a playwright, then go on to read everything by that writer you can find.

If the work of a particular writer doesn't appeal to you after you've got some sense of what it's like, put it aside for now and move on to something else. But try not to be vague about why you are rejecting a piece of writing. Is it because you find it difficult to imagine yourself in the character's shoes? Does the language seem alien to you? Are you looking for more humor, more action, more poetry, more pathos—what? Discovering what you do *not* find useful or effective is a major discovery. It will help you clarify your thinking about the type of theater, play, and role you really want.

If you're not sure how you feel about a piece of writing, try reading a bit of it out loud, just to see how it feels, or maybe work on a monologue or a scene in an acting class. Choosing material for yourself is a bit like picking out a dress or a suit in a clothing store: try it on, see how it feels on you; look in a mirror or ask a friend what it does for you. Eventually you will discover that certain material animates and energizes you, just as certain colors or lines bring out the best in your appearance.

• • •

The reading program I'm proposing may seem like an awful lot of work, but remember you have to read only one play at a time, and you have the rest of your life to read. Also you don't have to finish every play you start. In fact, you don't actually have to *read* everything. You can often get a surprisingly good feeling for a play just by leafing through it and sampling a speech or a few lines of dialogue here and there.

You'll probably find it helpful to set aside a particular time each day for your reading. Some people like to read just before they go to sleep. I do all my reading of plays on the subway. I pick up a batch every few weeks at a theater book store and always carry one or two in my bag. You might also want to set yourself a quota, so many plays or pages a week. If your goals prove unrealistic, cut back on them, but keep reading—regularly!

• • •

There's another way to get acquainted with plays, of course, and that's to see them in performance. If you don't go to the theater as often as you'd like, you may tell yourself that you just can't afford it. Theater tickets are expensive, true, but so are classes, so are pictures and resumes, so are a lot of other things that are essential to your career. Perhaps the problem may not be so much finding the money to go as getting organized to go. Take a pencil and paper again and make a list of all the plays currently running in your community that you've been wanting to see but somehow haven't gotten around to yet. Decide how much money you are able to include in your monthly budget for entertainment, and then set yourself a regular schedule. Buy a subscription ticket, for example, to a theater near you or in a neighboring city. (If you're not sure what theaters are close to you, consult Jill Charles' *Regional Theater Directory*, published annually in Dorset, Vermont 05251.) What I try to do in New York is go down to the TKTS booth at 47th and Broadway one Sunday a month and buy discount tickets for a matinee. Work out any plan you like, so long as it gets you to the theater regularly.

Of course it would be silly to go see a play only to look for monologues. Go to enjoy the play, follow the story, get involved in the lives of the characters, think about any new ideas that the play suggests to you—go for all the reasons you got hooked on the theater in the first place. You never know what may follow. I remember years ago seeing a double bill off Broadway by a then unknown playwright, David Mamet. I was stunned: here was a voice unlike any I'd ever heard in the theater before. Since then I have made a point of seeing or reading each new Mamet play as it comes out, not because I'm looking for material, but because I'm fascinated by that voice. Years later I got together a production of that first double bill, *Sexual Perversity in Chicago* and *Duck Variations* and played one of the two old men in the latter. Still later I did the same with *Reunion* and *Dark Pony*, playing the father in both plays, and I continue to use a monologue from *Reunion* as an audition piece. At this point I'm still looking for a chance to do the older actor in *A Life in the Theater*. I feel that Mamet is "my" playwright: he may not know it, but he writes for me.

• • •

Once you see material on stage that you'd like to perform, you'll want to get a copy of the script as soon as possible. You may be lucky enough to know someone connected with the production, or you can write the author or his agent and ask when it will be published. At the very least you can keep looking for the title in the regularly updated catalogs of the two main publishers of new plays, Samuel French and Dramatists Play Service. You can join a book club, the Fireside Theater (Garden City, NY 11530), which will send you a new play once a month unless you refuse it; often their editions come out a month or two before the play is available in bookstores.

By far the best way to keep up with newly published plays is to browse regularly in bookstores and libraries. I especially recommend that you try to find a bookstore that specializes in theater, such as Applause Theatre Books, the Drama Bookshop, and Theater Arts Bookstore in New York; a complete list of such stores throughout the country is given at the back of this book (List B, p. 283). Even if you don't live close enough to one of these stores to visit one in person, you may be able to get catalogs and order books by phone or mail.

When you go into a bookstore, how do you know what to look for? I try to catch at least two different reviews of plays that open in New York and in major regional theaters, I talk to friends about what they've seen, and I build up a mental "file" of plays that interest me. Even if I don't get to see a play, the title and author will usually stick in my mind. (For example, I never got to see John Patrick Shanley's *Women of Manhattan* when it played off Broadway, but I remembered from a review that it dealt with the relationships of three young women sharing an apartment on the upper west side, and I guessed, rightly, that it might contain good material for some of the actresses I coach.) Then, on one of my regular visits to a theater bookstore, I head first for the section where newly published plays are displayed. If I recognize a familiar title or author, I pick up the text and glance through it. If a speech or passage of dialogue intrigues me, I read further. If I find myself sufficiently involved, I buy the play and put it in my bag to read on the subway.

Most people's lives are organized for them by their bosses. As an actor you are your own boss, and unless you set yourself goals and schedules, it's all too easy to sit around waiting for the phone to ring. You may want to set up a monthly calendar, showing which days you're going to the theater, which days you'll drop into a library or bookstore, and what times you are setting aside for your reading. You could include in the same calendar other activities that further your career, such as making rounds, making phone calls, sending out pictures and resumes, taking classes. Once you've established the habit of doing these things regularly, you may begin to enjoy them. If you find that you resent doing them, it could be that you are pushing yourself *too* hard and need to ease up a bit. (Some of us are far more demanding of ourselves than any paying boss would be.) It could also be that, deep down, you don't really want to pursue an acting career in the theater as it exists today, and there's no law that says you have to. Your most important discovery may be that there's a whole other way to use your talents.

• • •

Let's say that you find a monologue from a new play that is just what you've been looking for. I would estimate that if the play is nationally known (which usually means a highly acclaimed New York production), you have from six to eighteen months from the New York opening before the best monologues from it start appearing at auditions. You can increase that time span considerably by getting to see plays *before* they become widely known. That's not as hard as it might seem. These days most new plays originate in off Broadway, off-off-Broadway, and resident theaters throughout the country. Later, some of them may be done on Broadway or in other resident theaters. In the appendix to the *Regional Theater Directory* mentioned earlier, Jill Charles lists those theaters that do mainly new works (see List C, p. 285). By frequenting such theaters in your community you may see a play that later becomes celebrated when it is done for a wider audience. You can also find good material in plays that *never* become widely known. Often there are passages of excellent writing in a play that doesn't quite work as a whole, or perhaps has not yet been properly produced.

There are still other ways to find neglected material. If you have access to plays that have not been produced or published yet, by all means read them. I suggest, too, that you pay special attention to one-act plays; for some strange reason very few people go to see them and even fewer people read them. I have found some fascinating material just by leafing though anthologies of one-act plays, such as the annual *Best Short Plays* series. Other out-of-the-way material can be found in scripts for film and television, more and more of which are being published or reproduced on videotape.

Although I emphasize new material, you can sometimes catch an auditor's attention by doing a piece from a play that is just old enough to have been forgotten. For example, when I was training as an actor, everybody did the same pieces over and over again from Williams, Miller, and Inge. For that very reason knowledgeable actors have been staying away from them in recent years, and I think we'll soon reach a point, if we haven't already, where some pieces of the 1940s and 1950s will seem fresh again. You have to know what you're doing here, however, because there are still a few old warhorses that just won't quit. For example, Carole Cutrere in Williams' *Orpheus Descending* has a speech (the one about being a "Christ-bitten reformer") that is still done a lot, but she has several other excellent speeches that are not done at all.

Even the old standards are sometimes appropriate: some casting people say they *prefer* you to do "an American classic" because it makes it easier for them to compare you with other actors. If you do decide to use a piece that's done a lot, you may be able to bring something new to it. Sometimes I have seen an actor do an old warhorse in such a fresh, original way, that I felt as if I'd never seen it before.

If you go back to the 1920s and 1930s you can feel pretty safe in using almost anything for audition material. Nobody does Philip Barry anymore, for example, or S. N. Behrman or Kaufman with his various collaborators: Connelly, Ferber, and Hart. And strangely enough, not many people do Odets or Hellman or Saroyan. O'Neill is a special case: his later plays, especially *Long Day's Journey Into Night*, are used a lot, but a piece from one of the earlier plays may go totally unrecognized.

And if you're looking for a "classical" piece, don't assume that Shakespeare is the only author who ever wrote one. He had some contemporaries who were pretty good, too: Christopher Marlowe, Ben Jonson, and John Webster, to name a few. If you move further ahead to the period between 1660 and 1800 in England, you'll find a wealth of material, mostly comic, by writers like Congreve, Etherege, Wycherley, Farquhar, Goldsmith, and Sheridan that is hardly ever used for auditions. Or if you move across to the continent in that period you'll find some brilliant writers, the first among them of course being Molière. (In fact, if you're looking for a classical piece that isn't overworked, I would look first at Molière.) A good way of getting started would be to buy an anthology of plays from a particular period, say the Elizabethan, or the Restoration and 18th century, and sample some of the writing. If you find a playwright you like, look up some of his other works, the ones that never make it into the anthologies, and you are likely to find a piece that will have your auditors exclaiming, "Isn't that wonderful! What's it from?"

• • •

The easiest way to find monologues, of course, is to look through the collections that are put out especially for actors. Unfortunately, a lot of actors just go to one of these books and pick something out, and after a time some of the monologues in them become rather familiar. Occasionally you can find a good piece in one of these collections that other actors haven't latched onto yet, or you may find one that has gone out of fashion and can be safely used again. If you'd like to know which monologues are most likely to elicit a groan from casting people at a particular time, see the list put out annually by Jill Charles in another of her publications, *Summer Theater Directory*. (I have quoted the current one here in List D, p. 288.)

Even though some of the material in collections becomes overused, I find these books quite useful and recommend that you add them to your library as they come out. (See List E, p. 290 for those presently in print.) The reason these particular monologues got into the books in the first place is that they are damned good. The best of them are done over and over again precisely because they work so well, and eventually some of them become what I have called the "classics" in the field. You can learn from them what a really good monologue can be.

But the principal reason for becoming familiar with monologue collections is that, like anthologies, they can help you discover a favorite author. Some years ago, in one of the standard collections, I came upon a piece by A. R. Gurney, Jr., that I liked a lot and was able to use for some time before other actors discovered it. It was the first thing of Gurney's that I'd ever read and, as with Mamet, I was so intrigued that I went out and got everything of his I could find. I've since used two other Gurney monologues myself and recommended several others to actors I coach. Gurney makes brilliant fun of a kind of upscale, WASPish, slightly repressed, very goodhearted, and terribly confused kind of character that I dearly love to play. He's become another of "my" writers.

Many of the things you look at will not be useful in themselves but will lead you on to other things. Think of your search as a kind of treasure hunt. Hidden away somewhere is your ideal role. There are hundreds of clues to be found, and if you know what you are looking for, after a time all clues will seem to point in the same direction. Your search will take its own unique form, and you will be led, step by step, sometimes by the most unlikely clues, to buried treasure.

3

Exploring Untapped Sources

You're sitting at home with a companion and you're reading something, not necessarily from a play, and you come across a passage that is so hysterically funny or so eloquent or so expressive of something significant in your life at the moment that you say to your companion, "Hey, listen to this!" and read it out loud. Now *that* is what you're looking for.

And if it happens to be from something other than a play, so much the better; chances are that nobody else will ever use it. I remember one summer years ago I was out of work and had absolutely nothing to do and so I took it into my head to read the complete works of Dostoevsky. I would go to the library, take out a fat volume, read through it in a week or two, then go back and get another one. I had no intention of doing anything with the material, I just wanted to read Dostoevsky. But at times I had the feeling that I was not reading words on a page but rather listening to a voice, an urgent, insistent voice, demanding that the listener *pay attention*. It was as if the words were leaping off the page, asking to be spoken aloud, and I found myself doing that. One short story, "The Dream of a Ridiculous Man," had this compelling quality throughout, and I began working on it, developing through improvisation a version that I presented one night at a meeting of a group I belonged to called Actors Alliance.

My fellow actors were as enthralled as I was, and so I came back a few weeks later with another piece, then another. After a few months I found I had more than enough material for a full evening, so I tied a number of pieces together with a chronicle of Dostoevsky's life and performed the work off-off-Broadway in an Actors Alliance production under the title *Dostoevsky's Forgotten People*. Later I got a grant from the New York Council for the Humanities to tour the show to branch libraries throughout the five boroughs of New York City, and I also toured schools and colleges outside New York. It was probably the most satisfying performing experience of my life.

• • •

You may or may not want to do a whole evening of your own, but it should be easy enough for you to find three minutes' worth of audition material simply by paying attention to what you enjoy reading anyway. What *do* you like to read? Take a pencil and paper and make a list of your favorite nondramatic authors, just as you did of your favorite playwrights. Again put down writers who genuinely appeal to you, even if they write detective stories or advice-to-the-lovelorn columns. Pick one writer and start reading. If you don't know many writers, try reading book reviews, talking with friends about what they're reading, perhaps joining a book club or taking a night-school course in something like the modern American novel.

You might want to look first at novels and short stories, since they lend themselves so readily to adaptation. Think of all the years of fascinating television that have been produced on Masterpiece Theater from adaptations of classics, near-classics, and even a few not-so-well-known novels. Think of the recent rash of mini-series on American TV. Think of all the Hollywood movies that come out every year based on recent Book-of-the-Month Club selections. Now instead of waiting for somebody else to produce the film version and cast Meryl Streep in it, why not get to the book first yourself?

Letters are another form of writing that can easily be adapted to the stage. A good letter can convey an amusing experience or a deep personal feeling to a close friend in language of peculiar clarity and force—and that's exactly what you're looking for in a monologue. Now every writer who ever published *anything* has also written letters. If you have a favorite writer of any kind, one of the first things I suggest you do is look up his or her letters. If you want to see how effective letters can be in dramatic form, take a look at Sylvia Plath's correspondence with her mother as adapted by Rose Leiman Goldemberg in *Letters Home*, or George Bernard Shaw's correspondence with Mrs. Patrick Campbell as adapted by Jerome Kilty in *Dear Liar*. But again you don't have to wait for somebody else to do an adaptation, you can go right to the source.

Diaries and journals also work well on stage. Anne Frank's is probably the best known, but you can find hundreds of other diaries that have never been used—for example, those of another holocaust victim, Etty Hillesun. Sometimes you can find fascinating material in the diaries of ordinary people. Take a look, for example, at this passage from the diary of a Gretchen Lainer, a young girl in Vienna in the early 1900s:

June 1
We've had such an experience today! It's awful; it's quite true then that one takes off *every stitch* when one is madly fond of anyone. We've seen it *with our own eyes*. I was just sitting and reading Storm's *The Rider of the Grey Horse* and Dora was arranging some writing paper to take to Fanzensbad when Resi came and said: "Fraulein Dora, please come here a moment, I want you to look at something!" From the tone of her voice I saw there was something up so I went, too. At first Resi would not say what it was, but Dora was generous and said: "It's all right, you can say everything before her." Then we went into Resi's room and from behind the curtain peeped into the mezzanine. A young *married couple* live there!!! At least Resi says people say they are not really married, but simply live together!!!! And what we saw was awful. She was absolutely naked lying in bed without any of the clothes on, and he was

kneeling by the bedside quite n—, too, and he kissed her all over, everywhere!!! Dora said afterwards it made her feel quite sick. And then he stood up and—no, I can't write it, it's too awful, I shall never forget it. So *that's* the way of it, it's simply frightful. I could never have believed it. Dora went as white as a sheet and trembled so that Resi was terribly frightened. I nearly cried with horror, and yet I could not help laughing, too. I was really afraid he would stifle her because he's so big and she's so small. And Resi says he is certainly much too big for her, that he nearly tears her. I don't know why he should tear her but certainly he might have crushed her. Dora was so terrified she had to sit down and Resi hurried to get her a glass of water because she believed she was going to faint. I had not imagined it was anything like *that*, and Dora certainly had not either. Or she would never have trembled so. Still, I really don't see why she should tremble like that. There is no reason to be frightened, one simply need not marry, and then one never need strip off every stitch . . .

For an actress young enough to be believable in this role and yet mature enough to play it without feeling uncomfortable, I think this would make a striking monologue. And yet, as far as I know, nobody has ever performed it, anywhere. I offer it here only as a sample of what's out there to be found.

• • •

Another place to look is in autobiographies. I especially enjoy, as I imagine you do, reading the lives of actors. There is a staggering abundance of them. The other day in just one section of a paperback book store I found accounts of the lives of Elizabeth Ashley, Julie Andrews, Lauren Bacall, Candice Bergen, Ingrid Bergman, Carol Burnett, Richard Burton, Sid Caesar, James Cagney, Sean Connery, Bill Cosby, Bing Crosby, Bette Davis, Frances Farmer, William Holden, Robert De Niro, Charlie Chaplin, Jackie Cooper, Errol Flynn,

Mel Gibson, Jackie Gleason, John Gielgud, Audrey Hepburn, Katharine Hepburn, Olivia de Haviland and Joan Fontaine (a dual biography), Rock Hudson, Burt Lancaster, Janet Leigh, Vivien Leigh, Jerry Lewis, Shirley MacLaine, Steve McQueen, Robert Mitchum, Marilyn Monroe, Mary Tyler Moore, Merle Oberon, Kim Novack, David Niven, Eddie Murphy, Jane Russell, Sylvester Stallone, James Stewart, Barbra Streisand, Meryl Streep, Liv Ullman, Orson Welles, Shelly Winters, Raquel Welch, Natalie Wood, and Jane Wyman. Most of these accounts are in the first person (sometimes "as told to" a professional writer) and some are by husbands, wives, or children of the actor. Just browsing through the shelves I came upon some passages that were quite moving, such as Liv Ullman's account of her failing her audition for admission to drama school (!) and some that were quite funny—David Niven, for example, tells one hilarious story after another.

Start from where you are. If you happen to be a baseball fan, you might enjoy such classic accounts of the game as Jim Bouton's *Ball Four*, Roger Kahn's *The Boys of Summer*, Donald Hall's *Fathers Playing Catch with Sons*, or any of the books of Roger Angell. If you're interested in women's studies you can probably find, as I did in one bookstore, lives of women aviators (Beryl Markham), folksingers (Joan Baez), scientists (Marie Curie), and saints (Teresa of Avila), as well as letters and diaries of women explorers, women physicians, pioneering women, and young girls. If you're a black actor you might want to perform excerpts from the works of Claude Brown, Maya Angelou, Toni Morrison, Gordon Parks, George Jackson, Dick Gregory, James Baldwin, and many other contemporary black writers. If you're Latino, I especially recommend that you look at Piri Thomas' *Down These Mean Streets*; it's one of the most fascinating autobiographies I've ever read, and I'd love to see a monologue from it some day.

• • •

Humor works especially well as monologue material. Two

useful anthologies are *The Best of Modern Humor*, edited by
Mordecai Richler, and *Laughing Matters*, edited by Gene
Shalit. You can find in these books a wealth of short pieces by
humorists ranging from Stephen Leacock and Robert
Benchley to Nora Ephron and Woody Allen. Just by browsing
through the "humor" section of most bookstores you can find
collections by Allen, Russel Baker, Roy Blount, Jr., Erma
Bombeck, Bill Cosby, Jean Kerr, Dorothy Parker, James
Thurber, Kurt Vonnegut, Jr., and many others.

Cynthia Heimel has written with great wit about the
plight of the single woman in the 1980s in *The Village Voice*
and other periodicals, and she has turned some of the material
into a play, *A Girl's Guide to Chaos*. But long before the play
appeared, much of her work was available in two collections,
Sex Tips for Girls and *But Enough About You*, and an alert
actress I know got a head start on using it as audition material.
Even now there are pieces in the books that were never
included in the play, and Ms. Heimel continues to turn out
new work.

My favorite among contemporary humorists is Garrison
Keillor. He also happens to be one of my favorite monologists,
but I would not suggest doing any of his monologues: they
tend to be rather long and rambling (part of their charm), and
those of us who have heard him on the radio would not want
to hear anybody else do his material. However, some of his
short essays in *Happy to Be Here* work well as audition pieces,
as some actors have already discovered, particularly his wicked
send-ups of Grimms' fairy tales.

Stand-up comedy routines provide perhaps the most
abundant source of humorous monologues, but they are not
often published. You can listen to material on records and
tapes, and you can sometimes find unpublished routines in
research libraries and museums, notably the Billy Rose
Theater Collection of the New York Public Library at Lincoln
Center, and the Museum of Broadcasting in New York.

• • •

Two brief warnings here: First, avoid any material that will evoke remembrances of a definitive performance. If you were to sing "Over the Rainbow" at a musical audition, for example, no matter how well you did it, you could never erase the memory of that other voice. Some monologues invite the same kind of comparison. But you don't have to avoid all material that stars have ever done. Hamlet is, after all, still up for grabs. And in many cases what a star has done with a particular passage in a play or film may not stick in our minds, even though certain other passages are unforgettable. For example, there are lines from the film *Casablanca* that we cannot think of without hearing Humphrey Bogart, Ingrid Bergman, and Claude Raines, but there are many other passages in films of these and other stars that we would not even recognize if we heard them out of context. It's a strange thing: if you tried to do Trudy the bag lady from Jane Wagner's *Search for Signs of Intelligent Life in the Universe* people might recognize that you were invading Lily Tomlin turf. But the society lady Kate in the same play is so different from our image of Tomlin (in fact the role was quite a stretch for her) that an actress who was more right for it might be able to do it without recalling the original performance at all. There is even a role for a man in *Search*, and I'd forgotten that completely until I read the script.

The second warning should be obvious: if you plan any kind of public performance of copyrighted material, you are required to get the author's permission and in most cases pay royalties. This is both a legal and an ethical responsibility. Of course if you do a three-minute piece for an agent or casting director at an audition, that's not a public performance, but if you were to do the same piece as part of a cabaret act, showcase, or one-person show, you would need to get permission, even if you didn't charge admission. If you're not sure what your responsibilities are, ask. In some cases authors or their agents may make special concessions when nobody is making any money on a show, but you do need to ask.

• • •

Poetry can also work for solo performances, as any number of poets have demonstrated by reading aloud from their own works. For a contemporary audition you'd probably want something in free verse without rhyme. A friend of mine uses T. S. Eliot's "Love Song of J. Alfred Prufrock" to great effect. For a classical audition the whole point is to demonstrate that you can handle traditional verse forms and language more extravagant than we are accustomed to in everyday life. Some actors have already caught on to the idea of using Shakespearean sonnets as classical audition pieces; they are complete in themselves, they usually provide an opportunity to express two contrasting feelings ending with a "punch line," and they happen to take almost exactly one minute to speak. But not many actors have thought of using the sonnets of other poets (Donne, Milton, Wordsworth, and Millay, to name just a few) or of trying different kinds of poetry. Satirical verse might work well for auditions—I'm thinking of certain pieces by Marvell, Swift, Pope, and Byron. Here, for example, is Marvell's "To His Coy Mistress."

Had we but world enough, and time,
This coyness, lady, were no crime.
We would sit down and think which way
To walk, and pass our long love's day.
Thou by the Indian Ganges' side
Should'st rubies find: I by the tide
Of Humber would complain. I would
Love you ten years before the Flood,
And you should, if you please, refuse
Till the conversion of the Jews.
My vegetable love should grow
Vaster than empires, and more slow.
An hundred years should go to praise
Thine eyes, and on thy forehead gaze:

Two hundred to adore each breast:
But thirty thousand to the rest;
An age at least to every part,
And the last age should show your heart.
For, lady, you deserve this state,
Nor would I love at lower rate.
  But at my back I always hear
Time's wingéd chariot hurrying near:
And yonder all before us lie
Deserts of vast eternity.
Thy beauty shall no more be found;
Nor, in thy marble vault, shall sound
My echoing song: then worms shall try
That long-preserved virginity,
And your quaint honor turn to dust,
And into ashes all my lust.
The grave's a fine and private place,
But none, I think, do there embrace.
  Now, therefore, while the youthful hue
Sits on thy skin like morning dew,
And while thy willing soul transpires
At every pore with instant fires,
Now let us sport us while we may;
And now, like amorous birds of prey,
Rather at once our Time devour,
Than languish in his slow-chapt power.
Let us roll all our strength and all
Our sweetness up into one ball,
And tear our pleasures with rough strife
Through the iron gates of life.
Thus, though we cannot make our Sun
Stand still, yet we will make him run.

You could easily do this piece as if you were addressing another character in a play, and it would give you an opportunity to display not only your ability to handle verse but also your wit and passion.

The "dramatic monologue," a popular form in the 19th century, might also be effective. I remember when I was in high school we used to have "poetry contests" in which we declaimed such monologues as Browning's "My Last Duchess" and Tennyson's "Ulysses." As I recall, we were pretty awful, but the material was wonderful and perhaps deserves a second chance.

The dramatic monologue has survived into the 20th century. Dylan Thomas' *Under Milkwood: A Play for Voices* and Edgar Lee Masters' *Spoon River Anthology* are the best-known examples. Thomas' piece was written to be performed, and Masters' has been adapted for the stage. Actors tend to use *Spoon River* a lot for auditions—and with good reason: the pieces are quite short and often quite powerful. However, if you go to the original poems you will find 244 different character sketches, and so your chances of picking one that has not been overdone are pretty good.

• • •

Anything written in the first-person singular is worth considering for monologue material. That includes public speeches, interviews, articles in newspapers and magazines, and transcripts of trials, public hearings, even private conversations. Wallace Shawn turned a lengthy talk with Andre Gregory to brilliant use in the film, *My Dinner with Andre*. Armed with tape recorders, Studs Terkel and other practitioners of oral history have collected and published many volumes of ordinary people talking about their lives. Terkel's *Working* is sometimes used by actors for audition material, but I don't believe that his *Hard Times: An Oral History of the Great Depression, "The Good War": An Oral History of World War Two,* or *The Great Divide: Second Thoughts on the American Dream* have yet been tapped.

Here is a sample from *The Great Divide*. The speaker is an Iowa farmer, Carrol Nearmeyer:

When I was really down and out, I couldn't find a job. You talk about prime of life, I'm forty-six years old. That went against me. I was already too old. If we're forced off the farm, we'll have to take jobs like ridin' on the outside of the garbage truck. Carrying garbage for a minimum wage. ... When they're coming down here after ya, you really feel what happens to a person on the inside. When you realize you're losing everything and be forced out of your home, you get mad. Damn mad.

I kept the whole problem to myself. She didn't know and the kids didn't know that I was having problems. There was times that I got suicidal. I would be driving and didn't know how I got there. There was several times that I had the gun to my head and she didn't know that. And then I got damn mad. I got to thinkin' about it and I got madder. These people don't have the right to do this to me! I have worked, I have sweated, and I have bled. I have tried out there to keep this place goin'. And then they tried to take it away from me! I worked out there to keep food on the table for the people over this whole nation. Nobody has the right to keep me from doin' that! I got so damn mad that I would have picked up arms to protect myself and my family. I would have shot somebody.

Then I got involved with this farm group, and there is people just like me. They get tagged as radicals right away. 'Cause we're supposed to be civilized now. It's all right for some S.O.B. in a white shirt and tie to come along and take our farms away from us on paper. But it's not all right for us to try to keep him from doin' that. The minute we say we're not gonna let him do that, we become radicals.

I got a reputation of talking. I'm trying to get them to understand. They will listen a little better than they did six months ago. ... Slowly, real slowly we got the American Ag Movement started in Iowa. I can see support coming faster and faster. Knowing what the administration has planned for us, we're going to see more people finally stand up and say, "Enough is enough. Let's change this thing."

You might want to do this speech as if you were addressing a rally of fellow farmers. In fact it has some of the fervor of the striking cab drivers in Odets' *Waiting for Lefty* and some of the down home eloquence of earlier dispossessed farmers in Steinbeck's *The Grapes of Wrath*. Again, it's only a sample of what's out there to be found.

An actress I coach turned up one day with a delightful piece from a column in that day's newspaper—the author is a well-known humorist, but I am sworn to secrecy. Other columnists who might serve are Erma Bombeck (already mentioned), Anna Quindlen, whose columns have been published in book form under the title *Living Out Loud*, and the various authors of "Hers" and "About Men" in the Sunday *New York Times Magazine*. I don't suppose anybody would think of doing a monologue from a column about etiquette, but the syndicated "Miss Manners" by Judith Martin has some delightfully sardonic comments to make about contemporary manners, and several collections of her material have been published in book form.

• • •

I have been suggesting some pretty unusual sources for monologue material, and I imagine that some agents and casting directors, upon being presented with a piece the likes of which they've never seen before, will not know what to make of it—or you. "You mean you're doing a *poem* for an audition?" I can almost hear them ask. "That's crazy, I don't want to hear you do *poetry*!" And under their breath they mutter, "Who is this, some kind of nut?" But then another auditor, hearing the very same piece, might glow with delight and compliment you on your resourcefulness.

There are few things that are certain in this business, but one thing you can be dead sure of is that anything anybody tells you will eventually be contradicted by somebody else. You can get a lot of useful feedback from casting people, but some of them turn their personal taste into a universal rule, and if you try to do everything they all tell you to do and avoid everything they tell you not to do, you will soon find yourself in a state of paralysis.

When anybody gives you feedback—whether it be a

casting person, a director, or a teacher—really listen to what they say. Never argue—that prevents you from hearing anything new. But then sift through what you've been told to find the truth in it (usually you can find at least a grain, sometimes a sizeable nugget); save what is valuable, and throw out the rest.

If you approach an audition with the desire not to prove yourself but to share material you love, then you can be free to try anything you like without being seriously disturbed by the reactions of anybody who doesn't happen to like it.

• • •

The more widely you read, and the more fully you live, the more material you will have to work with as an actor. But hopefully you can find some reason for reading and living other than to gather material for your work. You wouldn't want to pass over certain experiences in your life just because you don't see how you could use them on the stage. (Some experiences, of course, you might prefer to do without, but then these are the ones likely to provide the most grist for your mill.) Enjoy a book, too, for its own sake; don't suffer through it just to see if there's a good monologue in there somewhere. You might want to leaf through a book quickly to see if it might have any attraction for you. If it doesn't, put it down and pick up something else. But if it grabs you and tugs at you, then dip right in and keep reading and don't concern yourself with what use you might make of it.

4

Making a Monologue of It

Don't expect to find a perfect monologue ready-made for you right there on the page. Most of the time you will have to *make* a monologue out of the text by cutting, editing, and piecing material together. In this chapter I will first consider some questions you might have about what to look for in an audition monologue, and then I'll describe some techniques for adapting material to come as close as possible to your ideal.

HOW LONG SHOULD IT BE?

Three minutes used to be a kind of standard length, but a few years ago, when Actors Equity Association began scheduling "EPA's" (originally "Equity Principal Auditions," later changed to "Eligible Performer Auditions" when some nonmembers were made eligible), requests for two-minute monologues became common, probably because several hundred actors show up each day, two or three days in a row, for these calls. I've even heard of some calls for *one*-minute monologues, but they're pretty rare. Usually you can count on two or three minutes. If you're asked to do two contrasting pieces, or a monologue and a song, you'll probably have three to four minutes altogether. The simplest solution to the time problem is to have pieces of different lengths or different versions of the same piece. I have one monologue that I can do in either two minutes or three, depending on which sections I choose to include.

You can almost never find a piece that's too short. You may feel that you can't possibly show what you can do in less than three minutes, but the truth is that most people form their impression of an actor in the first few *seconds*. I'd be willing to bet that you do the same: when an exciting new actor steps on stage you sit up in your seat before a word is spoken. Flipping the TV dial, suddenly you stop, arrested by the presence of some actor you've never seen before. You can command that kind of attention at an audition. If you finish a piece in sixty to ninety seconds, you can then follow it with another very short, contrasting piece, and strike a double blow. The same principle holds for cutting a piece: don't be afraid to pare it down to the bone or do just a part of it. Remember you're only showing samples, you're not modelling the whole line. Above all, if you have a choice between cutting and rushing, by all means cut!

SHOULD I DO THE KIND OF THING I DO MOST EASILY OR TRY TO SHOW HOW FAR I CAN STRETCH?

At a general, "getting-to-know-you" type of audition, especially if it's for film or television, it's best to use a piece that clearly exploits the qualities you bring most readily to the stage. If you have time, you can then add a piece that shows an unexpected side of you. If you want to prove to an agent that you can do a kind of role you never get submitted for, or if you want a casting director to consider you for a particular role, you might want to stretch pretty far.

When you are doing a monologue out of context, you can sometimes ignore certain aspects of the character to bring the role closer to you. If the character is much younger or older than you, for example, you may be able to cut any mention of age and do the monologue within your own age range. Of course if the age is inherent in the content or style of the speech, as it is for example with Kit Carson, the old prospector in William Saroyan's *The Time of Your Life*, you'll either have to play the age or not do the piece. Sometimes you can change the gender of the character too. Any of the monologues in Beckett's *Waiting for Godot* could easily be done by a woman, as I believe the whole play has been.

Often you can ignore ethnic background too. Nontraditional casting is becoming more and more widely accepted. Eric Bogosian included some black characters in his solo performance, *Drinking in America*, and I found his work in good taste—and utterly convincing! James Earl Jones has played the owner of a Southern plantation, Big Daddy, in William's *Cat on a Hot Tin Roof*. I didn't see him in it, but I feel he's very right for the role: he has the size, the voice, and the temperament—what difference should the color of his skin make?

IS IT ALL RIGHT TO DO A MONOLOGUE IN WHICH THE CHARACTER TELLS A STORY ABOUT SOME PAST EVENT?

Some people say such pieces are not "active" enough for auditions. It's true that they present special problems, but sometimes they can be quite effective. The main problem is one of time. Speeches that express a feeling directly in the present tense can generally make an impact in less time than those that recall past events. You can say "I'm so ashamed!" in a second or two; you could also make the same point, perhaps more fully, by telling a story about a humiliating experience, but it's going to take you longer.

Narrative writing makes its effect through the accumulation of detail. The greater the weight of the accumulation, the greater the potential effect, as in *War and Peace* and *Moby Dick*, but the less likely that the individual details will hold up out of context. Tolstoy's theory of history and Melville's descriptions of whaling techniques, fascinating as they are on the page, are wisely cut from stage adaptations of their work. Dramatic writing has the advantage of being able to make a powerful impact in a short time, but it can only suggest the kind of rich background detail that gives to certain stories a peculiar resonance.

That doesn't mean that narrative writing has no place on stage—if you have the time for it. A really good story, like those of Spalding Gray, may take a whole evening to tell. Even a fairly brief story told by a character in a play may take five minutes or more and may depend a great deal for its effect on the context; for example, it may reveal something about the speaker that we (and the other characters) have been waiting for two acts to find out! At the end of Act Two of Pinter's *The Caretaker*, we come to understand the rather strange behavior of Aston when he tells a long story about being subjected against his will to electric-shock treatments in a hospital. No part of the speech would work on its own. Even if you had fifteen minutes to do the whole monologue at an audition, it would not have the same meaning and force that it does in the context of the play.

Some stories can make a considerable impact in only two or three minutes, but you need to know what to look for. Try to find a piece with a minimum of background detail—stuff like, "It was June, 1973. I was twenty-three years old at the time, and I was living in Chicago with my brother Mike, my sister Edna . . . " and so on. Or try to cut out as much of the background detail as possible. If you're doing the whole play you have time for some exposition, but if you only have three minutes you can't afford to spend two of them *leading up* to what you want to say. The detail that remains should carry as much emotional weight as possible. For example, look at this letter written by Sherry Matulis of Peoria, Illinois, to President Reagan. (It has been cut and edited by Susan Baum, an actress who uses it to great effect as an audition monologue.)

In early 1970 I was very brutally raped and this act resulted in pregnancy. I went immediately to my doctor, but of course he couldn't help me. To have performed an abortion would have meant risking up to twenty years in prison for both of us.

So, I went to the only man in town who had nothing to fear from the police because he was paying them off.

The thing I remember most vividly was walking up those three flights of darkened stairs and down that dirty corridor and knocking at the door at the end of it, not knowing whether I would ever walk back down those stairs again. More than the incredible filth of the place, more than the fear that I would become infected, more than the fact that the man was an alcoholic and drank throughout the procedure, more than the pain, more than the humiliation of being told, "You can take your pants down now, but you should've (heheheh) kept 'em up before," more than the offer of a $20 refund if I would perform oral sex on him afterward, more than the hemorrhaging and the peritonitis and the hospitalization—more than all those things, those stairs and that dank, dark hallway and the door at the end of it stay with me and chill my blood still.

Almost twenty years later, I still have nightmares about that door. I *had* to walk through it because *not* doing so would have meant giving birth to the offspring of a beast. I resent more than any words can say what I had to endure to terminate an unbearable pregnancy. But I resent even more that ANY WOMAN should, for ANY REASON ever again be forced to endure the same.

Every detail in this narrative carries its own weight, nothing is there just to set something else up. The same principle holds in selecting a comic story: look for humor throughout, not just in the punch line.

The reputation that narrative monologues have acquired for being "inactive" may be due in part to the way they are frequently performed. They can easily seduce you into a kind of lethargic reverie, like the song of the sirens that lures sailors onto the rocks. Be careful not to get so caught up in "reliving the past" that you lose awareness of your listeners and of the point you're trying to make with the story. *All* monologues should take place in the present, and all of them can be "dramatic" if the speaker is engaged in communicating something that matters here and now.

I certainly would not eliminate stories from consideration as audition pieces. For one thing, there are so many of them available. Leaf through any play at random and you'll find that most of the long, uninterrupted speeches are narratives. The fact is that people love to tell stories. Sometimes that's the only way to convey some deep feeling or, as in the case of certain Zen and Hasidic tales, some striking insight. Why start your monologue search by ruling out some of your richest resources?

Besides, stories are more or less complete in themselves, and they are fairly easy to do at auditions. There's something quite simple and natural about getting up in front of people and telling them about something that happened to you. But when you have to imagine that you are engaged in a dramatic confrontation with somebody who isn't really there, a certain awkwardness may set in, both for you and your listeners.

Rather than following any "rules" about what makes a good monologue, look at each piece independently and try to get a sense of what excites you in it and what leaves you cold. You can then choose it, reject it, or adapt it to make it work for you.

ARE COMIC MONOLOGUES BETTER THAN SERIOUS ONES?

Not necessarily. We all like to laugh, true, and auditors hearing monologues all day long are usually grateful for a little comic relief. But what really captures an auditor's attention is a piece that is exceptionally well done, whether it happens to be comic or serious or somewhere in between. Why not have several monologues of different kinds in your repertoire? Sometimes you will get a call for a particular kind of monologue, "contemporary comic," "serious classical," whatever. Usually you can just select from your repertoire the piece that seems most appropriate for whatever is being cast. Or you can just do whatever you feel like doing that day.

Certainly you should do what you do best—after all, it's your show. Some actors are innately "comic"—almost everything they do comes out funny. Or they may be possessed by an irrepressible urge to turn everything, however grim, into a joke. Other actors seem to be drawn more to serious roles—they love to break down and cry or to make an impassioned plea for justice.

No matter which way you lean, keep working to develop the opposite side. Both sides are essential, sometimes even in the same piece. A sense of humor can enrich a serious piece, and a serious point of view can make a comic piece more believable. The distaste that some casting people express for what they call "depressing" pieces may come from having heard too many actors do serious monologues without any awareness of the irony in the character's plight. (Irony is such an important ingredient in acting that I'll consider it at length in Part Two.) But it can be just as upsetting to see a comic piece done without being grounded in a recognizable situation.

Some auditors, subjected too often to torrents of verbal abuse, heartrending sobs, and screams of agony, advise actors to stay away from serious material out of sheer self-preservation. Pieces of extreme emotional intensity, which may be quite effective in the context of a play, are in fact nearly impossible to do in isolation. They can become embarrassing in a small audition room, especially if the actor seems intent on displaying a capacity for grand passion. Remember that the purpose of an audition is for the casting people to get to know you, acquire some sense of how believable and interesting you can be on stage, and see how well you match up with their idea of what they're looking for that day. You don't have to pull out all the stops.

IS IT ALL RIGHT TO DO A PIECE THAT'S IN QUESTIONABLE TASTE?

Not if it's your taste we're talking about. If the language or content of a monologue makes you uncomfortable, don't do it. But what if you yourself feel comfortable with a speech but are afraid that it might offend somebody else? That's a difficult question. Writers with something new to say must often expand the boundaries of what is permissible on stage. At one time Eugene O'Neill's plays were shocking to many people, just as some of David Mamet's are to some people today. But the propensity of Mamet's people to use the word "fucking" as a kind of all-purpose adjective and to speak of sex in crude terms makes a comment about a crass, insensitive culture. To avoid such material simply because it might give offense to some people would be to limit your range as an actor. On the other hand, I can understand the objections of some casting people who describe certain kinds of audition material, particularly graphic descriptions of violence, as an "assault" on their sensibilities. If you're passionate about doing a piece, if it says something that matters to you, if you're not just out to shock or titillate, by all means do it. You'll probably get different reactions from different people: a piece that turns one person off may captivate another by its wit and boldness. You'll never please 'em all anyway, so you might as well please yourself.

WHAT ABOUT PIECES IN DIALECT?

You can sometimes get away with ignoring the dialect of the character provided it isn't too deeply embedded in the syntax and rhythm of the writing. An Alan Ayckbourn piece, for example, is less likely to sound incongruous in American speech than a Pinter piece. If you do decide to use a dialect, make sure you can do it accurately and effortlessly, without having to concentrate on it, and look for an opportunity, either in an interview or contrasting piece, to display your native speech.

If you're doing a general audition for a casting director for film or television, you're probably better off choosing a monologue that allows you to use your everyday speech, since that's the kind of thing you're most likely to be cast in. (Roles requiring dialects are usually given to a native speaker of the dialect or to a star who is then assigned a dialect coach.) But if you're auditioning for a resident theater that is casting the entire season, you might want to demonstrate your mastery of certain dialects. Standard British is particularly in demand these days, along with several of its variants (Irish, Cockney, etc.). Among American dialects the most useful are the various Southern patterns, simply because of the popularity of Tennessee Williams, Beth Henley, and Horton Foote.

DOES A MONOLOGUE HAVE TO FOLLOW ANY PARTICULAR STRUCTURE?

Some people will tell you that an audition monologue needs to have a certain dramatic shape: the beginning should draw us in, there should be a "build" of some kind, and then a clear-cut ending. Also the monologue has to have at least two contrasting "colors" or emotional tones. All this would be wonderful if you could ever find it in a single monologue. The hard truth is that a monologue extracted from a larger source will almost never have an ideal shape. (If you want variety, you will usually have to do two different pieces.) However, if you find a piece that was written to be complete in itself, or if you write your own, that's another story. Here, for example, is the A. R. Gurney piece I mentioned earlier; it's one of a number of short sketches, each complete in itself, that make up his *Scenes from American Life.*

MAN: (*Dictating.*) **Dear Brad.** (*Pause.*) **Thanks for your note.** (*Pause.*) **I'm very sorry, but this year I don't think I'll cough up another nickel for Yale. I'm distressed that** the library was burned but why should I keep Yale up when even its own students persist in dragging her down? (*Gets angrier.*) Indeed, why do people like you and me and Snoozer, Brad, have to keep things *up* all the time? It seems to me I spend most of my time keeping things up. I keep the symphony up. I keep the hospital up. I keep our idiotic local theatre up. I keep my lawn up because no one else will. I keep my house up so the children will want to come home someday. I keep the summer house up for grandchildren. I keep up all that furniture Mother left me because Sally *won't* keep it up. I even keep my morals up despite all sorts of immediate temptations. (*The* SECRETARY *glances up at him.*) I keep my chin up, I keep my faith up, I keep my dander up in this grim world. And I'm sick, sick, SICK of it. I'm getting tired supporting *all* those things that maybe ought to collapse. Sometimes all I think I am is an old jock strap, holding up the sagging balls of the whole goddamn WORLD! (*Pause.*) Strike that, Miss Johnson. Obviously. And excuse me. (*Pause.*) Strike out the whole letter, Miss Johnson. (*Pause.*) Begin again. (*With a sigh.*) Dear Brad. Enclosed is my annual check for Yale. I wish it could be larger. Sally joins me in sending love to you and Jane. Sincerely. And so forth.

The Gurney piece has just about everything I could ever ask for in an audition monologue. First, it's a useful length, just under two minutes. Second, it's the kind of role I might be readily cast in. Third, it's written in highly expressive language in which every detail counts. Fourth, even though it's not a story, the conceit that I am dictating a letter makes it simple and natural to perform at an audition. Fifth, I think it's very funny and at the same time quite touching. Sixth, it's in good taste, with the one line about the jock strap being just enough to give it a little zing. Seventh, it requires a kind of "cultivated" American speech that comes quite readily to me. And finally, being complete in itself, it has a definite build, a sharp turning point, and a contrasting finish. It's like a little mini-play, able to stand entirely on its own. In short, it's as close as I've ever come, or may ever come, to an ideal monologue. I performed it for several years until other actors started using it and I'd done it so often that it grew stale on me. Too bad! I wish I could call up Gurney and order a dozen more.

• • •

You'll be lucky if you come across an ideal monologue once in your lifetime. But if you have an ideal in mind, you can cut, edit, and piece together material in order to come as close as possible.

Sometimes you may find a role that you like a lot but can't seem to find any speech in it that's more than a few sentences long. That doesn't necessarily mean you can't make a monologue out of it. If you'll look closely at a page of dialogue, you'll sometimes discover that it is actually a kind of interrupted monologue: one speaker keeps going along the same track, and the other mainly prods, prompts, or lends a sympathetic ear. Take a look, for example, at the following exchange between Murph and his buddy Sal in Jane Willis' *Men Without Dates*. An actor I coach pieced this material together by leaving out the lines I have enclosed here in brackets.

MURPH: **I can't do that, Sally—Me an' Tracy—**
[SAL: Don't marry her, Murph! Don't do it!]
MURPH: **I have to!**
[SAL: YOU DON'T HAVE TO DO ANYTHING, MURPH!]
MURPH: **GODDAMN IT SALLY! I HAVE TO! ALL RIGHT?! I HAVE TO MARRY HER!**
[SAL: What're you talking about?]
MURPH: **Think about it, Sally—SHUT THE FUCK UP FOR TWO SECONDS AND THINK ABOUT IT?**
[SAL: (*Thinks for a beat.*) Oh. You're in trouble? You got her in trouble?]
MURPH: **Good thinking. Your mental capacities are overwhelming to me.**
[SAL: When'd you find out?

MURPH: Right before we decided to get married.
SAL: Sorry Murph. I'm sorry.
MURPH: Thanks.
SAL: And congratulations too?]
MURPH: (*Whispering urgently.*) I don't even know her, Sal.
Here I am marrying somebody I don't even know that
well? (*Pause.*) No wonder I'm dying! No wonder I'm
dying!
[SAL: You never know anybody, Murph. You just never
know, I dunno.]
MURPH: I just—I'm looking at her across the table in
the Injun food restaurant? And I just wonder. I'm
thinking, boy she smells good. And she's pretty—it's
not like I'm stuck with a dog—
[SAL: God knows I love her like a sister. The woman is a
saint.]
MURPH: (*Cont.*) Her eyes are done up in colors and her
hair's doing that thing? (*Demonstrates.*) You know, that
thing it does?
[SAL: (*Nodding.*) That thing.]
MURPH: And she's very good to me. She always looks
out for my better interest. I could do worse?
[SAL: (*Without enthusiasm.*) Yeah, I spose.]
MURPH: And she's very good in other ways, which I will
not name by name.
[SAL:Obviously.]
MURPH: Then how come I don't like—*feel* anything for
her? How come I don't love her?
[SAL: (*Calling down to the bartender.*) Two more of these
please—(*Holds up glasses.*)]
MURPH: And I'm wondering to myself—if I can't love
this woman sitting across the table from me. This
woman who has given me the world, her time, her heart
and her soul to me. This woman who is having my kid.
. . . Is there something—like—wrong with me?

Like a miner working a vein of gold, you can use this
method to extract monologues out of material that others pass
by without noticing. Often all you have to do is cut your
partner's lines and those of your own which are direct

responses to them—your remaining lines may then flow along in a natural sequence. Sometimes, however, you run into a snag. Take Murph's fifth line, "Good thinking. Your mental capacities are overwhelming to me." Clearly this is a direct response to Sal's realization that Tracy is pregnant, and it cannot be cut. The solution is to take a moment to "look" at Sal, "hear" what he supposedly says (just as you would in a telephone conversation on stage), and then react with your own line. This is a technique that needs to be used sparingly—no more than once or twice in an entire monologue. If you have to react too many times to nonexistent stimuli, your monologue is going to look like one of those pictures in children's books that show a stove without a chimney, a mop without a handle, and a chair with three legs, all under the prominently displayed caption, "What's missing?"

Sometimes the only way to proceed with one of your lines is to supply the sense of your partner's line yourself. Suppose your partner interrupts a story you've been telling by asking, "Why on earth did you do such a stupid thing?" and you respond, "I have no idea. I must have had a thousand reasons. First . . ." And then you go on to give your reasons. You can't really cut your partner's line, because it leads you into a whole new train of thought. And you can't just pretend to hear it, because your next line would make no sense. What you can do is to say something like this: "I sometimes wonder why I did such a stupid thing. I must have had a thousand reasons. First . . ." And then you're home free. Try not, however, to say things like, "You're asking me why I did such a stupid thing?"—again you don't want to call too much attention to your absent partner.

• • •

When you're building a monologue out of pieces of dialogue, don't feel that you have to limit yourself to lines that are arranged consecutively in a scene. You might find a line from a page before or a page after, or even from a different act altogether, that you like a lot and can fit into the passage you've chosen.

In fact, a good rule of thumb, both in piecing material together and in cutting material, is always to start with what you want to save, not with what you want to discard. If you come across a really striking line in a play, even if it lies on the page all by itself, surrounded by rather dull material, mark it with a pencil. Or if you like only one small part of a monologue, mark just that part. You may be able to put a lot of different pieces together and create a kind of mosaic.

Let's say you've got a monologue that runs three or four pages. You like it so much that you don't know where to begin to cut. Look first for the one passage you feel you couldn't possibly live without. Mark the passage, preferably with one of those handy yellow highlighters. Now, highlight the passage that would be next most painful for you to cut, even if it isn't connected with the other. Keep highlighting your favorite parts until you have enough to make a monologue of about the right length. Then use only as much of the material in between as you need to connect these parts together. If you tried to go about it the other way, cutting what you think is not necessary, you might find yourself reluctant to perform any surgery at all.

• • •

Perhaps the easiest way to cut a monologue is through improvisation. Pick a fairly long monologue, about half a page to a page and a half in an acting edition. Read it through silently once, and as you're reading try to get the gist of what the character is saying. Then put the book down and do the monologue, or as much of it as you remember, more or less in your own words. You may happen to remember only ten or twenty percent, and that's fine. What is interesting is *which* ten or twenty percent sticks in your mind. Now repeat the procedure several times. Each time you are likely to remember more of the piece, but there may be passages that you consistently leave out or abridge severely. That can be for one of three reasons: 1) you don't really understand them, 2) you have an emotional block against them, or 3) they're really not that important to you. If you can rule out the first two reasons, then these are passages you can most readily cut.

It may be helpful to divide a long monologue into "blocks," or units of thoughts that seem to hang together. Mark these blocks in your script and give a "key word" to each to help you remember them. You can improvise on one block at a time if you like. Or if you're going through the whole speech you may suddenly realize that you can jump directly from block 3 to block 5 without any great loss, and there again is a possible cut.

Each time you do this exercise you will probably get closer and closer to the author's words, not because you're trying to memorize them, but simply because they express the thought or feeling so well. Eventually you may memorize the whole speech, or those portions of it you decide to keep, without ever having set out to do so. You will also have done a large part of your work as an actor by getting in touch with the thoughts before you speak the words. And finally you will have come up with a cutting of the speech that works for you.

• • •

When adapting material for an audition, have respect for the author's intentions. If you were performing the material in public, you would of course need the author's permission to change or cut even one word. Inside the confines of an audition, you still have an obligation to present the material as faithfully as possible. I like to think, when I am building an audition monologue out of the author's material, that I am making the choices the author would make himself if I were able to ask him to create an effective piece for me within the given time limits.

• • •

So. You've found a piece you like a lot, you've cut and edited it to your satisfaction. Now wouldn't it be nice to think that at last your search for monologue material is over? Actually it's only beginning. You're probably going to want more than one monologue in your repertoire. How many exactly depends on what kind of projects you will be auditioning for. If you are going mainly for film and TV, two contemporary monologues are probably enough, both pretty close to you but showing somewhat different sides. If you're auditioning for stage work, particularly for resident theaters, you'll probably need at least one classical piece as well.

You'll need to keep replenishing your repertoire. A favorite piece may grow stale on you, and you'll have to put it aside for six months to a year till you can come back to it afresh. Other actors may discover a piece you thought was your private domain. You may need to develop a new piece to meet the special requirements of a particular audition. Or you may want to try out a piece that intrigues you but seems a bit beyond your reach at the moment. Experimenting with new pieces will keep you stretching and growing as an actor. You don't have to use a piece at an audition if you find it doesn't work for you, but unless you try it you'll never know. Find a place where you can afford to take a big risk—maybe a workshop or class—and try a piece that seems far beyond you. You may discover, to your astonishment, a whole new range of possibilities opening up before you.

Searching for new monologue material is something you'll need to keep doing for the rest of your career, at least until your work is so well known that you will always be allowed to go directly to a reading from the script—or perhaps not have to audition at all! Even then you'll want to keep a lookout for new material for performance. It's a lot of work, but if you do a bit at a time, regularly, you can keep an everchanging repertoire of three or four pieces at your command at all times. Then when you get that call, instead of wondering what on earth you are going to do, you can simply select from your current repertoire the piece or pieces that would be most satisfying for you to perform on that particular occasion.

5

Writing Your Own Monologues

There's a very simple way to find a piece that is uniquely suited to you, that nobody else ever does, and that can stand entirely on its own: write it yourself. And yet when I suggest that to actors, they usually look at me sideways and say, "You mean it's *all right* to do that?" They seem to feel there's some kind of eleventh commandment, "Thou shalt not write thine own material." I don't know where they get that idea.

Some casting people, it's true, say they don't want to see actors do monologues they've written themselves. Ask them why, and they'll probably tell you, "That's not acting; anybody can do their own words. I want to see you do something where you have to become somebody else, that's what acting is all about." If we accept that somewhat peculiar definition, then we would have to say that at least two of the finest artists of our time, Charles Chaplin and Woody Allen, are not really actors. All they do is their own material. *Anybody* can do that, right?

Can you imagine Shakespeare or Molière, both of whom acted in their own plays, appearing before a modern-day casting director and being told, "You mean you wrote that yourself? Well, it's very nice, but come back with something that's more of a challenge"? I find the whole argument ludicrous, and I'm tempted to tell you just to go ahead and write your own stuff and not worry about what people will say. However, given the power that some casting people wield in this crazy business, you may want to protect yourself against their prejudices. The simplest way is not to announce the title of your piece, or to announce a title without an author, or perhaps give yourself a pen name. If you are asked directly, "What's that from?", as you may well be, I recommend telling the truth. You don't have a great deal to lose: by this time you've already done the piece, and you may get some useful feedback on how well it works for you. Some actors equivocate, saying things like, "It's from a new play" or "It's by a friend of mine." If you want to do that, fine, but you may suffer some embarrassment if you're asked a lot of follow-up questions.

• • •

If you're intimidated by the prospect of writing your own monologue, think instead about "talking" one. Almost anybody, when speaking spontaneously about something that really matters to them, can achieve a kind of eloquence. You can discover for yourself the power of everyday speech just by listening to people talk, by reading oral history, or by watching documentary films and television. (I once had to play a scripted role, a doctor, in an industrial film in which real patients talked, in their own words, about their actual problems. It was a humbling experience: they were *really* spontaneous. And what they had to say sounded so much better than what was written in my script!)

Talk first, write later. That's how two friends of mine, David Wysocki and Jim Denton, created a piece. Jim, a writer, had often heard David, an actor, tell about the night he learned of his father's death. Jim felt he knew the story so well that one day he sat down and wrote it out and gave it to David, who has since used it with considerable success at auditions. Here it is as David usually performs it:

I think the hardest thing to accept was that it happened without me. I had nothing to do with it. When I learned about it he was simply gone.

I remember the floor was sticky and it crackled

each time I took a step. It was the first fraternity party
I'd ever attended. . . . November of my freshman year
and I had only been away from home for two months.
Everyone was fairly wasted. There was a lot of grass
and five kegs for the occasion. They had spilled beer all
over the place and the floor was sticky from the foam
and slime. I was being very independent. I had a lot of
hits and I drank a lot of beer. And I danced. Oh, how I
danced.

Then this girl, this P.K. came running over to me.
P.K.—that's Preacher's Kid! There were a lot of them
at my school. They were famous partiers, all of them,
and they usually hung out with the theatre kids. She
came running up to me and grabbed me and started
dancing with me. She had this drunken, startled look in
her eyes; frightened . . . scared of something. I was
talking or singing—I'm not sure which. But I was
having a terrific time. And she kept saying something to
me, but I couldn't hear her. The music was at
brain-destruct level and I was too stoned to understand
what she was saying. Finally I caught it: she was saying,
"Have you talked to Tom? Did Tom find you?"

No, I hadn't talked to Tom. All I could think was
that Tom had told me he was going to break up with
her soon and, Oh Shit, had he done it today and was she
about to dissolve on my shoulder right here while I was
having such a fantastic time?

She pulled me toward the door and out into the
cold. I was hollering, "No, no, I don't want to go." I
saw Tom a block away running toward the frat house.
She threw her arms around me and she hugged me
tighter than any girl had ever hugged me. I could hear
her crying. She held on until Tom ran up and pulled me
back inside and down the hall past the room with the
sticky floor to the row of pay telephones. He said, "Call
home." I looked at him and thought why the fuck
should I call home? Nobody's supposed to be having a
baby. (There were four Catholic girls in my family—
somebody was always giving birth.) Tom placed a dime
in my hand and said again, "Call home."

The operator wanted a dollar-fifty to put the call

through! I had forty cents in my pocket, Tom had seventy-five cents. We had to get the rest from the P.K. who was sitting on the steps of the frat house crying.

The line was busy. I tried my sister's house and her line was busy. I tried my aunt's house and her line was busy. I tried my house again. It rang through and my mother answered.

My mother and father were sitting in the bleachers on a silver-blue November afternoon watching a football game in which my younger brother was playing. There were only two minutes left in the game when my father fell onto her, heaved his immense body on top of her. My brother noticed the commotion in the stands from the field, but he continued to play out the last two minutes of the game. Then they told him it was his father. He ran to the hospital in his football uniform, but by the time he got there the man was dead. Cardiac arrest. Massive. Instantaneous.

That's when I realized that independence isn't what it's supposed to be. You think you'll be master of your own life; you think that when you finally leave home and you're finally on your own, you'll have the power to MAKE things happen . . .

No. Independence is discovering that things will happen without you. Without even asking your permission.

And it takes a long time to get over that awful feeling of impotence.

This story works for three reasons: it sounds like an individual talking, it deals with a powerful emotional experience, and it has a point to it. The point is suggested in the first few lines and articulated more fully at the end. If you wanted to sum it up in a single sentence—a technique you'll be hearing a lot more about later—it might be something like this: "I thought I was grown up and free at last, but I was wrong."

There's a good deal of background detail, but it's vivid and striking, and it serves the purpose of establishing David's feelings of being "grown up." There's also an appealing, self-mocking humor in the way the present-day David looks back at his younger self, a kind of irony that helps to lighten an otherwise serious piece. There's even a bit of outright comic relief, the comment about his Catholic sisters. Finally, the detail creates a certain amount of suspense: we sense what has happened, but David doesn't know yet, and the account of the familiar frustrating experience of searching for change for an urgent phone call actually helps to move the piece along.

• • •

You may not be lucky enough to have a professional writer for a friend. You could seek one out of course, or you could work with somebody you know who happens to have a way with words. There are also a few writers who do monologues for actors for a fee. You may be able to find them by reading advertisements in the trade papers or on bulletin boards where actors congregate. In choosing a writer you need to take as much care as in choosing a photographer. Ask to see samples of their work, talk with them and see how well they are able to draw you out. Their job, just like that of a photographer, is to catch you at your liveliest—which often means off guard. They need to get to know you and create a piece especially for you, not just hand you something ready-made. You need to be clear too about what you're getting for your money (is coaching included, for example?) and what happens if you're not satisfied with the initial results.

• • •

There's a simpler and cheaper solution: create monologues through improvisation and record them on tape. It will be easier if you have at least one other actor to work with, preferably a group. That way you can improvise together, like jazz musicians, and listen later to what you did. You don't have to sit there all alone with that machine, which can sometimes be as intimidating as a typewriter.

Start by taking a journey in your mind back to a school you once attended. Picture yourself on the way to school, approaching the building, walking down the hall and into a classroom or lunchroom or auditorium. See yourself meeting your old friends there, or a favorite teacher. Sit somewhere in the building for a time, look out the window, listen to the sounds around you. Take a walk around the grounds or athletic fields, maybe get involved in a game.

Once you feel you are sort of "back there," pick one thing that happened to you there that you remember quite vividly. It could be a painful or embarrassing experience, an astonishingly happy one, or simply something funny. Recall as much of the sensory detail of the experience as possible: sights, sounds, tastes, colors.

Now come back to the present. Start the tape recorder and tell the story to the group you're working with. If you are working alone, imagine you are talking to your best friend. Naturally a lot of feelings from the past are going to come back to you, but try to stay in the present and keep connected with your listeners. Don't "act," just tell what happened.

Now listen to the tape. You may be surprised at how full and complete the story is. You may even be able to take a first improvisation like this, transcribe it, cut and edit a bit, and then present it as a monologue. If you need to make revisions, here are some questions that might be helpful, but ask them only *after* you've done your improv, not before or during it: What works in the story for you? Is there anything you're especially pleased with? Is there anything that doesn't work as well as it might? Did you leave out anything essential? Are there details that could be cut or condensed? Are there things that could be said more colorfully, or perhaps with more humor? Is there a point to your story? Does it say anything about how you got to be what you are today or about teachers or children or schools or "the system"?

Get feedback from your listeners. But ask them to observe a very strict ground rule: they are not to direct or criticize or tell you what to do; they are only to describe their own reactions to the story. For example, how vividly and clearly did your experience come across to them? Did they understand exactly what happened? Were they amused or touched by the story or perhaps reminded of something in their own experience? What were the highlights? What point, if any, did the story make for *them*? So long as they describe their reactions in the first-person singular, their feedback can be helpful. Even if somebody says, for example, "I was bored and restless during this part of the story," that might be useful for you to know. But it's usually not helpful to be told how to "fix" a problem. It's your job to rewrite, taking into account how your audience was affected by your first draft.

You can "rewrite" either by taping successive versions of the story or by transcribing your first improvisation and making changes on paper. Unless you have a major overhaul to do, the second method is usually better. Sometimes an improvisation loses something by repetition. When you do transcribe your improv, write down exactly what you said, with all the hesitations and rough edges.

Don't be afraid to stretch the truth a bit. Most of us have the capacity, in remembering our past, to "improve" upon it considerably, and those who are especially gifted that way often become writers. You may want to add details to your story that are not true but give it more color. You may even want to report, with a straight face, something absolutely preposterous. That's what stand-up comics do all the time. Also great monologists: Garrison Keillor is particularly good at starting off in a world that is rock-solid real and then gradually ascending into a world of total fantasy. He does it so skillfully that we're never quite sure exactly when he took off!

Now, try inventing a dramatic context for your story. Pretend, for example, that the incident was a turning point in your life. Then imagine that you are telling the story to somebody in the present for some particular reason. Suppose, for example, that you are breaking up with somebody, and you need to tell the story of an early love affair as a way of showing how you came to be incapable of sustaining a long-term relationship.

This kind of fantasy journey can be used to explore your entire past, not just a single event in school. You can revisit the neighborhood where you grew up, a favorite vacation spot, your first apartment on your own, maybe a summer theater where you began your acting career. You can play endless variations on this game of recalling—and rewriting—your past.

• • •

You can also create monologues by imagining a dramatic confrontation in the present. Think of a person towards whom you have strong feelings, either positive or negative. Lovers, best friends, parents, children, and siblings usually work well, or you may be able to use a boss, teacher, therapist, or mentor. You could pick somebody you don't actually know, such as a famous actor or writer, or somebody who is no longer living. The point is to think of a person or kind of person with whom you feel the strongest possible emotional connection.

There is something important that you want to say to this person, preferably something that's been building up for some time and is difficult to say. Now write down one simple sentence that conveys the gist of what you want to say. Here are some examples by actors in my monologue workshops:

—It's crazy, underneath the anger and hurt is the real truth: I miss you, I want you to come back, and I love you very much.

—I'm afraid one of us is going to die before either of us has a chance to say I love you.

—I could tell you where your lack of confidence comes from if you want to hear it.

—I never had a chance to say good-bye.

—I think I don't want to change myself enough to marry you.

—I'll love you always, but we have to go different ways now, and you have to learn to love yourself more.

—I always hated clowns when I was little.
—I wish you could accept me for what I am and not
keep putting your expectations on my behavior.

The next step is to say your sentence out loud. If you're working with other actors, "cast" an actor from the group as the person you have in mind and speak directly to him or her. If you're working alone, imagine the presence of your listener. But I would not recommend using the actual person you have in mind. Not just because that might get you into hot water. The point of this exercise is to think of something you *might* say, and to allow yourself to express it more freely and fully than you'd ordinarily be able to manage in a real-life encounter.

Again and again I've noticed that this simple exercise, one actor speaking one sentence to another, brings about an incredibly powerful or extremely funny interchange. The actor addressed may be deeply shaken or may break up. The moment becomes a kind of mini-drama, with the whole history of the relationship becoming immediately clear.

At the same time most actors don't feel satisfied with saying just the one sentence. They've made their point, but they haven't made it fully, and they feel "unfinished." If you feel satisfied, fine, but if you don't, then go on to the next and final step of the exercise: do an improvisation in which you express the whole feeling to your satisfaction. The only rule is that your original sentence must appear somewhere in your improv: at the beginning, in the middle, or at the end. Again, of course, tape record and transcribe your improv, then cut, edit, and rewrite as necessary.

For example, Tamra Shaker, the actress who wrote "I always hated clowns when I was little," used that as the first sentence of her improvisation. She went on to describe how terrified she was of clowns as a little girl. Then she told how, as a young woman, she watched a clown come to entertain some children in a hospital. She described how loveable and funny the clown was, how he was able to go up to children with the most appalling injuries and diseases and say or do just the right thing to make them squeal with laughter. And she ended with this sentence: "And I said to myself, I'm going to marry that clown!" The whole speech became a very touching declaration of love for her husband.

Another actress, Joanna Brown, used her one-sentence summary as the final sentence of her improvisation. The whole thing went as follows:

I know I'm unconventional, and I'm really not like everybody else's mother. I don't play mah-jong, I'm bored with playing ladies' doubles every Wednesday morning—all those ladies talking about their dinner parties the night before, or whatever their hairdresser said. I mean, those things are not important to me. I know you're disappointed in me because I'm not like all your friends' mothers. But I am me. I wish you could accept my unconventionality. You know I come from a totally different background. . . . And I didn't bring you into this world to make your life miserable. I'll never forget when you were born, how filled with joy I was. A beautiful little girl! You were . . . you were the most beautiful, beautiful child that had ever been born. And you were always so special to me. . . . And I tried all the other routes, I was PTA, and you know I was the volunteer in the health room, so that whenever the kids skinned their knees or something I was always there for them. I always tried to be all of that, but deep down, I'm just me—a human being. I wish you could accept me for that and not keep putting your expectations on my behavior.

After you have improvised a monologue, look back on it and see if you can discern its underlying structure. In the piece just quoted, for example, the speaker first admits to being unconventional and asks that her daughter accept that. Second she makes the point that she really wanted and cherished her daughter. Third, she says she tried to be a certain kind of mother but couldn't, and again she asks that she be accepted for who she is. The speech could be reduced to a few key phrases:

—not the conventional mother
—loved and cherished you
—tried but couldn't,
  wish you could accept me

Although most speeches can be outlined like this after the fact, you may not be conscious of following a particular structure at the time. Usually you will recognize, however, that the idea was prepared ahead of time and existed in a kind of vague, ill-defined form before it took final shape in words. Next time you find yourself making a long speech in life, or listening to one, see if you can trace the path of the thoughts. The ability to discern the underlying structure of a speech will be of immense value to you when you start working on monologues that you encounter on the page.

• • •

So far the examples of original monologues we've looked at have been pretty serious. How do you create something comic? Same way, really. Just don't be so serious. J. Brandon Hill, an actor in one of my workshops, was once asked by a friend if he would like to attend a wedding with her. She was surprised when he said yes, and she told him, "I didn't think you were the type that would enjoy these things." J. B., as he is usually called, didn't think so either. At the time he had no ready comeback, but after a few days he composed this response:

> I don't know why I like going to weddings. I guess I'm like those people who like to watch houses burn down or slow down on the highway to get a good look at a car crash—they find them fascinating, but no one wants it to happen to themselves.
>
> As for marriage itself, I think it's a disease. I myself don't have any of the symptoms. I don't feel the need

for a "meaningful" relationship. I don't want to grow old with someone. I don't even want to do that by myself so why would I want some old lady watch me do it?

I think the disease is released with the hormones that become active during puberty. It incubates in the body and in about 15 years you get married. After getting it, one of two things happens: the condition is terminal and you die (sometimes undergoing counselling to help cope with the affliction) or you get cured. This is called divorce. It is frequently a long and painful cure and in some cases very expensive. Perhaps someday a more humane cure will be found.

Right now the best cure, of course, is prevention. Just say no. Avoid breeding grounds of the disease such as singles weekends and the highly infectious (especially for women over thirty) family gathering.

Marriage should be a thing of the past like TB or The Plague. The main thing keeping it alive is the money it generates. Churches, catering halls, lawyers, and magazines sold at supermarket checkout counters would go bankrupt.

Marriage isn't natural. If it were, we wouldn't need to learn how to stay married or work at marriage, it would just come to us.

Marriage is a perversion of the human spirit: I'll watch it being done, but beyond that, count me out.

Now create a monologue for a character very different from yourself. Start by taking pencil and paper and jotting down a list of twenty character traits that you think of as opposite to your own. If you are normally very trusting, for example, write down "highly suspicious." If you are quiet or shy, write down "boisterous or domineering." If you are basically kind, write "cruel and sadistic." You could also include in your list political or religious beliefs that are opposite to your own. If you happen to be an atheist, write down "born-again Christian." If you are a pacifist, write "ardent militarist." If you're a member of an ethnic minority, write "white supremacist."

It may help if you think about people you actually know who get under your skin because their attitudes, beliefs, or behavior are so bizarre that you can't possibly understand how any human being could act that way. These are the people who invariably provoke you into argument or flight. You might think about what drives you crazy about your parents, if you haven't forgiven them yet, or what you can't tolerate in your children, if you haven't let yours go yet. Or you might think of roommates, bosses, other actors, people current in the news—anybody who acts in a way that seems incomprehensible to you—and write down those traits that are especially maddening.

Don't try to evaluate your ideas as they come to you, just keep jotting them down until you have twenty character traits. Then go back over your list and try to pick a trait, or perhaps a combination of several, that would be fun for you to play. You might create a character, for example, who is totally self-absorbed, constantly complaining, seeks out advice and help from other people and then rejects it. Next, set up a situation for improvisation that will allow you to play this person in confrontation with a "normal" person, i.e., somebody very like yourself, who will be played by another actor. For example, a teenage actress asked another actress to play herself coming home at 2:00 a.m. after a date, and she played her own mother, lecturing the daughter on all the terrible things that were bound to happen from leading such a dissolute life. If you're playing somebody whose political or social views seem to you outrageous, you might want to invent some kind of public forum, such as a trial, a rally, or a television interview, where you can expound these views. Tell the other actor or actors what the situation is and if you want them to instigate something or give you a particular kind of feedback. Turn on the tape recorder and give it a try. The improvisation that follows may be more dialogue than monologue, but don't worry about that; you can probably make a monologue out of it by the familiar method of piecing together material. You may need to tape several different versions of the improvisation, perhaps giving different instructions to the other actors, until you are able to bring out what you want.

• • •

Some actors are reluctant to do improvisations. "I'm not good at thinking on my feet," they say, or "I love working with a script but I hate to make up my own words." I understand these feelings because to some extent I share them. I need time to develop my ideas. I'm writing this book slowly, hammering out one sentence at a time, frequently tearing out a page with only three or four lines on it and inserting a clean sheet to give myself a fresh start.

If you don't want to improvise a monologue, you might feel more comfortable sitting down with a pen and paper or at a typewriter or word processor and writing one. You could easily turn any of the above improvisations into a writing exercise. For example, instead of improvising a speech to somebody you feel strongly about, you could write that person a letter that you never send. Or you could keep a journal in which you record conversations you've had with people or conversations you would *like* to have. At one point in my life, for example, when I was having difficulty communicating with my teenage son, I would write out in my journal exactly what I wanted to say to him, and when the rare moment came when we were able to talk, I was somewhat prepared by my "rehearsal." Of course something always came up that I hadn't anticipated, but the wonderful thing was that he picked up the habit himself, and sometimes when he was indignant at something I'd done, he would rip out a page of his journal, hand it to me in sullen silence, and retreat to his room. I would at long last be able to see his side, and we would be able to work things out.

• • •

Keeping a journal is a habit that can be enormously helpful even if no monologues emerge from it. When you're working on a role, try keeping a day-to-day account of your thoughts about the character, your struggles in rehearsal, your questions, doubts, and fears, your blocks and breakthroughs. Looking back over it later, you may come to understand better how you work, and you may be able to solve similar problems when they come up again, or at least take comfort in the knowledge that this too shall pass.

I also use my journal to keep a record of the auditions I do. I describe how terrible I feel when I've "blown" one or how elated when I feel I did well. I try to record exactly what I did as I prepared for the audition and during the audition itself, and that helps me to understand why some worked well for me and some didn't. I'm also able to recognize those times when it was not anything I did but rather how the auditors behaved that made for an unpleasant experience.

I also listen to the various ways I talk to myself and record what these different "inner voices" have to say. There's one voice, for example, that is always belittling me and putting me down. I call this voice C.T., that's short for Critic-Taskmaster. When I find that I am talking to myself in a disparaging way, saying such things as, "I don't really have the stature to play this role, there's no point even in going to the audition, I'd be very weak and ineffectual in it," I rewrite such a comment as a line of dialogue coming from somebody else, changing "I" to "You." For example:

CT: You don't really have the stature to do this role. Don't even bother going to the audition. You'd be so weak and ineffectual in it people would wonder how you had the gall to show up.

I find it helpful just to "listen" to such a speech objectively and realize it is expressing only one aspect of myself. Often I feel I want to respond as my reasonable self, whom I call "ME":

ME: Well, my agent submitted me for it, so *she* must think I could do it.
CT: What does she know?

ME: Well, she's been wrong before; but you know I played a role just like that once—I'd almost forgotten it—and I was very strong and forceful on stage.

I don't always argue with C.T., sometimes I just listen to him, acknowledge whatever is true in what he says, and decide how I can cope with the difficulty. Sometimes a third voice intervenes, often that of a frightened child who says something like, "I don't want to go to that audition, I'm scared!" I try to let the child have his say too. Sometimes my dialogues with C.T. go on for pages, each of us interrupting the other and trying to score a point. Often I end by telling him to shut up and stop bothering me.

• • •

Starting a journal is the easiest thing in the world. Get yourself some writing materials, sit down every day about the same time, and write. If you don't know what to write, put down that you don't know what to write. Keep "freewriting" like this, recording whatever thoughts and feelings you're experiencing at the moment. You may start a session believing that you have nothing much to say, or you may begin by describing some mundane event, and then then all of a sudden you'll discover something in the back of your mind that you very much want to write about.

Some of this material may develop into monologues, some of it may be indirectly useful to you in your career, some may be emotionally therapeutic for you, and some may have no practical use whatever. But just as you did with your reading, value everything for its own sake.

6

Creating Your Own
One-Person Show

Doing a monologue for an audition is one thing. Doing a
solo performance in a theater may seem like a different
experience altogether. But the only essential difference, aside
from the length of the presentation, is how you think of your
audience. I suggested earlier that if you could think of the
casting people at an audition not as your judges but as people
you'd like to entertain, then an audition can become a kind of
mini solo performance, valuable for its own sake and not just a
means to an end. Now I'm going to suggest how you can break
down the boundaries even further by using the same
techniques you've learned for developing audition material in
order to create your own full-length one-person show.

Of course that's not something that you *have* to do. You
can have a perfectly satisfying career as an actor without ever
spending an evening on stage by yourself. In fact the only
people crazy enough to do that seem to be driven from within
by some irresistible urge. They just can't help themselves.

Perhaps it seems narcissistic, but I think the urge can be a
healthy one. Sometimes it arises out of a fascination, an
obsession even, with a particular author or historical figure.
The classic examples are Emlyn Williams as Charles Dickens
and Hal Holbrook as Mark Twain. They have been followed
by Julie Harris as Emily Dickinson, Henry Fonda as Clarence
Darrow, James Whitmore as Will Rogers, Laurence

Luckinbill as Lyndon Johnson, Olga Bellin as Zelda
Fitzgerald, Zoe Caldwell as Lillian Hellman, and countless
others.

Sometimes the urge is simply an itch to tell a story.
Storytelling is the oldest form of solo performance—it actually
predates theater—and it has been a continuing tradition in
every culture I know of. And storytellers are not always actors.
Spalding Gray happens to be a professional actor, but
Garrison Keillor is a writer and host of a radio show; Mike
Feder is a former social worker who now makes a career out of
doing a kind of public free association about his life; Roy
Blount, Jr., is a humorist; and Laurie Anderson a performance
artist. The differences in their styles of presentation are
striking. Feder and Blount, who make no bones about being
amateurs to the stage, have a certain rough-hewn simplicity
and endearing awkwardness about them. Gray and Keillor
speak mainly in a simple, conversational tone, though
occasionally they depart from it and become almost like high
priests at a theatrical ritual, casting a spell over their audiences.
Anderson mixes music, singing, and lighting effects with her
narrations to make rather complex performance pieces.

A third stimulus to performing alone is a passion to play a
number of different characters. Ruth Draper was the first
person I know of to perform, all by herself in a single evening,
a wide range of characters of her own invention. What I have
heard of her few recordings makes me heartsick that I never
had the good fortune to see her in person. Cornelia Otis
Skinner did a similar kind of solo tour de force about the same
time. Lily Tomlin and Jane Wagner happen to be great
admirers of Draper, and their *Search for Signs of Intelligent Life
in the Universe* follows very much in her tradition. If I didn't
know better, I'd say that the work of Eric Bogosian does too,
but Bogosian appears to have developed more out of the
experimental theater of the 1970s.

• • •

If you are already possessed by one of the urges I've described, gathering material will be a simple matter. If you want to adapt the work of a favorite author, you can use exactly the same techniques I described earlier for cutting, editing, and piecing together material. If you want to tell stories or create a variety of characters, you can try some of the exercises in writing original monologues.

The big difference is that you no longer have to limit yourself to two or three minutes, you have an hour or two at your disposal. If you find that prospect daunting, I suggest you simply collect one piece at a time. That's how Wagner and Tomlin put together *Search for Signs of Intelligent Life in the Universe*; they tried out early versions of some material to invited audiences in a storefront in Los Angeles; later they toured and kept adding new pieces, getting feedback from each audience after the show. Bogosian also develops a piece at a time, sometimes improvising into a tape recorder. By the time he is ready to put a show together he has more than enough material and has to leave some of it out.

Gray develops his stories in performance. He describes how he created his first monologue, *Sex and Death to the Age 14*, in the preface to the published version: "I sat behind that desk with a little notebook containing an outline of all I could remember about sex and death until I was 14 years old. . . . The first night maybe fifteen people came to the Garage and the monologue ran about forty minutes. The next night the audience was a little larger and so was the monologue. I tape-recorded each performance, played it back the following morning and made adjustments in my outline. . . . The monologue grew to an hour and twenty minutes." Since then Gray has continued to improvise from notes and diaries. His published monologues are transcribed and edited from the tapes.

I used a somewhat similar approach in developing *Dostoevsky's Forgotten People*. I would pick an episode from a novel or story and first go over the Russian text with the help of a dictionary and my Russian tutor, the late Lydia Karakasch. When I felt I understood it well enough, I would rehearse by reading a passage silently in Russian, getting the gist of it, and then improvising my own translation out loud. I never wrote anything down, I always worked directly from the Russian text, allowing for slight changes in my English version even in performance. In the process of improvising I naturally condensed material or took a giant leap from one section of the text to another, so I was always editing and cutting. My first performance of the Marmeladov piece from *Crime and Punishment* played almost an hour, and that was already severely abridged from the Russian. Gradually I got it down to forty minutes, but as I kept adding new pieces to the program I had to cut it even further, and eventually I arrived at a version that lasted eighteen minutes. I kept developing new pieces during the three years that I performed the program, and if I had ever done all my material in a single session it would probably have lasted six to eight hours. My solution was to select for each performance those pieces I wanted to do, based in part on the particular audience I was playing to and in part on how I happened to feel that night. Sometimes I made up the program as I went along.

• • •

Once you've collected your material, your next task will be to arrange it in a particular order and provide connecting links, if needed, from one piece to another. If you're telling a story or doing a piece about somebody's life, a chronological order is natural but not inevitable; Gray and Feder occasionally jump back and forth in time. If you're playing unconnected characters, as Tomlin and Bogosian do, or presenting random fragments of an author, as I did with Dostoevsky, you'll have to experiment by trying pieces in different combinations, like playing with blocks, to see what the total effect becomes.

If you want to insert connecting links to provide continuity between the various pieces, you can deliver these as the author of the material, as one of the characters you're playing, or simply as yourself, the narrator. The tradition in adapting the work of a writer is to put on costume and makeup and pretend to be the author, as Williams did with Dickens and Holbrook with Twain. Since both those authors used to do public readings of their work, it was easy enough to pretend that the performance was one of these occasions, and the performer was able to tie the various "readings" together with a running commentary.

With other figures you may need to invent other circumstances. In adapting the writings of Zelda Fitzgerald for Olga Bellin in *Zelda*, William Luce suggested that Zelda is waiting for her psychiatrist in his office in the sanitarium and talking to herself; soon, however, she turns and addresses the audience directly, assuming that they are somehow in the office with her. Occasionally she speaks to "Scott" in her mind's eye or responds to taped voices from her past. Zelda's mind shifts abruptly from one episode in her past to another, and Luce makes no attempt to supply connecting links.

Luce used a similar device in adapting Lillian Hellman's autobiographies for Zoe Caldwell in *Lillian*. He suggested that Hellman is in a waiting room in a hospital where her lifelong lover, Dashiel Hammett, is dying. Again he has her address the audience as if they happen to be there. Occasionally, in the course of telling the story of her life, she acts out scenes between herself and Hammett or other figures from her past, playing both parts. The material is arranged more or less chronologically, and transitions from one episode to another are made quite naturally, as they would be if indeed she were talking to a stranger or group of strangers in the hospital.

Of course you don't have to impersonate anybody. Ian McKellen, in putting together an evening of selections from Shakespeare called *Acting Shakespeare*, was simply Ian McKellen. He came on in casual clothes and talked directly to the audience about his experiences acting Shakespeare. He would perform a piece, chat some more or give a brief demonstration of how he worked, and then do another piece. I found it a wonderfully refreshing experience. I decided (actually before I'd seen McKellen) on a similar approach to Dostoevsky. Despite my admiration for his work and my fascination with his life, I had little sense of the man as a person. I was loathe to put on a beard and frock coat and pretend to be somebody I'm not sure I would care to spend an hour with in private. (What on earth would we talk about? With Chekhov, by contrast, I feel I'd get along famously.) So I simply wore a black turtleneck and tweed jacket, came on carrying a complete set of Dostoevsky (in Russian), and began talking about how I became fascinated with his work. I would alternate between telling about an incident in Dostoevsky's life and playing characters from his fiction. The biographical inserts sometimes had a direct relationship to the fictional pieces that preceded or followed them and sometimes did not. Rather than provide connecting links between the pieces I simply tried to present a collage of Dostoevsky's life and works, maintaining my identity as Jack Poggi but of course slipping in and out of the various characters I played.

• • •

If you're doing an evening of storytelling your role is pretty clear: you are the storyteller. Spalding Gray never pretends to be anybody but Spalding Gray, although occasionally he will act out a dialogue between himself and another person. Mike Feder is always Mike Feder, Roy Blount is Roy Blount. There is no "conceit" here, nothing to imagine. These people are who they are, they never pretend to be anywhere but in the performing space, and they simply tell about things that really happened to them. Gray admits that sometimes his memories are "slightly embellished," but Feder claims to tell everything exactly as it was. (I take these gentlemen at their word, but I must say they seem to have had more than their fair share of bizarre experiences in life.)

Another interesting difference is that Gray keeps developing his stories until they become more or less fixed, whereas Feder tries never to tell the same story exactly the same way. Feder likens his storytelling to the free association of psychoanalysis, and he always begins with what is foremost in his mind at the moment. That will remind him of something in his past, which in turn reminds him of a third thing, and so his stories seem to follow the leaps of his consciousness, usually returning at the end to the theme he started with—a process he calls making "loops." When he repeats a story he may have vaguely in mind the series of "loops" he followed before, but he tries to describe things each time from a fresh perspective: since he has changed, he feels the story should change too. When he does a story for the first time he may write out a brief outline, but then he throws the outline away. He says there were times when he went on the air at WBAI, where he first began telling stories, without the slightest notion of what he was going to say. By his steadfast refusal to "enhance" his stories in any way or to repeat what worked before, Feder achieves a level of spontaneity that professional actors may well envy.

Feder could legitimately claim, like Polonius in *Hamlet*, to "use no art at all." Garrison Keillor may seem to make the same claim, but don't believe him for a moment. As the host of the radio show, "A Prairie Home Companion," he is who he really is, but the stories he tells are an intriguing blend of familiar realistic detail and fantastical invention. I find it astonishing that he is able to spin such fanciful tales with no apparent premeditation. The differences between an extemporaneous speech and one that has been written down and memorized become pretty obvious to anybody who listens carefully to both, although a consummate actor can sometimes fool you, and to my ear Keillor's pieces certainly sound improvised. Perhaps he has some kind of scenario in his head, but I remember several nights towards the end of the run of his weekly show when I would have sworn that he had gone on the air, like Feder, totally unprepared. He is also like Feder in that frequently he starts off on one subject, goes off on a tangent, then on a tangent from that and so on, but with Keillor I'm not always sure he's going to find his way back. At times he seems genuinely to have forgotten where he is or where he's headed, and those moments are gripping. To be lost in the middle of an improvisation is a terrifying experience for a performer, and can be unnerving to an audience that senses what is happening—it's like watching a high-wire artist teeter at fifty feet above the ground—but often what follows is a stroke of brilliant invention. (At least it does if you're as gifted as Keillor.)

• • •

If you're playing a number of different characters, and you have not established yourself either as the author or the narrator, you may want one of your characters to tie the pieces together. Trudy the bag lady performs this function in *Search for Signs of Intelligent Life in the Universe*, often commenting on the other characters. Also Tomlin sometimes becomes just "Lily" addressing the audience. Transitions between one character sketch and another are marked by sound and light changes.

Eric Bogosian makes no attempt at continuity. He is *never* himself on stage; he is a Bowery bum or a manic disk jockey or a Texas cowboy or a Harlem drug addict or a death-row convict or the proprietor of a Greek restaurant. On television he sometimes deigns to make a slight change of costume, but on stage he goes swiftly from one character to another, without even a sound or light cue, and the changes are breathtaking to watch. Here is how he describes his approach in the preface to *Drinking in America*:

Individually the characters might be repulsive, unnerving, pathetic or melodramatic, but taken together a larger picture could be seen. Like a collage. ... I had enjoyed watching performers like Andy Kaufman and John Wood make lightning changes during a performance, but disliked the presence of the

> performer "himself." So I just cut out all the in-between stuff. Like you were turning channels: first this guy, then that guy. Fragments. Chunks of personality. There was no need for me to be up there.

Bogosian is a very different kind of actor from Spalding Gray: he is never himself on stage and Gray seldom pretends to be anybody else. I have enormous respect for both ways of working, but as an actor myself I lean very much towards the second. I always like to work out of my own "center," and although I'm capable of assuming beliefs and attitudes that are alien to me, I'm not very good at impersonating people whose speech patterns and body language are markedly different from my own. If you want to learn from a master character actor, go see Bogosian. If you want to see how much artistry can exist in a performance without impersonation, go see Gray.

• • •

Once you have your material selected and arranged, how do you go about getting your show produced? Probably the same way you created it: by yourself. That may sound like quite a challenge, but one of the great advantages of solo performance is that you are free to do your own thing. You don't have to wait for somebody to write the ideal role for you, you can create it yourself. You don't have to get an agent to submit you or a casting director to call you in for a reading, you cast yourself in it. You don't have to suffer the imperfections of other actors, there are no other actors. You don't even have to submit to the will of a director (unless of course you want to, and then you can pick your own); you can do your own blocking, make your own interpretations. You can design your own sets and costumes and lighting if you like, or you can pick designers with whom you feel compatible.

You don't even have to raise a lot of money. How much does it cost to costume yourself and pick up a few pieces of furniture and some props? Of course you have to have a place to work and an audience willing to listen to you. But you can start anywhere, in your own living room with a few friends if you like. You may be able to get yourself connected with a group that has a space, however small and remote. Bogosian started by going to work at The Kitchen, a loft in Soho, "as low man on the totem pole (a step up from gofer)." Gray began about as far off Broadway as you can get with his own group, the Wooster Group, at the Performing Garage. Tomlin and Wagner just invited people to come in off the street and watch some of their early work.

I tried out my Dostoevsky material at meetings of my fellow actors in Actors Alliance. I also experimented on my students at C. W. Post Center of Long Island University, letting them off work in exchange for listening to me and giving me feedback. My first public performances were produced by Actors Alliance in a school auditorium on West 60th Street that we got for free in exchange for conducting workshops for the students. Later I performed in a tiny second-floor studio of a brownstone called "The Troupe" on West 39th Street. Andy Milligan, the proprietor, lived on the fourth floor and had another small theater on the first, and a costume and prop shop on the third. Andy let me use the space for free in exchange for the meager box-office receipts. I made nothing, of course, but Andy probably spent more for rent and utilities than he took in. Even when I got a grant from the New York Council for the Humanities, my budget for space was still zero: I give free performances in public libraries throughout the five boroughs of New York City. I designed and built my own set, including a table that I could take apart and reassemble, and traveled with it in the back of my Honda hatchback.

• • •

Perhaps, like Bogosian and Gray and Feder, you will create solo performances that will get you rave reviews in *The New York Times* and induce agents and casting directors to call you up and plead with you on the phone. But I think that's the last reason why you should set out to do a one-person show. If you're not motivated primarily by a passion for the work itself, the work probably won't be any good. And you won't be able to sustain the hard labor and endure the anguish that it takes to get the work together. I don't see doing solo performances as a means to a career in the commercial theater, but rather as an alternative to it.

To be quite frank, I don't even see auditioning as a means to a career in theater. It's something you have to do, of course, and occasionally you may get work as a result, but chances are that ninety-nine percent of your auditions will bring about no immediate discernible benefit. That's why I have been saying all along that you need to look at an audition primarily as an opportunity for a satisfying performing experience. Any practical benefits will be cumulative and long-term. In short, *all* work should be for its own sake.

If fame and fortune are all that you want in the theater, you probably will never get them. Or if you do, you'll be miserable. Why be miserable? Enjoy your life. Enjoy acting—wherever and whenever you can. If somebody decides one day to pay you a lot of money and put your name up on a Broadway marquee or above the title of a Hollywood blockbuster, fine, you just might allow that. But cherish the work first.

Part Two:

REHEARSING

7

Improvising on the Content

Let's say that (finally) you have in front of you the text of a monologue that you want to work on for an audition, class, or solo performance. Or maybe you have just been handed the script of a role you have been cast in, and you find, to your mixed terror and delight, that you have a speech two and a half pages long. How do you begin?

First read the speech silently and try to make the content vivid and "real" to you. Let the words evoke pictures and images in your mind. Try to "see" each thing the character is talking about—almost as if you're making a film of the monologue. If the speech contains concrete images, such as "We shall see the sky all diamonds" (from Chekhov's *Uncle Vanya*) your task will be fairly easy. But even a more abstract statement, "You've never loved me, you only played at being in love with me" (from Ibsen's *A Doll's House*), may suggest some kind of image, however vague—such as a grown-up man playing a kind of "love-game" on a school playground—or perhaps a fleeting memory of somebody who once treated you that way or even *might* have treated you that way. Go through the whole speech this way, letting the words suggest the reality that lies behind them.

Now put the text down and do an improvisation in which you try to convey, more or less in your own words, as much of the content of the monologue as you happen to remember. If you're working with a group (always an advantage with these exercises), pick an individual to address or talk to the group at large; if you're working alone, imagine the presence of somebody you know in your own life. Don't try to "act," just deliver the sense of the monologue as if you really meant it. And don't struggle to remember every detail—this is not a memory test, it's more like an artist's rough sketch. Just convey whatever stuck in your mind from that first reading as best you can.

Now pick the text up again and read the monologue silently a second time. You may realize that you left out certain sections, misunderstood others, or got some things out of sequence. Pay particular attention to those sections: try to get clearer "pictures" of them or more meaningful associations.

Put the text down and improvise a second time. If you happen to remember some of the text and feel like using it, fine, go ahead, but don't force yourself to use the exact words. So long as you have a clear sense of *what* you want to say, you can use your own words, the author's, or some combination of the two.

Keep alternating between silent reading of the text and improvising aloud till you can convey the content of the whole monologue in some detail and with some assurance. You may find that after a few times you have memorized the speech word for word without even trying. That's fine—this exercise is great for learning lines. But that is not its main purpose. The purpose is to force you to grasp the content before you find the words to express it, just as we do in life. First we are aware, however dimly, of what we want to say (we may "see" it or "feel" it or have a "sense" of it), and *then* we find the words that will best convey it. The great advantage of improvisation is that it allows you to follow this natural process. You may have noticed that your first improvisation was quite spontaneous. Try to keep that feeling always of "making it up." If, as you get closer to the text, you find yourself repeating the words mechanically, try to refocus your attention back to the pictures, pretend you don't know the words, and start out *as if* you are going to improvise.

In other words, trick yourself. One of the greatest inhibitions to acting is the obligation we feel to the words, the fear that we'll forget them or not speak them the way they're "supposed" to be spoken. Telling yourself that you are *not* going to use the text is similar to the remedies prescribed by some therapists for sexual inhibitions: couples are told to show affection by kissing and fondling but under no circumstances to have intercourse. (Of course, if after a time, you can't help yourself . . .)

• • •

I call this exercise "words and pictures." You may recognize it as a form of what many acting teachers call "sense memory." In your silent reading of the text you may "hear," "smell," "taste," and "touch" things as well as "see" them, but I single out the sense of sight because for me (and for most actors I've worked with) a visual image is the easiest way to grasp a thought in what might be called its "pre-verbal" stage. However, images do not work for everybody. Some actors seem to grasp ideas more readily through verbal cues, such as "key words." Still others tend to pick up on the "flow" or "movement" of a speech. My wife, who has a very strong kinesthetic sense, tells me that she grasps the sense of a speech by feeling as if she is "moving" through it, and I don't understand that at all because I don't think that way. I worked with one actor who discovered that the best way for him to learn a speech was to turn it into a song.

The point is to grasp, by whatever method works best for you, the thoughts that lie behind the words and give rise to them. If you also get a kind of visceral sense of the *feeling* of the speech, so much the better. As Stanislavski taught us all, sense memory tends to evoke "affective" or emotional memory. For example, recalling the sunlight filtering through the curtains of a hospital window on a particular occasion may bring back the feeling of grief that you experienced then.

• • •

But I would like to take our work beyond both sensory and affective memory. I suggest that you ask yourself not only "What was I feeling in the past?" but also "What exactly do I, as the character, want to express here and now?"

Quite often the two questions will lead to different, even opposite answers. Let me illustrate by quoting a monologue that has been done so often in classes and auditions that it has become a kind of "classic": Lila's "roses" speech from William Inge's *A Loss of Roses*. (It's funny, nobody ever does the play any more, but the monologue is done all the time.)

LILA: I remember *my* first day of school. Mother took me by the hand and *I* carried a bouquet of roses, too. Mama had let me pick the loveliest roses I could find in the garden, and the teacher thanked me for them. Then Mama left me and I felt kinda scared, 'cause I'd never been anyplace before without her; but she told me Teacher would be Mama to me at school, and would treat me just as nice as she did. So I took my seat with all the other kids, their faces so strange and new to me. And I started talking with a little boy across the aisle. I din know it was against the rules. But Teacher came back and slapped me, so hard that I cried, and I ran to the door 'cause I wanted to run home to Mama quick as I could. But Teacher grabbed me by the hand and pulled me back to my seat. She said I was too big a girl to be running home to Mama and I had to learn to take my punishment when I broke the rules. But I still cried. I told Teacher I wanted back my roses. But she wouldn't give them to me. She shook her finger and said, when I gave away lovely presents, I couldn't expect to get them back ... I guess I never learned that lesson very well. There's so many things I still want back.

I have often seen this speech done as if the actress is trying to "relive" as fully as possible all the terror, pain, and anger

that Lila experienced when she was six. I know that many acting teachers tell their students to do just that, but the attempt
often results in a kind of stage cliché. I begin to wonder why
Lila is working so hard to suffer all that agony all over again—
what is she, some kind of masochist? Or perhaps she forgot
what happened, she is making such an effort to dredge it up.
But the most unsettling thing is the realization that the actress
is so far into her private world that she seems totally unaware
of where she is, who she's talking to, or why she's telling the
story. If she behaved like that in my living room I would reach
for the phone and dial 911.

In life when we talk about the past we need make no effort
to "recreate" it. It already exists, and we simply tell *about* it. Of
course as an actor you may need to take some time at first to
make Lila's past experience vivid and "real" to you—that's the
whole point of the words and pictures exercise. But then you
can just assume that all that has *already* happened and give
yourself over to the task of communicating what the character
wishes to communicate in the present. What that is depends of
course on the immediate context out of which the speech arises. What makes you want to tell this story here and now? Is
there a point you want to make with it? In the play Lila has
given in, the night before, to the sexual importunings of a
young man, out of a mistaken sense of "generosity." This
morning she realizes that once again, as so often in the past,
she has let herself be used by a man. Sitting on the front porch
with a friend, she sees a young girl on her way to school, and
the sight prompts her to say how foolish she has been all her
life to give away what she can never have back.

If you place yourself in Lila's present situation, you will
probably want to tell the story as a way of expressing your regret, a regret that is perhaps tinged with irony, for your lost
innocence. As you tell the story shades of other feelings from
the past—the fear of the unknown, the sting of the slap, the
fury at the teacher—may still hover in the air and may glow
with life for a moment, but spontaneously, not because you
conjured them up. And they will be transformed and integrat-

ed from the perspective of the present. Things that were painful then might even seem funny now, as when you tell how you demanded your roses back.

Just before telling the story, try to focus on the point that Lila wants to make by it. There are a number of ways of doing that. The simplest is to repeat silently a one-sentence summary of the gist of the speech. In this case you might use what Lila herself says at the end, "I guess I never learned that lesson very well; there's so many things I still want back." That sentence conveys the main feeling that Lila sets out to express: regret that once again she has acted so foolishly. If the words in themselves don't stir up that feeling for you, you might try beginning the speech by picturing the shining face of that other little girl on her way to her first day of school and realizing that you can never be like that again. Or you might try imagining what it would be like if you had stupidly given away something precious that you can never recover; it doesn't have to be literally roses or even your virginity, it could be anything dear that you have given away irrevocably: suppose, for example, that you had pushed your lover into the arms of your best friend, or had given up your child for adoption. One final way to grasp the essence of a speech before embarking on the first sentence is to "see" it as a single dominant image, perhaps something like the face of a little girl as she reaches out for roses that are being drawn away from her. You may need to experiment until you find what works best for you, and if that wears out for you after a while you can always try something else. Nobody can tell you ahead of time what will work for you. And once you have found something that works, never tell anybody else what it is.

• • •

If you're working on a fairly long monologue, doing the words and pictures exercise for the whole thing at once may be more than you can manage. You may want to break the speech down into parts and work on one part at a time. Let's use as an example a speech from Sam Shepard's *Suicide in Bb.* Louis and Pablo are detectives investigating the case of a famous jazz musician who may or may not have been murdered. I have broken the speech down into four parts by drawing a line across the page at points where I feel Louis starts out on a new tack, and I have written a key word or phrase in the margin to identify each part. I have also enclosed in brackets Pablo's lines and those of Louis that I would cut.

LOUIS: **I have a theory. Do you wanna hear it?**

[PABLO: (*Pausing, catches his breath.*) What theory?]
(PIANO PLAYER *begins to play, accompanying* LOUIS *as he speaks.* PABLO *keeps going through the papers, half listening to* LOUIS.)

LOUIS: (*Piano behind.*) **A boy hears sound. He hears sound before he has a name. He hears gurgling, pounding underwater. He hears an ocean of blood swimming around him. Through his veins. Through his mother. He breaks into the light of day. He's shocked that he has a voice. He finds his voice and screams. He hears it screaming as though coming down through ancient time. Like it belongs to another body. He hears it that way. He hears the crack of his own flesh. His own heart. His skin sliding on rubber mats. Squeaking. He hears his own bones growing. Stretching his skin in all directions. Bones moving out. Organs expanding. The sound of cells booming through his brain like tiny intergalactic missiles. Atoms. Nuclear rushes of wind through his nose holes. Toenails rubbing blankets in the dark. Books falling on pianos. Electricity humming even when the lights are off. Internal combustion engines. Turbo jets.** Then one day he hears what they call music. He hears what they call "music" in the same way he hears what they call "noise." In the same stream. Music as an extension of sound. An organization. Another way of putting it. He's disappointed. He's disappointed and exhilarated at the same time. Exhilarated because he sees an opening. An adventure. A way inside. He sees that putting any two things together pro-

Margin notes: ① Sensitive to sounds — in womb — at birth — in crib ② sound = music

duces sound. Any two things. Striking, plucking, blowing, rubbing, dropping, kicking, kissing. Any two
things. He has a revelation. Or rather, a revelation
presents itself. Stabs at him. Enters into him and becomes part of his physiology. His physiognomy. His
psychology. His paraphernalia. His makeup. He puts it
to use. He's driven toward it in a way most men consider dangerous and suicidal. His production is abundant.
Nonstop. Endlessly winding through un-heard-of-
before symphonies. Concertos beyond belief. He orga-
nizes quintets. Soloists rush to him just to be in his
presence. The best ones are rejected. He only takes on
apprentices. He only plays nightclubs although he
could pack out the Garden in a flash. He shakes the
sidewalks with his compositions. Every city in the world
is calling his name. He invents totally new chord pro-
gressions and scales. New names for notes that not
even the Chinese have heard of. Instruments that he
makes in the bathtub. His music is sweeping the country. And then one day he disappears. Just like that. He
goes. Not dead. Just gone. No one can figure it. Rumors are spread that he's kidnapped. Abducted and tak-
en to Sweden. Then it switches to murder. Talk of him
being involved with particular ladies of particular gentlemen. Then his body is found. His body is found but
his face is blown off. His fingerprints are tested and
they check out completely. His one-of-a-kind fingerprints. The case is closed.

[PABLO: (*Short pause, still looking through papers.*) Is that it?
LOUIS: No.
PABLO: There's more?
LOUIS: Yes.
PABLO: Well what is it?]

LOUIS: He's fooled them all.

[PABLO: How do you mean?]

LOUIS: He's just laying low.

Like so much of Shepard's writing, the language here is highly evocative, not only of sights and sounds, but also of vague, dream-like feelings, half-forgotten fragments of some uncertain past. I wouldn't worry too much about what all this "means"; it may mean different things to different people, and anyway that's the critic's concern, not the actor's. Go instead for the plain sense of what Louis is saying here: he has a theory about what happened to the jazz musician. I think you'll see that the theory consists of four assumptions, which are set out in the four sections of my breakdown, and a conclusion, stated in the very last sentence. The argument could be summarized as follows:

1. Suppose that a boy is born with an extraordinary sensitivity to sound.

2. Then suppose he makes the great discovery that *any* kind of sound can be performed as music.

3. He has a highly successful career doing this.

4. And then one day (possibly because success was too much for him?) he disappears and goes into hiding.

Conclusion: He isn't really dead, "He's just laying low."

You might want to break the speech down differently, but for the sake of demonstration, let's use my four-part analysis. First read section one silently, from the beginning through "Turbo jets." Try to make the content vivid and real, put the text down, and paraphrase as much as you can remember. You may well find that even this one part of the speech is too much for you to grasp at once. If you find yourself struggling to remember what comes next, try breaking down this section into subsections. Notice that Louis describes first the sounds the boy hears from inside the womb, second the scream he hears at the moment of his birth, and third all the sounds he hears as an infant lying in his crib. Work on each of these subsections separately, and then try all of the first section together.

When you have a fair grasp of the first section, go ahead

to the second (again subdividing if necessary), and then the third and fourth. Remember you're not trying to memorize the words, you're just trying to get a clear sense of the content. And now comes the moment of truth: try an improvisation in which you touch upon the main ideas of the whole speech in sequence. That may seem like an awful lot, but actually all you have to remember are a few key words or phrases:

1. sounds in womb, at birth, in crib

2. sound = music

3. success

4. disappearance

   Conclusion: laying low

As long as you have the general sense of where you're headed you can say anything you like. You can use some of the examples within each section and leave others out. Or you can invent your own examples. You don't have to worry about forgetting your lines, you haven't learned them yet. Anyway, if you understand Louis' theory, what is there to forget? Even if you memorized the speech and then went up on it in the middle of a performance, you could easily improvise your way out of the jam.

If this were a real situation, Louis would have no more in mind before he opens his mouth than the vague outline of his theory. He could, if he wanted, present the whole thing in four well-chosen sentences. Why then does he go on and on? I think he's improvising, spinning variations on a theme, playing "riffs" like the jazz musician he's talking about. All the more reason to approach the speech through your own improvisation. Even after you've memorized the text you should keep a sense of playful improvisation, pretending to find all these wonderful words as you go along.

On the page the words look so intimidating. There are so *many* of them. My teacher, Mira Rostova, used to say, "If anybody ever handed us in the morning the script of everything we were going to say that day we'd never get out of bed." But of course we manage. And the reason we manage is that we *like* talking. And what could be more fun than to talk as well as Shepard's people?

• • •

When you break a speech down like this and try to make everything vivid and real to you, there's a danger of getting bogged down in detail. You need to start out knowing where you are headed and keep moving, however slowly, towards the conclusion. To get a feeling of the movement of the speech, it might be helpful to try an improvisation that follows a similar structure. For example, Louis' speech reminds me very much of the kind of speech we have heard over and over again in detective movies of the 1930s and 1940s. At the end of the film Humphrey Bogart, or somebody like him, presents the "theory" that solves the whole case. It usually goes something like this:

Let's just suppose here for a minute that there's a dame who has a grudge against her husband. Pretends to adore the sap, but secretly she can't wait to ditch him. Suppose she hops a plane to Frisco. Buys herself a lot of new duds. Goes to a beauty saloon and has her hair dyed. Redoes her makeup, her fingernails, her whole personality. She checks into the St. Francis under an assumed name, starts an affair with the bellhop. Has the time of her life. Then does herself all over again and comes back to Chicago looking just the way she did when she left, and nobody is the wiser. Her hubby thinks she's been off visiting her sister in Cranston, Rhode Island. And all of a sudden this San Francisco bellhop shows up at the front door—out of uniform of course—whips out a .45 and blows away her old man. The cops pick him up and grill him, he breaks down and spills everything, tries to implicate the dame, but she proves conclusively it's a case of mistaken identity. No resemblance at all. Her sister in Cranston backs her alibi completely. She's free and clear. The case is closed.

And then, turning to Mary Astor (or somebody like her), he adds, "Isn't that what really happened, sister? Only you forgot one thing. You forgot that tiny little birthmark on the inside of your right thigh. Didn't think I noticed that, did you, doll?"

Can't you just *hear* Bogart doing the Shepard speech? Talk about an ideal role! What a shame he never lived to play it. Of course I'm not suggesting that you imitate Bogart or anybody else. But if you're doing a speech that's a parody—and whatever other reverberations Shepard's language sets off in our heads, surely the echo of the thirties movie detective is among them—it may help you to know what you are parodying. Improvising on a parallel theme will also help you to capture the flow of the speech, the way that Louis keeps moving relentlessly, even while he is spinning endless variations on each of the four steps of his argument, towards the inevitable (and brilliant) conclusion. What motivates Louis is the desire to show how *wise* he is. Maybe he saw a few Bogart movies himself.

• • •

Now that you've done these preliminary improvisations, getting the text down word for word should come easily to you. Use whatever method works best for you: some actors like to cover the text with an index card and slide the card down the page a sentence at a time, some put the monologue on tape and listen back to it, some write it out. However you work, I suggest that you memorize backwards: that is, commit the conclusion and section four to memory first. Then memorize section three and run three and four in sequence. Then two, three, and four, and so on. It may seem like an odd approach, but every actor I've suggested it to tells me it makes the process go more quickly and with less anxiety. Once you know the ending you are always heading towards familiar territory and reinforcing what you already know. If you were to start from the beginning, you would have all that unfamiliar ground in front of you, and that can be scary. As one actor put it, he prefers to clamber up a mountain from the bottom rather than slide down into what seems an abyss.

• • •

When you're working on a monologue by yourself, set aside fifteen to thirty minutes a day, the same time every day, to practice some of the exercises I've suggested here. Regular short rehearsals are usually more productive than infrequent lengthy ones. Besides, if you wait till you have an hour or two at your disposal, you may wait forever! You may be surprised at how quickly the monologue takes shape. I have known actors to get a monologue ready for an audition within twenty-four hours by using only the techniques described so far.

When you're doing a first rehearsal of a play with a company, or a cold reading for an audition, you can probably find a few minutes ahead of time to practice the words and pictures exercise and, if necessary, break a long monologue down into manageable chunks. If you can also come up with a one-sentence summary, a single dominant image, or a parallel improvisation, that may help you get a clear sense of the whole. Having that whole in mind, you can embark on the first sentence knowing where you are headed. You will have a kind of nonverbal sense of what you want to say, and when you need to find the words to express it, you can glance down at the paper and come up with them. To quote Mira Rostova again: "Don't be a slave to the words: they are there to serve you, not the other way around."

8

Finding the Structure
of the Speech

In both monologues that we've just examined, the speaker keeps heading towards a point that is made in the very last sentence. Are all monologues like that? Not at all. In the first place not every monologue conveys just one idea. Sometimes, if we have nothing in particular to say, we ramble on from one topic to another. Sometimes we set out in one direction and then stop and reverse ourselves. We may start to deny an accusation, for example, realize that there is some truth to the charge, and then admit to it. Or we may get caught up in expressing a feeling and then suddenly become aware that we are acting inappropriately, perhaps boring or offending the listener, and so we back off and apologize. A good example of the latter is the Gurney piece in which the businessman gets carried away while dictating a letter.

Even when we stick with one thought, we may express the whole thought in the very first sentence and then develop the idea. Or we may finish developing the thought, realize that we haven't expressed it fully enough, and set out to restate it, perhaps with additional examples. As we saw in one of the exercises for writing original monologues, it's possible to place a kind of one-sentence summary statement at the beginning, in the middle, or at the end of a monologue. But you won't always find a summary or topic sentence in the text itself: often the point of a monologue is implied rather than stated.

Every monologue has its own unique structure. And yet on paper they all look alike: a string of words running continuously across the page, with only an occasional guidepost, such as a paragraph break, an ellipsis (. . .), or a stage direction to alert us to the stops and turning points. As an actor you need to be able to uncover the underlying structure of a text.

• • •

If you find yourself struggling with a speech, try writing a brief one-sentence summary of the main idea that the character sets out to convey. Pick a sentence out of the text or make one up. Then mark with a double slash (//) the first place in the text at which the character has completed that idea. If the speaker starts up again, perhaps to repeat or develop the idea, perhaps to embark on a whole new thought, mark with another double slash the next point of completion. These are the places at which you could conceivably stop, having made your point. If in fact you were to cut the speech at that place, it would make perfect sense, but if you cut it off any earlier it would seem to dangle in mid air.

In both Lila's and Louis' monologues, for example, the idea they set out to convey is not really completed until the very last sentence, and so the double slash would be appropriate only at the end of the speech. With Louis' speech we found it helpful to break the text up into manageable chunks and attach key words to each, but none of these chunks is complete in itself.

With some speeches, however, a point of completion is reached in the middle of the text. Let's look at a monologue from Edward Albee's *Who's Afraid of Virginia Woolf?* George and Martha are in the middle of a knock-down, drag-out marital brawl. Martha has just accused George of taking a kind of masochistic pleasure in the abuse she dishes out, and George has been trying to make the point that Martha is, as he says, "deluded."

GEORGE: I'm numbed enough . . . and I don't mean by liquor, though maybe that's been part of the process—a gradual, over-the-years going to sleep of the brain cells—I'm numbed enough, now, to be able to take you when we're alone. I don't listen to you . . . or when I *do* listen to you, I sift everything, I bring everything down to reflex response, so I don't really *hear* you, which is the only way to manage it. But you've taken a new tack, Martha, over the past couple of centuries—or however long it's been I've lived in this house with you—that makes it just too much . . . too much. I don't mind your dirty underthings in public . . . well, I *do* mind, but I've reconciled myself to that . . . but you've moved bag and baggage into your own fantasy world now, and you've started playing variations on your own distortions, and, as a result . . .

In this case we can arrive at a one-sentence summary just by doing some editing. If we cut out all of George's circumlocutions, the speech could be reduced to read: "I'm numbed enough now to be able to take you when we're alone, but you've taken a new tack lately that makes it too much." If we wanted to reduce that even further, to a kind of gut level, it might be something like "I can't take it any more!" or "I've had it!"

The impulse for the speech originates of course at the gut level. But before he can say that he's had it, George seems to want to establish that until now he *has* been able to take it, thus making Martha's recent behavior appear all the more insufferable. In the first sentence he seems to be saying, in effect, "Don't underestimate me, I'm not thin-skinned, I'm capable of shutting out an awful lot of crap." In the second sentence he says *how* he shuts her out—by not listening. Only in the third sentence does he finally arrive at the point: Martha has changed and now it's "too much . . . too much." On the way towards this point George keeps going off on detours, qualifying what he has just said, explaining it, giving examples, but all the while he is headed towards saying it's "too much," and so that's the first place in the speech that I would mark with a double slash.

In other words, at the time that he opens his mouth to speak George *already* has in mind to say that Martha is "too much," and if you tried to cut the speech at any time before that, both you and your listeners would have a sense of something left unfinished.

Where is the next place where George could conceivably stop? There isn't one. Beginning with "I don't mind your dirty underthings in public," he again seems to anticipate a possible misunderstanding, then he adds another qualification ("well, I *do* mind . . . ") and he seems to be heading towards saying again that Martha has gone over the edge and is now impossible to take. But he never makes it all the way home this time, because Martha interrupts him with a succinct "Nuts!" If she hadn't, he might have completed the last sentence by saying "and as a result I can't take it anymore!" In that case we could have added a second double slash, but even then there would be no guarantee that George wouldn't start up again.

I call the point at which the double slash occurs a "full rest." It's a bit like the point in a song where the melodic line comes back to the first note of the scale. One has a sense of completion: the melody might start up again, or it might not. Of course there are other points where you can pause, but if you were to stop altogether, your listeners would find it rather odd. The difference lies not so much in the length of the pause as in what you do *before* the pause. Certain choices make it clear that you are moving on, others that you have made your point. There is yet a third kind of choice: one that makes it clear that you are finished for good, that you have no intention of starting up again. I'm not sure if that's what Pinter means by his stage direction "silence," which he uses sometimes instead of "pause," but I like to use that term to describe that kind of moment. The distinction between a "full rest" and a "silence" is quite subtle: with the former you might or might not go on; with the latter you are definitely finished. (I suggest using a triple slash if you want to indicate a "silence.")

• • •

There are very definite practical uses for this kind of textual analysis. Focusing on the structure of a speech is another way, like the words and pictures exercise, of getting your attention off the words and onto the content. You might want to make a kind of "outline" of George's speech, using key words. You could do that a number of different ways, but one way might look like this:

> numbed enough (not liquor)
>> don't listen
>>> changed . . . *too much//*
> not dirty underwear (actually yes)
>> bag and baggage
>>> result: CAN'T TAKE IT!//

Another technique, already mentioned in examining Lila's speech from *A Loss of Roses*, is simply to repeat your one-sentence summary silently before you start. This technique is particularly useful when you must launch into a speech out of context at an audition. You could picture "Martha" in front of you, say silently, "Martha, I've had it! Now don't misunderstand me. . . . [*and then aloud*] I'm numbed enough . . . and I don't mean by liquor . . . " and so on into the speech.

For some actors, however, one-sentence summaries and key words are not very helpful. They tend to think more creatively in images than in verbal abstractions. One very imaginative actor I worked with found his own unique way to grasp the structure of the monologue from Horton Foote's *Valentin'e Day* reproduced on the cover of this book: he pictured the woman whose love has brought him happiness for the first time standing quite prominently in the foreground of a kind of "cyclorama": in the background there was a circular series of images from his past: the mother killing the chickens, himself lying in bed sick, and so on; these images curved around in a spiral leading back to the central figure. In this way he was able to grasp both the whole and the parts simultaneously without any verbal analysis of the speech.

Use anything that helps you embark on the speech with your destination in mind and some sense, however vague, of the route that might take you there. It's like having a kind of "map" in your mind, but the map is not the territory. You may find yourself "lost" at times, or going off on detours. George doesn't know ahead of time, for example, that he's going to insert all those qualifying remarks, it's just that it keeps occurring to him in mid-sentence that he might be misunderstood. Also, as I can't say often enough, *he doesn't know the words yet.* Take your time, discover how you can make yourself clear, find satisfaction in the discovery of each telling phrase and apt example. You can pause as often and as long as you need to, and so long as you keep a sense of heading somewhere, the pauses will hold.

Understanding where you're headed will also prevent you from making too much of a preliminary remark. The words "dirty underthings in public," for example, might tempt you to express great disdain, but actually George wants to say that this is the kind of thing he can take in stride. It would be somewhat like a cynical, burnt-out high-school teacher saying, "I'm numbed enough . . . and I don't mean by twenty years in the classroom . . . though maybe that's part of the process, all that chalk dust in my veins . . . I'm numbed enough to put up with the obscenities on the walls, I don't mind the falling plaster and the turgid textbooks, the knifings and rapes I can close my eyes to, but this new hotshot principal is too much! I can't take it any more, I'm getting out!"

• • •

Here is an example of a speech with a very different kind of structure. It's the opening monologue of Chekhov's *Three Sisters.*

OLGA: It was just one year ago today that Father died, the fifth of May, your birthday, Irina. It was cold then, and snowing. I thought I'd never live through it, you were lying on the floor in a dead faint. But now look, a year has passed and we can think about it easily, here you are in a white dress, your face shining. (*The clock strikes twelve.*) And the clock struck then too. (*Pause.*) I remember when they carried Father away, music was playing, and they fired a salute over his grave. He was a general, a brigade commander, but still not many people came. Of course it was raining then. Heavy rain mixed with snow.

[IRINA: Why think about it?]

OLGA: Today it's warm, we can keep the windows open, though the birches haven't come out yet. Father took command of the brigade and left Moscow with us eleven years ago, and I remember distinctly at this time in Moscow, at the beginning of May, everything was in blossom, it was warm, all flooded with sunshine. Eleven years have gone by, and I remember everything just as if we left yesterday. My God! This morning I woke up, I saw a mass of light, I saw the Spring, and joy stirred in my heart, and I wanted so much to be back home.

What exactly does Olga set out to say here? The words can easily mislead you. The very first sentence on the page looks like a statement of fact. Olga appears to be informing her sisters of the date of their father's death. But why on earth should she do that? Surely they were there too, and they can hardly have forgotten that it happened just one year ago today, on Irina's birthday.

Olga must intend to convey with those words not the facts but some feeling. What feeling is it? Many actresses who attempt this speech assume that it has to be grief. Olga does go on to describe the events of that day in rather vivid detail. Surely she must be back there in her mind, experiencing everything she went through. And so the actress, especially if she has been well schooled in "reliving the past," tries to do just that. A one-sentence summary of what she sets out to say, whether she realizes it or not, would read "Wasn't it awful the day that father died!" or "I can't endure the pain!"

You might want to experiment to see what happens when the speech is approached that way. Try to feel as sad as you possibly can. Maybe imagine somebody you love lying in a coffin. Feel that wet, cold snow on your face, picture Irina on the floor, really believe that you cannot possibly go on living. If you are successful, you may find yourself deeply moved, tears may even stream down your cheeks, and the first few sentences may go well for you. But then, all of a sudden, you have to say, "But look, a year has passed and we can think about it easily." How can you possibly say that sentence? You would have to contradict everything you have just been acting.

Let's look for a moment at the larger context out of which the speech arises. Years ago three young women lived an exciting and promise-filled life in Moscow. Then they were uprooted to this dull little village with streets of mud, where there's nothing to do and nobody to talk to, and all they can hope for is that one day their father will be transferred back to Moscow. Meanwhile they try to keep going, but Olga hates her job teaching school, she knows that at 29 she is already past marriageable age, and Irina sleeps all morning and does absolutely nothing with her life, and Masha, a woman of enormous passion, is married to an excruciating bore, and their brother Andrei is betraying all his early promise, and then one morning they wake up and find their dear father, the single source of meaning and hope in their lives, lying cold in his bed. They must have reached a point, Olga in particular, at which life really *stopped*. It was no longer possible to go on living. But somehow the sisters do go on, and gradually the past recedes and then one morning a year later Olga looks out the window and sees that "mass of light," the birches about to burst into leaf; she feels the warm air streaming through the sunlit curtains, and suddenly it occurs to her, to her utter astonishment, that life is starting up again.

Of course she still grieves for her father. But the dominant feeling, the one that possesses her at the moment and seeks to find expression in words, is not grief. And it's not joy either. I think it's wonder. The speech is not about how awful it was then, not about how great it is now, but about how incredibly *different* it is. A one-sentence summary might read, "Strange! . . . life is stirring again!"

If we take Olga's first sentence, "It was just one year ago today that Father died, the fifth of May, your birthday, Irina," not as a statement of fact, not as a cry of grief, but as an expression of wonder, that in itself would convey the whole idea: such a short time, and so much has changed! If Olga were to stop here, I feel the thought would be complete, and so I would place a double slash at this point. However, Olga has only stated the theme, as a composer might in the opening bars of an orchestral work; she hasn't really developed it yet, and so she goes on to give some examples of how it was then and how it is now.

Where is the next place she could stop? When she says it was cold and snowing? When she recalls Irina lying on the floor in a dead faint? I don't think so. Even while she is saying these things she *already* has in mind to say that today is warm and sunny and Irina looks quite radiant. This is one whole idea, not a series of separate thoughts, and I don't think Olga completes it till "your face shining." That's where I would put the next double slash.

Olga "rests" at this point for a moment, but then the striking of the clock prompts her to make the same point again: "And the clock struck then too." In other words, it's exactly the same and yet totally different.

After that line Chekhov indicates a "Pause." You can afford to ignore the stage directions of some playwrights, but when Chekhov gives you one of his very rare and terse directions, pay attention. Put at least a double slash here, perhaps a triple. I have the sense that Olga might, for the moment, have no intention of continuing, and so this could be one of those pauses I described earlier as a "silence."

When she does start up again she seems to set off on a slightly different tack, and so we need a new one-sentence summary. It might read, "They buried him with full military honors, and yet so few people came." Again that seems to me one whole thought, followed by an afterthought: "Of course, you couldn't expect people to come in such bad weather." Olga seems torn here: she is awed by the signs of renewed life, and at the same time she doesn't want to let go of her father. She seems to want to dwell on the funeral, afraid perhaps that they didn't do him justice then.

At this point Irina says, in effect, "Why dwell on the past?" But Olga, apparently still caught up in her own train of thought, does not respond. The warm air and bright sunlight prompt her to speak once again of how different it is today. But that sets her going on a related thought, "It's been so long since we left home, and yet I can see it all so clearly!" That leads her directly to the culminating thought: "My God! I want to go home!"

We have broken the speech down into units, beginning where the impulse to say something takes over and ending where that impulse seems to have been satisfied, at least for the moment. In a sense, however, Olga is never completely satisfied because everything she says is part of a still larger thought that has possessed her ever since she woke up this morning and looked out her bedroom window, a thought that might be summarized as "It's a new day, maybe we'll get to Moscow after all!" Each time she completes the expression of the theme one way, the need to express it again begins to fill her, for it has all been prepared ahead of time.

It's as if her glass is brim full; she empties it, waits for it to refill itself from an inexhaustible source, then empties it again. You might want to start this speech by allowing yourself to be filled with a sense of wonder at the sunlight, the warm earth burgeoning with new growth, your sister's radiant face—all the signs that life is stirring again out of the dead earth . . . . When you are filled, begin to express your wonder. Each time you embark on a new thought or a restatement of the present thought, keep moving, without rushing, always finding the words as you go, until you have completed it. When your glass is empty, wait till it refills itself, then start again.

• • •

Notice that George's speech seems to roll right along, whereas Olga's seems to flow more slowly, with more frequent resting places. The pace and rhythm of a speech are almost built into the writing, and if you look closely at a text you can often find clues to performing it.

Let's look at a third monologue that is different still. It's from Stanley Eveling's *Dear Janet Rosenberg, Dear Mr. Kooning*. Alec is a fiftyish novelist of middling repute who has come to meet Janet, his adoring teenage pen pal; only Janet is not home, and Alec finds himself stuck with her mother, with whom he has absolutely nothing in common.

ALEC: **Yes ... er ... I'm a writer. I write ... novels, mainly. (***Pause***.) Yes. (***Recklessly***.) Of course, there are other literary forms, epic, lyric, tragic, comic ... other genres ... tried my hand at all of them ... yes ... but, when the chips are down it's the novel that gets my vote, the art of Austen, Trollope, if you'll pardon the expression, Conrad, Foster, Virginia Woolf, James ... Joyce and others too numerous to mention ... Dostoevsky, for instance, ... *The Idiot* and Tolstoy ... great spirits, those, imaginations in the upper-imagery bracket ... don't you think so?**

What does Alec want to say here? Not very much, really. His glass is empty, but he has to say *something*, so he pours out each little dribble as it accumulates and then waits in agony for more water. "I like my work" is the sum and substance of the whole speech. He says it all in the very first sentence, "Yes ... er ... I'm a writer," as if that were the most fascinating profession in the world. And then he rests, giving Mrs. Rosenberg a chance to pick up the ball. When she doesn't, he is compelled to add, "I write . . . novels, mainly." This exhausts his conversational store. Still not getting any rejoinder, he adds, "Yes," expressing for the third time his satisfaction with a life well spent. Again, silence. After a time, in sheer desperation ("recklessly" as the stage direction suggests), he sets out on a new tack: "Of course there are other literary forms . . . " I feel he could come to a definite stop after "It's the novel that gets my vote," even though the author places only a comma here. Then he sets out to give a series of examples, ending with absolute finality with "and others too numerous to mention." Period. Finished. Done. But the silence becomes so intolerable that he is compelled to add "Dostoevsky, for instance," as if all this while he had been still caught up in the same train of thought. And so it goes through the whole speech. Lots of double slashes, even triple slashes if you like.

The great fun in doing this speech is to give the impression that you have finished and then start up all over again. If you can manage to "dwell" on each thing after you have said it, still expressing your satisfaction nonverbally, you will be able to pause for a very long time. Anything might happen: Mrs. Rosenberg might actually say something. Janet might mercifully walk in, or you might continue to sit there in silence. Nobody knows, least of all yourself. Of course the pauses will feel awkward—that's the joke of the scene—but I would not try to *act* as if you are uncomfortable. On the contrary, in such situations we pretend to be having a great time. Just stay occupied with the fascinating thing you have just said, perhaps nodding slightly and smiling, for as long as you possibly can. Then start up again as if you have a fresh contribution to make to a scintillating conversation.

• • •

Here's another speech that seems to start and stop with every line, but for a different reason. It's from "Request Stop," one of Harold Pinter's *Revue Sketches*. You don't have to worry about marking the full rests: Pinter has done that for you with his characteristic stage direction, "Pause." (Like Chekhov, he writes infrequent but significant directions.) The speaker is a woman at a bus stop who apparently feels that she has been insulted by the man standing next to her. Since this is the beginning of the sketch, we don't know what, if anything, he did to set her off, but she seems to react as if he had made some kind of lewd advance.

A queue at a Request Bus Stop. A WOMAN *at the head, with a* SMALL MAN *in a raincoat next to her, two other* WOMEN *and a* MAN:

WOMAN: *(To* SMALL MAN.*)* I beg your pardon, what did you say?
Pause.
All I asked you was if I could get a bus from here to Shepherds Bush.
Pause.
Nobody asked you to start making insinuations.
Pause.
Who do you think you are?
Pause.
Huh. I know your sort, I know your type. Don't worry, I know all about people like you.
Pause.
We can all tell where you come from. They're putting your sort inside every day of the week.
Pause.
All I've got to do, is report you, and you'd be standing in the dock in next to no time. One of my best friends is a plain clothes detective.
Pause.
I know all about it. Standing there as if butter wouldn't melt in your mouth. Meet you in a dark alley it'd be . . . another story.

Obviously the woman feels outraged. "How dare you!!!" is the essence of what she wants to say, and I feel she says it in the very first line. Even though there's a question mark after the line, I don't think she is literally asking him what he said, I think she is saying, in effect, "I can't believe my ears!!!" You know how it is when somebody says or does something that shows they think of you as stupid or worthless or cheap: you seethe with rage, you say one thing, are temporarily at a loss for words, and then start up all over again. *Nothing* you can say is adequate to the injury. I see the first four lines of this speech as a kind of continuous expression of incredulous outrage, occasionally erupting into words.

Then, beginning with the line, "Huh, I know your sort . . ." I feel she sets out to say something different. And so we need a new one-sentence summary, perhaps, "You may look innocent, but you don't fool me for a minute." This thought is expressed verbally four times by my count and again nonverbally between the lines. The whole sketch goes on this way. Each time the woman appears to be finished she isn't really, for she is still full of indignation. Each time she empties her glass it quickly refills to overflowing. Interestingly, at the end of the sketch the man leaves and she approaches another man in a very seductive manner, asking directions to Shepherds Bush in a way that invites the same kind of "insult" that she just seemed so indignant about. As so often happens with Pinter's people, there is something quite strange going on under the surface, but I think it's best to play the indignation as genuinely as possible and leave it to the audience to guess at what might lie beneath it.

● ● ●

After you have taken a speech apart like this, let it all come back together. Wipe your mind clear of all the analysis, place yourself in the character's position, and become aware of the source for the first thing you say. You might look in silence for a moment at the person you're addressing, as we suggested with George's speech, or you might "hear" what that person supposedly says, such as the rude remark in the Pinter piece, or you might immerse yourself in sensory impressions, such as the signs of Spring in *Three Sisters* or the silence in *Dear Janet Rosenberg* . . . . When you are filled with what you want to say, set out to express it, finding the words as you go.

Never start speaking until you are in touch with what you want to say. But once you start never stop until you have said it. Then, if you can stay with what you have just said by continuing to express it nonverbally, the next thought will occur to you freshly. You will not only appear to speak spontaneously you will *actually* speak spontaneously: that is, the words that you had previously memorized will pop into your head as if you'd never seen them before. In fact, the first time this happens to you, you will have the momentary impression that you have forgotten your lines.

It's a scary feeling, but that's precisely what you want: to act dangerously. Beginners feel that their main problem is to remember all those lines. Actually the main problem is to forget them. Of course in order to do that you have to know them quite well.

If you have done your homework, if you know what you want to say and when you have said it, you can simply ride each thought until it plays itself out, like a wave on the surf, then wait for the next one to pick you up and sweep you along. If you've ever felt that the text is playing you, rather than the other way around, you know what I mean.

9

Grasping the Whole Idea

When we embark on a monologue in life we usually have in mind a whole idea that cannot be adequately expressed in just a few sentences. We may be able, as we've seen, to convey the gist of what we want to say in a single summary sentence, but in order to express it in its full force and clarity, we need to flesh it out with examples and illustrations. We may need to lead up to the point gradually, as George does in *Who's Afraid of Virginia Woolf?*, or we may state the point and then develop it, as Olga does in *Three Sisters*. The kind of monologue in which we just keep repeating one simple point, either because we don't have much to say, like Alec in *Dear Janet Rosenberg ...*, or because we're not satisfied with saying it once, like the woman in the Pinter sketch, is comparatively rare, both in life and in dramatic literature.

Even when we have a rather large and complex idea to expound (Louis' speech in *Suicide in Bb* is perhaps the best example we've seen so far), we tend to know already, at the moment we open our mouths, the whole of what we want to say, although we may know it in a kind of foggy, nonverbal way. We may even have "rehearsed" various versions of the speech in our heads well before we have occasion to deliver it—though of course the "performance" may not go exactly as "rehearsed." Often we feel brim full of something that absolutely *has* to be said, and if anybody interrupts before we have said it all, we instantly say, "Wait—I'm not finished yet!" How can we know that we are not finished unless we have some sense of where we're headed?

In life grasping the whole idea before we speak is seldom a problem. But on stage it frequently is. When we read words on a page, we take in one sentence at a time. Often we cannot really understand the individual sentences until we have read a whole cluster of sentences, sometimes a rather large cluster. Does that seem strange to you? Perhaps you were taught in grammar school, as I was, that "A sentence is a group of words having a subject and a predicate and expressing a complete thought." Well, I maintain that that definition is flat wrong. Sometimes sentences convey complete thoughts, and sometimes they don't.

Take, for example, the sentence "I'll never forget how gentle you were when we first met, how sensitive to my needs." Take a moment to make those words "real" to you and then say the sentence as if you really mean it. You will probably feel that you have expressed a complete thought.

But now put the same words into a larger context. Suppose now that it is only the first sentence of a speech that continues as follows: "I adored you, I thought you were kinder and wiser and more loving than any human being I'd ever met. But now I've come to realize you're not who I thought you were at all. I invented you in my own head. You never really loved me, you only made a game out of being in love with me. You're a stranger to me, and I can't stay another minute in this house. I'm leaving!" Begin with the first sentence again, but this time do the whole speech.

Once you've read the entire passage that I just made up (actually I stole most of it from Ibsen's *A Doll's House*), you cannot possibly say the first sentence the way you did when you treated it as a separate entity. In the larger context it means something entirely different. It is not a complete thought, it is only part of a thought, a kind of "prelude" to the main theme. Your intention is not to say how gentle and sensitive your lover is but, on the contrary, how you were deceived by appearances. The speech is not about tenderness, it's about disillusionment. To convey the whole idea in one sentence you'd have to say something like, "Once I adored you, but now I see you're not who I thought you were, and I have to leave you."

• • •

We may also have been taught in school to memorize sentence by sentence. We may have painful memories of being made to "recite" a speech or a poem line by line—God help us if we left one out!—without any awareness of the function that each bit serves in the larger context. Later on, in acting classes, we may have had it drilled into us that we must make everything "real," and so we come to feel that we are required to *act* everything, even if it's only a bit of background detail or a prefatory remark that is there to lead us up to a point.

It's not surprising then that actors are inclined towards what Mira Rostova has called "acting on the installment plan." They may invest so much importance in the individual moments that they lose or distort the sense of the whole and fail to get caught up in the momentum of a speech. Not having started with their destination in mind, they never get there. They get bogged down in the swamps of their own acting.

Let's look at a monologue that positively *invites* you to get bogged down. It's full of traps for the unwary actor. It's called "Demigod," it's by Richard LaGravanese, and it's from *A . . . My Name Is Alice*, a revue conceived and directed by Joan Micklin Silver and Julianne Boyd. The monologue is a complete sketch in itself.

WOMAN: I know you're gonna go. . . . I know it. I've been thinking a lot about what you said and I believe that you love me too. . . . And I understand that she gives you something else, something you need I guess is what you said. I wanted to apologize for yesterday. I was so confused, you know. I didn't know what to do with myself. . . . I mean, two years . . . what does a person do? Do I have a nervous breakdown? Do I start a new career? Do I go and have an affair with O.J. Simpson? I mean what do I do? I felt so ugly, Frank, and I don't mean just looks, I mean ugly . . . you know? Then you held me and touched the back of my neck and kissed me and said the things you said, and I felt a lot better. So, I did our laundry, like I always do on Sundays. And in the middle of folding our bedspread, I noticed your jock strap in the washing machine. Drowning in the wash cycle. It was twisting and turning, being mangled and manipulated into all sorts of painful positions. It looked as if it were crying out for help, poor little thing. Then the strangest thing . . . I imagined you were still in it . . . the jock strap I mean. I got hysterical. I mean I couldn't stop laughing. I thought it was the funniest thing I ever thought of. . . . People started staring at me. . . . A woman came up to me and said I should be careful not to inhale too much of that fabric softener. . . . Then all of a sudden I heard your voice. So I ran over to the machine, lifted the lid, and I could hear you in there, choking on the Clorox 2 and the Lemon Fab. But I couldn't make out what you were saying, so I yelled, "Frank, what is it, what are you saying?" And the manager of the laundromat yelled back, "I'm gonna call the police if you don't stop screamin' at your wash, lady!" It made me think, Frank. It made me think that maybe I'm not handling this too well. I can't drop two years of being lovers and go back to being friends. We never were friends, Frank. We slept together on the first date, remember? And I know you wanted to leave on good terms, like telling me you still love me and all, but I really think it'll be easier for me if we break up as enemies. It'll be better for me just to hate you openly instead of being so adult about it, don't you think? I mean, why be adult about it? So we can meet for lunch and laugh about all this? So you can tell me about your lovers and I can tell you about my lovers? So we can sleep together for old times' sake? I don't want to be your friend, Frank. I loved you, but I never said I liked you. And if being adult means throwing *me* away for that slut-rag your picked up on the goddamned train platform, then the most mature thing I could do for you would be to rip your face off.

(She mimes doing so.)
Oh, yes! That feels much better!
(Blackout.)

Since this is a rather long piece, let's again make a kind of "outline" of the structure:

1. I understand that you're leaving me for another woman.

2. Yesterday I acted like a fool, I felt so devastated.

3. But then at the laundromat I saw your jock strap in the wash and imagined your genitals being mangled in it.

4. And I realized that I don't want to part as friends, I want to rip your face off!

You may want to break the speech down differently, but however you do it, the crucial question is how much of what this woman says is on her mind at the moment she first opens her mouth to speak. Are these four separate ideas, or are they parts of one whole "cluster" or "gestalt"?

When you read the words on the page it may seem that all she wants to say at first is that she knows he's leaving, and then it occurs to her to talk about how devastated she was yesterday, and then she happens to remember the incident at the laundromat, and then it occurs to her that she really wants to rip his face off. But if you don't know from the beginning, at least at some level, that today you really want to rip his face off, how can you possibly find the motivation to do that in the middle of the speech? There is no indication in the text, as there is in the Gurney piece about the businessman dictating a letter, that a whole new idea suddenly dawns on you. Nor is there any suggestion that the man you're talking to does something *during* the speech to make you suddenly angry with him. My guess is that you have been furious with him for years, only you suppressed your true feelings and played the role of a dutiful, subservient wife. Even yesterday, when he told you about the other woman, instead of standing up to him, you became pathetic and helpless. But then, at the laundromat you had a blinding revelation: the sight of his jock strap provoked a fantasy in which you saw his balls being mangled and crushed. Just as dreams often reveal our true feelings to us, that image got you in touch with the depths of your anger. That *already* happened. Yesterday. By the time you begin the speech you already know that you are going to tell him off.

Why then, you may well ask, don't you just come right out and say you want to rip his face off? In the first place, that's not easy to do. Besides, he would have no idea what you were talking about. You have undergone such a startling change overnight that you need to present him with the whole picture: how you felt yesterday, what happened at the laundromat to change you, and how you feel today. When you break up with somebody you love you usually need to make clear, before walking out the door, exactly where you stand.

If you were to improvise the whole speech at this point I don't think you'd have any difficulty making it all fit together. But when you pick up the text, watch out! The words are full of traps. The very first line, for example, "I know you're gonna go . . . I know it," would entice almost any actress to play how devastated she is by his leaving. Sure it hurts, it hurts unendurably, but you don't have to *play* the hurt. In the context of the whole speech the best choice is to admit as calmly as possible to the truth, painful as it is. Yesterday you were not able to face the truth and today you are. That's a big change. It's important that he understand that.

Then you have to say, " I wanted to apologize for yesterday." Actors are funny, they see the word "apologize" on the page and they immediately feel that they are required to *act* apologetic. And the more abjectly the better. But of course it's possible just to *say* that you want to apologize. You needn't feel terribly ashamed about how you acted yesterday. It would be no different if, in a fit of totally justified anger at your boss, you had yelled and screamed incomprehensibly and then left the office dissolved in tears. You are only sorry that you did not instead tell him frankly what you think of him, which is precisely what you are about to do.

Apparently you went into a fit of hysteria yesterday when Frank first told you he was leaving you for another woman. He needs to understand now that you reacted that way because he made you feel so "confused" and "ugly." You were still stuck then in your old role of being completely dependent on a man for your future and your sense of self-esteem. Now you want to make clear to him exactly what he put you through. But again, don't feel that you have to *act out* how "confused" and "ugly" you felt then. Even when you say how much better you felt when he held you and touched the back of your neck and kissed you, I think it would be a great mistake to act as if you are deeply touched by his tenderness. Today you realize that this was just one more example of how you (typically) let yourself be manipulated by him. *Yesterday* you may have been deeply touched (in the head!), but since then you have been to the laundromat and you have seen the light.

• • •

Perhaps you feel that you have been keeping yourself in check all this time, stifling the expression of any passion. But if you simply keep trying to give a clear account of what you went through yesterday (knowing of course what it would mean to be abandoned by a man you've loved), some of the feeling is likely to come through in spite of yourself, like steam escaping from the rim of a covered pot. (In acting you need to know when to leave the lid on and when to let the pot boil over.) At the same time you will keep the sense that you are moving on towards the expression of what you feel most deeply today.

Now you are ready to describe that moment of enlightenment in the laundromat. This section should be easy enough to play (no traps). All you have to do is imagine that it really happened—to you. Just picture that jock strap, with his balls inside it, being twisted and mangled. Don't be troubled if you feel that you would never believe in the vision as strongly as she seemed to. She wasn't really hallucinating, it's just that the fantasy became so vivid that she got carried away. Allow yourself a little poetic license here. And don't be afraid to appreciate the humor in the situation either—at the time it may have been terrifying, but surely in telling about it the next day you would be aware of how absurd it was.

Absurd, of course, but illuminating too. When you start the section beginning, "It made me think, Frank," you are ready to tell him everything that was revealed to you in that startling fantasy. You have arrived at last at the point of the whole speech: you don't want to part as friends, you want to twist his balls off, kick him in the guts, rip his face away.

But first there's one final trap you have to get past. The sentence, "It made me think that maybe I'm not handling this very well" may look on the page like another apology. But I think the statement is ironic: according to *Frank* the way to handle this situation is to be calm and friendly and understanding, that's how adults are "supposed" to behave (and of course that would make things a lot easier for him), but the truth is you don't *want* to be calm and friendly and understanding, and so you're not doing a very good job of meeting *his* standards. Tough! You prefer, as you say, "to hate you openly instead of being so adult about it." You go on to say how silly it would be to meet for lunch or sleep together occasionally. You are showing disdain for his expectations, refusing to play his game. Instead you tell him what *you* want to do. For the first time in your life, perhaps, you are standing up to a man.

It may seem hard to believe that this woman was transformed so completely by one Zen-like moment in the laundromat. Of course her new insights must have been incubating for some time, perhaps through reading or talking with friends. But enlightenment does tend to come suddenly when it comes. Anyway things usually happen in less time on stage than in life. At least it's easier for you to assume that it happened yesterday than to try to make it happen in the middle of the speech.

You can assume that you've had time on the way back from the laundromat, and perhaps while you lay awake during the night, to think through everything you want to say. This is the kind of speech we tend to "rehearse" in our heads rather thoroughly, knowing that we will soon face a significant encounter. It's all prepared ahead of time, bursting to be told. This is the liberating truth you have finally attained. And how wonderful to let it roll out! Of course you're angry with him, but it's not a helpless, painful kind of anger. On the contrary, there's a tremendous satisfaction in being able to express your feelings so directly. Even when you say you want to rip his face off and then mime the action, I think you should do this not so much in anger but with enormous *relish*. Let yourself go. The author wrote this as a solo piece, knowing there's nobody on stage who might actually get hurt, and so the gesture is meant to be symbolic, not literal. You are showing Frank what you would *like* to do to him. It's a bit like hitting somebody with a pillow in an encounter group: what counts is not the damage you inflict but the gusto with which you attack. This whole speech is an act of joyous assertion, not a cry of pain.

• • •

You may not agree with the particular choices I've suggested, and that's fine. I do think it's important that you *make* choices and that you are aware of the consequences of your choices. Actors go wrong more often by slipping into a pattern without being aware of alternatives than by deliberately choosing badly. And if they persist in their error it's because they do not realize the effect that it produces—on themselves, on their stage partners, and on the audience. Let's look first at the consequences for yourself. If you choose to play separate moments of agony and humiliation and loving tenderness in the first part of the speech, you may feel that you are acting up a storm, but I think you will find it impossible to launch yourself with any impetus into that final joyous declaration. I could be wrong, try it and see. But you might think also of the effect you want to have on Frank: do you want him to see you as pathetic and helpless or as liberated and free? Finally, there's the audience. Although I don't think it's wise to base your choices solely on audience reactions, it is helpful to get feedback from a director or somebody else you trust. If you play the separate moments, some people in the audience (including some directors and casting people) may tell you how marvelous you are at portraying all those different feelings. But others may react differently. I know that when I see this monologue done piecemeal (and that's how I almost always see it), I don't believe a word of it, and I get bored and irritated, impatient for the actress to get on with it. The few times I've seen it done by an actress who sees everything in the context of the whole I remain on the edge of my seat. I am certainly aware that this woman has been deeply wounded, but I sense all along that she is moving towards the act that will heal her, and I am rooting for her all the way. When she gets there I want to cheer. And I believe that most people, if they had the opportunity to see the monologue done both ways, would much prefer the second.

• • •

My analysis of the speech makes it seem more complicated than it really is. The way you arrive at the kinds of choices I suggested is simply by feeling your way into the character's situation. Sometimes you make all the right choices intuitively at the first reading, and then you spend the rehearsal period working your way back to what you did then. More often rehearsal is a process of trial and error. You sense vaguely that something is "off," and having learned from experience to pay attention to that feeling, you try something else, and then a third thing, until suddenly, perhaps in the heat of a runthrough, perhaps while you're doing the dishes or out walking the dog, the way to play a moment dawns on you, and at that point no other choice seems worth considering. (Unfortunately that sometimes happens six months after the play has closed!) Eventually you have a kind of "score" of the whole role. You know at each moment exactly what it is you want to convey to your partner, and your task becomes to convey just that. It's like a "note" that you play, and if you have a well-tuned instrument and all the notes fit together a lovely melody will emerge. Once you have learned the notes you don't have to relearn them each time you do the piece. You just play it. Of course you may need a moment to collect yourself, gather your forces before you start, just as a pianist takes that moment before lifting her hands to the keys. That's the moment in which you can focus on where you're headed.

The notes are not the words, the notes are what the character intends to convey with the words—what I call the "content" of the words. In different contexts the same words can convey a different content. In fact the content is determined by the context. You have to arrive at it by immersing yourself in the situation created by the author—the whole situation, including everything that has led you up to this particular moment. The broader the context you examine and the more intimately acquainted you become with it, the surer you can be of your choices. That's why it's important to read the whole play. With some plays it helps to know also the cultural and political background out of which the play emerged.

The choices are not arbitrary. There are right notes and wrong notes. Of course a single note played in isolation can never be off key. Even a string of wrong notes played in sequence may sound perfectly fine for a time, but sooner or later they will jar the ear. Some actors are better than others at finding the right notes—often they surprise us by doing something totally unexpected that turns out to be exquisitely right. Different actors have different ways of searching for the notes. Also each actor has a unique instrument. The same note will sound somewhat different coming from a different actor. Inevitably an actor taking over a role brings something different to it, but that doesn't necessarily mean making a different interpretation. Every actor plays some notes better than other notes, and every actor has a "range," like a singer, some wide and some narrow. And some actors have such incredibly expressive instruments that they can make music sweeter than any we have ever heard before.

• • •

Before ending this chapter I want to add a qualification to my main point. In your effort to keep moving towards your destination without getting bogged down, you have to be careful not to plough through the speech pell-mell, paying no attention to what is being said, just so that you can get to the "point" as quickly as possible. I cannot emphasize strongly enough that knowing the whole of the speech is necessary only for *deciding* what the individual moments mean. The very choice of one thing over another is going to make it clear that you are not finished, that you have something larger in mind. (If indeed that is the case: in the last chapter we looked at some speeches in which you *are* finished, several times within the same speech.) You don't have to rush. You don't even have to keep the main point constantly in mind, you only have to accept, when you start out, that it is already prepared for you, ready to be released when the time comes. First you have other things to attend to. You need to give your attention to laying out the steps that will lead you to the point, you can't just skip over them.

Moreover, you have to find the words that are going to convey each step as clearly and forcefully as possible. An unspoken thought, like a fetus in the womb, is not fully shaped until it finds birth in words. Sometimes the birth is difficult. If you watch people being interviewed in documentary films or on television, it's fascinating to see how they struggle sometimes to find the right words to express something they feel quite strongly. An actor handed the transcript of the same speech might rattle it off glibly. When you're repeating memorized words, you need to allow for the fact that the character doesn't know them yet. You have to "make them up" as you go along.

Back in the 1950s Marlon Brando, Geraldine Page, and a few other actors found a way to do that more believably than was customary in the acting of the time. I met Page a few years before her death, and I told her how, when I'd first seen her in

Strange Interlude, she was the only one in a company of distinguished actors who made me believe that she really didn't know what she was going to say next. I could literally *see* new ideas dawning on her, and I watched in utter amazement as she seemed to pick just the right words out of the air. (That's hard enough with any text, but with the sometimes turgid prose of Eugene O'Neill it was downright miraculous.) I had never seen acting like that before, and I've seldom seen it since, except in improvisation. Page told me that she had been profoundly affected by a remark Uta Hagen made once in class: "The words haven't been written yet." That was a startling revelation to her, and from then on she tried to base her work on that premise. But other actors, she said, began to imitate the result without going through the process, and so "groping for words" became a kind of cliche.

The difference between Page and her imitators is this: she managed to become so thoroughly involved in the situation that when thoughts and feelings came to her she was innocent of the words and had to find them on the spot, whereas they become absorbed in *how* they are saying the words, deliberately stumbling and faltering to give the impression that they don't know them. Actually what they are doing is just another form of slavish attachment to the words.

You need to arrive on stage in a state of innocence. You need to trust that you have already been through whatever the character has experienced to this point. Then, when your cue comes, a thought will actually come with it. It may be a fairly simple thought requiring only a sentence or two, or it may be a complex idea that sets you going for three pages. It may be a totally new thought that takes shape with considerable struggle, or it may have been so thoroughly prepared that it tumbles out pell-mell. In any case you have to give up control and let the words arrive in their own time.

10

"What's It Like?": Improvising on a Parallel Situation

A one-sentence summary of everything I've tried to say in the last three chapters of this rather lengthy monologue I'm delivering here might go something like this: before you open your mouth to speak, you have to have some sense of what you want to say. In life we are always in touch, however tenuously, with the thoughts and feelings that give rise to the words. At times we may set out with only a vague notion of where we are headed and grope our way towards a point; or we may start to say one thing and then become aware of another, less accessible thought that has been there all along, struggling towards the surface. At other times we may have a firm grasp on a whole complex idea, though we don't have the words yet to articulate it. But always we are possessed by *something* that seeks to find expression in words. And so our task is to find the words that will best satisfy existing wishes.

Unfortunately when we act it's the other way around. We don't have the wishes yet, but we do have the words—they are handed to us on neatly bound sheets of paper, and we know that eventually we're going to have to memorize them all and hopefully find a way of speaking them that will satisfy first our director and then the critics and public—or perhaps a panel of stone-faced casting people. And so, lured away from their source, we are made to dance attendance on the words themselves. Most of us have to struggle constantly against that perilous fascination with the sound of the words in our own ears. Other actors, more favored, are led immediately, by some secret path, to the source of the words. They don't need to consider the process, they may even prefer not to. "All I do is memorize my lines and pray to God," Bette Davis once said, and her method worked fine for her because God was always on her side. The rest of us may be endowed with grace from time to time, but when we are not we need a more deliberate approach. For me the approach that works best is to ask questions. The answer may or may not come, or it may come in its own sweet time, arriving perhaps long after we have any use for it. But at least the questions can be learned.

• • •

I have already suggested the question, "What am I setting out to say here?" In this chapter I want to propose a somewhat different question, "What's it like?" Both questions are ways of getting at what I have been calling the "content" of a speech. The first leads to a kind of frontal attack on the content, while the second sneaks up on the content and catches it when it isn't looking. If one way doesn't work for you, try another.

Asking "What's it like?" is simply a way of making a personal connection to the situation created by the author by relating it to a familiar, more recognizable experience. Here is an example from a role I once played, Colonel Redfern in John Osborne's *Look Back in Anger*. The Colonel has come to collect his daughter, Alison, who is leaving her husband Jimmy. He has just said that he couldn't understand how a daughter of his could have married a man like Jimmy in the first place. But he catches himself and adds,

No. Perhaps Jimmy is right. Perhaps I am a—what was it?—an old plant left over from the Edwardian Wilderness. And I can't understand why the sun isn't shining any more. You can see what he means, can't you? It was March, 1914, when I left England, and, apart from leaves every ten years or so, I didn't see much of my own country until we all came back in '47. Oh, I knew things had changed, of course. People told you all the time the way it was going—going to the dogs, as the Blimps are supposed to say. But it seemed very unreal to me, out there. The England I remembered was the one I left in 1914, and I was happy to go on remembering it that way. Besides, I had the Maharajah's army to command—that was my world, and I loved it, all of it. At the time, it looked like going on forever. When I think of it now, it seems like a dream. If only it could have gone on forever. Those long, cool evenings up in the hills, everything purple and golden. Your mother and I were so happy then. It seemed as though we had everything we could ever want. I think the last day the sun shone was when that dirty little train steamed out of that crowded, suffocating Indian station, and the battalion band playing for all it was worth. I knew in my heart it was all over then. Everything.

When I first read this speech I found very little connection to it. I couldn't remember ever feeling, as the Colonel apparently does, that I was out of touch with the younger generation. But what would it be like for me if I did? Could I at least *imagine* a parallel situation? Suddenly I remembered several years earlier having been the object of a revolt in a college theater department by students who complained that I was so attached to "realistic" acting and to "old-fashioned" playwrights like Tennessee Williams and Arthur Miller that I was completely out of touch with what was going on in contemporary theater. Actually they were wrong, but at the time the accusation really stung. What if it were true? What if I had indeed become the old fogey they took me for? I might even have had good reasons, just as the Colonel did. Suppose, for example, that I had been away from New York for a long time . . .

And so I began to improvise on my parallel situation, trying to make the improv follow as closely as possible the structure of the Colonel's speech. It went something like this:

No. Maybe my students are right. Maybe I am—what was it they called me?—an old relic left over from the days of David Belasco, and I can't understand why the theater isn't realistic any more. You can see what they mean, can't you? After all, it was March, 1959, when I left New York, and except for a weekend visit every few years, I didn't see much of the New York theater till I came back in '73. Oh, I knew things had changed, of course. People told me all the time how it was going— all nudity and grunts as the matinee ladies are supposed to say. But it seemed very unreal to me out there in Colorado. The theater I remembered was the one I left in 1959, and I was happy to go on remembering it that way. Besides, I had the ski school to run—that was my world, and I loved it, all of it. When I think about it now it seems unreal. I can't help wishing it had gone on and on. Those long schusses down the slopes at sunset, the air so quiet and clear. Your mother and I were so happy then. It seemed as though we had everything we ever wanted. I think the last day of my life was when that TWA turboprop took off from the Denver airport, our friends all standing there, waving. I knew in my heart my life was over then. The whole thing.

Actually, I've never even been to Colorado, let alone run a ski school. The details that I invented for my improv were no more real than the ones Osborne invented for the play. Still, improvising along parallel lines did a number of things for me. First, it made me more aware of the humor in the speech: I couldn't refer to myself as a relic of the David Belasco days— my substitution for the "Edwardian plant"—without a certain wry amusement. Second, I was able to recount the whole long chronicle of events (when I left, when I came back, and so on) effortlessly, for I recognized that the Colonel wasn't *telling* Alison any of this (why should he, she was with him the whole time) but merely acknowledging known facts in order to make a point. Third, it forced me to get in touch with what I wanted to say before I found the words to say it.

Once I had the thoughts going for me I found I could switch in midstream from my parallel improv to the text and keep that sense of making it all up. In fact, I *wanted* to use Osborne's words, since they expressed the thoughts so much better than mine. Of course I must have had some sense of the content of the speech even before doing my improv, otherwise I could never have come up with this particular parallel, but putting it in a familiar context somehow made it *mine*. I came to feel that there was essentially no difference between me and the Colonel, even though I'd never been to India or commanded a maharajah's troops. Of course I had to work also on his speech patterns and military bearing, but that's another story.

• • •

In some cases it may be easier to picture the situation in the play than to invent one of your own, and then of course there's no need for the exercise. If you can readily imagine yourself in the character's shoes, why make the effort to imagine yourself anywhere else? Improvising on a parallel theme is just another tool that might be useful if you find yourself stuck, if, for example, you feel no empathy for the character at first or find the situation alien to you. It's also useful for freshening up a speech if you find yourself repeating the words mechanically.

If absolutely no parallel situation comes to mind, it is usually a sign either that you don't really understand the speech or that you are taking the words too literally. Take a look, for example, at the first few lines of the opening monologue of Ionesco's *The Bald Soprano*. Mr. Smith sits reading the newspaper, Mrs. Smith is darning socks, and after the clock strikes seventeen times Mrs. Smith remarks, "There, it's nine o'clock. We've drunk the soup and eaten the fish and chips, and the English salad. The children have drunk English water. We've eaten well this evening. That's because we live in the suburbs of London and our name is Smith."

How on earth do you find a connection with *that*? If you ask what it's like to eat English salad or drink English water you will come to a dead end. Of course you could always substitute "American" for "English," but what good would that do you? What you need to look for is not a literal parallel to the words but a recognition of what is familiar in the situation. All that Ionesco did was to take a very common situation and carry it to an extreme: the husband is reading the newspaper in silence and the wife is talking just to hear herself talk, expressing great satisfaction with everything in their ordinary domestic lives. Once you've recognized what that's like, it should be easy enough to improvise a speech in which you pretend to be extremely satisfied with a whole series of mundane things. I tried a paraphrase of this speech while sitting at my typewriter with my beloved cat Simplicity on my desk watching me work. In the left-hand column I quote the Ionesco speech, in the right my paraphrase:

MRS. SMITH: **There, it's nine o'clock. We've drunk the soup, and eaten the fish and chips, and the English salad. The children have drunk English water. We've eaten well this evening. That's because we live in the suburbs of London and our name is Smith.**

(MR. SMITH *continues to read, clicks his tongue.*)

MRS. SMITH: **Potatoes are very good fried in fat; the salad oil was not rancid. The oil from the grocer at the corner is better quality than the oil from the grocer**

MR. POGGI: **There , it's two o'clock. I reread chapter one, revised chapter two, and got started on chapter three. You have sat here watching. I wrote well this morning. That's because I live in the suburbs of New York and my name is Poggi.**

(SIMPLICITY, *a black and white cat, continues to look at* MR. POGGI *and blinks.*)

MR. POGGI: **This looks very good in black ink; the ink hasn't faded on this ribbon. The ribbons from the stationery store on the corner are better than the** across the street. It is even better than the oil from the grocer at the bottom of the street. However, I prefer not to tell them that their oil is bad.

(MR. SMITH *continues to read, clicks his tongue.*)

MRS. SMITH: However, the oil from the grocer at the corner is still the best.

(MR. SMITH *continues to read, clicks his tongue.*)

MRS. SMITH: Mary did the potatoes very well this evening. The last time she did not do them well. I do not like them when they are well done.

(MR. SMITH *continues to read, clicks his tongue.*)

MRS. SMITH: The fish was fresh. It made my mouth water. I had two helpings. No, three helpings. That made me go to the w.c. You also had three helpings. However, the third time you took less than the first two times, while as for me, I took a great deal more. I ate better than you this evening. Why is that? Usually it is you who eats more. It is not appetite you lack.

(MR. SMITH *clicks his tongue.*)

ribbons from the stationery store down the street. They're even better than the ribbons at the stationery store six blocks away. But I'd hate to tell them that their ribbons are bad.

(SIMPLICITY, *continues to look, blinks her eyes.*)

MR. POGGI: But the ribbons from the store on the corner are still the best.

(SIMPLICITY, *continues to look, blinks her eyes.*)

MR. POGGI: Jeanlee did a good job vacuuming this room yesterday. The last time she didn't do it so well. I don't like it when she vacuums.

(SIMPLICITY, *continues to look, blinks her eyes.*)

MR. POGGI: The air outside was fresh. It invigorated me. I went outside twice. No, three times. That made me sleepy. You went out three times too. But the third time you didn't stay out as long as the first two times, whereas I stayed out much longer. I've been out more than you this morning, Simpy. Why is that? Usually it's you who is out more. It's not that you don't want to.

(SIMPLICITY *blinks her eyes.*)

What I did was to abstract the *essence* of the Ionesco speech. I took it out of one concrete situation and put it into a totally different concrete situation, but the essence remains the same. If you have difficulty thinking of parallels you are probably still rooted in the concrete. Just as the Colonel's speech is not about post-war England, this speech is not really about salad oil. Sometimes, in order to break away from the concrete, it's actually easier to invent something rather farfetched. In *Method or Madness* Robert Lewis tells the story of how the famous actor Jacob Ben-Ami captured the moment of terror a man might feel just as he is about to pull the trigger of a revolver he is holding to his temple: he remembered what it was like just before turning on the cold water in the shower. That may sound absurd, but for Ben-Ami that was the emotional essence of the moment, and Lewis said it was a stunning moment to watch.

It's important too that you find the essence of the situation as the character sees it, even though you might see it quite differently. Take the line, "Once . . . I've been wanting to tell someone this, Eileen . . . once I came *this* close to committing suicide." Now *you* might feel distressed or ashamed saying that. But when you see the line in context—it's from *Search for Signs of Intelligent Life in the Universe*—it's clear that Chrissy finds the thought of suicide absolutely *fascinating*. That she even thought of doing it makes her such an interesting person. She's not talking about how awful it was but how exciting. So you might want to try something like, "Once I came *this* close to working as a call girl!"—anything that strikes you as exciting and somewhat dangerous and makes you a fascinating case study. Again, it doesn't have to be anything you ever really did.

If you feel that you would never act as the character does in the situation, just ask yourself in what situation you *would* act that way. For example, in Oscar Wilde's *The Importance of Being Earnest*, the butler, Lane, when asked if he had heard his master playing the piano in the adjoining room, replies, "I didn't think it polite to listen, sir." It's a delicious line, but if you're troubled by the fact that *you* would never react that way, think of some other situation in which you might feel reticent to listen in on something. Suppose, for example, you are working as a secretary and your boss comes out of his inner office and asks if you overheard his telephone conversation. You wouldn't even have to paraphrase, you could say exactly what Lane says, and it would make perfect sense. To play somebody very different from yourself you don't need to change yourself, you need only change the way you look at the situation.

If you were playing Algernon in the same scene you might want to try an improvisation about an actor walking off the stage, quite pleased with himself. It might go something like this:

ALGERNON: **Did you hear what I was playing, Lane?**	ACTOR: **Did you see that scene I just did?**
LANE: **I didn't think it polite to listen, sir.**	APPRENTICE: **I thought it might upset you if I watched.**
ALGERNON: **I'm sorry for that, for your sake. I don't play accurately—anybody can play accurately—but I play with wonderful expression. As far as the piano is concerned, sentiment is my forte. I keep science for Life.**	ACTOR: **Too bad for you. I don't say the lines right— anybody can say the lines right—but I say them with extraordinary feeling. As far as the stage is concerned, feeling is my thing. I leave accuracy to computers.**

Trying a parallel improv like this may help you realize how playful Algernon is being here. You don't have to make yourself "believe" something that is patently absurd. Nor do you have to adopt an affected manner simply because this is a "stylized" piece. Of course, you have to master upper-class British speech, and you have to become comfortable with the clothes and objects of the period, but the style comes directly out of the content. What the parallel improv does, in effect, is help you make the appropriate choices. You discover through the improv what to do, and you do precisely that with the text.

• • •

If you are required by the play to speak in an idiom that is unfamiliar to you—say O'Casey's Dublin brogue or Shakespeare's iambic pentameter—you need to become fluent in a new "language." Partly, of course, that's a matter of sheer technical drill, practicing over and over until you can speak comfortably in the idiom even while improvising. But once you have learned the "language," you must still be able to utter these strange new sounds as if they expressed your own thoughts and feelings. Paraphrasing first in your own language may help you accomplish that. Let's see how that might work with a fairly simple speech from *As You Like It.* The shepherdess Phebe is clearly smitten with Rosalind, whom she thinks to be a man, but apparently doesn't want to admit to her passion.

PHEBE:
Know'st thou the youth that spoke to me erewhile?
· · ·
Think not I love him, though I ask for him.
'Tis but a peevish boy, yet he talks well.
But what care I for words? Yet words do well
When he that speaks them pleases those that hear.
It is a pretty youth—not very pretty.
But sure he's proud, and yet his pride becomes him.
He'll make a proper man: the best thing in him
Is his complexion. And faster than his tongue
Did make offense his eyes did heal it up.
He is not very tall, yet for his years he's tall.
His leg is but so-so, and yet 'tis well.
There was a pretty redness in his lip,
A little riper and more lusty red
Than that mix'd in his cheek. 'Twas just the difference
Betwixt the constant red and mingled damask.
There be some women, Silvius, had they mark'd him
In parcels as I did, would have gone near
To fall in love with him. But for my part,
I love him not nor hate him not; and yet
I have more cause to hate him than to love him,

> For what had he to do to chide at me?
> He said mine eyes were black and my hair black,
> And, now I am remitting'red, scorn'd at me.
> I marvel why I answer'd not again.
> But that's all one: omittance is no quittance.
> I'll write to him a very taunting letter,
> And thou shalt bear it. Wilt thou, Silvius?

If the words do not at first come easily to your tongue, try putting the exact same thoughts into contemporary American English. You might begin, for example, by asking, "Do you know that boy who spoke to me just now?" Once you experience the wish to ask that question, you can just as easily ask it in Shakespeare's words—it's no more "unnatural" than asking it in French if you happen to speak French. You could then add, "Don't think I like him just because I asked about him," and so on through the speech, first expressing each thought in your own words and then going immediately to the text.

A fairly literal paraphrase like that, helpful as it may be in clarifying the thoughts, may still leave you feeling somewhat removed from the character. If you tend to think of Phebe as a ditzy young girl (which she may be, though *she* doesn't think she is), if you can't even remotely imagine yourself behaving in such a silly fashion, that is a sign that you have not yet entered her world, learned to see through her eyes. If that's the case, I suggest trying a more imaginative kind of parallel. Ask yourself what it would be like to be attracted to something and at the same time deny the attraction—not literally to a boy but to something else. What else might it be? Suppose, to choose a rather silly example, you are sitting in a restaurant with a friend who knows you are on a very strict diet. You see a waiter bring a luscious-looking French pastry to a neighboring table, and you can't help remarking, "Did you see what that waiter just put down over there?" You might continue to paraphrase as follows: "Don't think I'm going to order one because I asked about it. It's just a silly little dessert. . . . Still, it does look creamy. . . . But what do I care for whipped cream? . . . Yet whipped cream is pretty tasty when they make it in a place like this." And so on.

An improvisation of this kind may help you discover how Phebe seems to be absolutely finished with almost every sentence. She is not interested. Period. . . . But then of course she can't help starting up again. Lots of double slashes here, triple slashes actually. You would need to do with this speech exactly the opposite of what I advised with the monologue from *A . . . My Name Is Alice*: you need to do each thing as if it is complete in itself, with no idea that you are going to go on. You have to "surprise yourself" in a sense by saying each thing quite decisively, staying with it for a moment, and then letting the next thought come to you freshly.

You could probably go through a good deal of this speech using what might be called the French pastry connection. At some point, however, you will need to be work with a different parallel. For example, when Phebe asks Silvius (who is in love with her) to carry a letter to Rosalind, you might try what it would be like to ask a roommate who is up for the same part as you to drop off your picture and resume for you.

• • •

Here's another example from Shakespeare. In *Taming of the Shrew* Petruchio is waiting for his first confrontation with the notorious Kate.

PETRUCHIO:
 I will attend her here,
And woo her with some spirit when she comes.
Say that she rail; why then I'll tell her plain
She sings as sweetly as a nightingale:
Say that she frown; I'll say she looks as clear
As morning roses newly wash'd with dew:
Say she be mute and will not speak a word;
Then I'll commend her volubility,
And say she uttereth piercing eloquence:
If she do bid me pack, I'll give her thanks,
As though she bid me stay by her a week:

If she deny to wed, I'll crave the day
When I shall ask the banns, and when be married.

Once, when I was coaching an actor on this speech, we both got stuck. He understood the speech perfectly, he could sum the whole thing up in one sentence, he could outline the steps, he could even paraphrase the exact thoughts in contemporary language. The only problem was he wasn't having any fun with it. I couldn't think of anything to say that might help him. And so I asked what I usually ask when I get stuck: what is this situation like? At first neither of us could think of a parallel, but we kept trying. Kate is so notorious for dishing out abuse that no other suitor even dares go near her, but Petruchio is going to beard the lion in her den. Who else might this lion be?

Almost simultaneously it occurred to us that Kate is exactly like a power-mad producer who cuts actors up into little pieces and eats them for breakfast. Other actors are terrified even to ask for an appointment. But this actor is now waiting in the producer's outer office without an appointment, having made a bet with his friends, who are now watching in amazement, that he can disarm the producer and win the part. His parallel improv, as I recall, started out something like, "I'm going to wait right here for that sonofabitch and go after him with some balls when he comes out."

For each thought in the text the actor found a close parallel: "If he starts yelling at me, I'll tell him he has a voice as mellifluous as Richard Burton's. If he scowls, I'll tell him he has a face as open and clear as an alpine lake." (Notice, by the way, that where Shakespeare's language is somewhat extravagant, the actor found an extravagant parallel.) He continued that way through the whole speech, ending with "If he tells me to get out, I'll tell him thanks, I'll be delighted to stay for lunch. If he refuses to give me the part, I'll ask what day we sign the contract and when rehearsals start."

Both of us kept cracking up during the improv. The actor discovered how much fun it would be to do what Petruchio does, and he was able to have the same kind of fun with the text.

The possibilities for parallel improvisations are endless. In one of my monologue workshops an actress came up with a totally different parallel for this same speech of Petruchio's: she did an hilarious improv, line for line, about a babysitter who decides to take on a five-year-old hellion whom nobody else dares go near.

Anything you can come up with to help you get to the heart of the matter is fair game. You don't have to limit yourself to things you've actually experienced. Often fantasies provide richer material than reality. You may never have been in a serious automobile accident, for example, but surely it has occurred to you at times, perhaps in rather vivid detail, what would happen if the car approaching you from the opposite direction at 65 miles per hour were to swerve suddenly across the double line and plough directly into yours. If that thought or something like it has never crossed your mind while driving, you will never be an actor. (You probably won't make a very good driver either.)

• • •

Once you've picked a parallel situation, begin to improvise on it, perhaps loosely at first, just to get a sense of the whole. Do not write your improvisations down; I've had to do that here, of course, but once you write an improv down it becomes just another text. Try with each improvisation to come closer and closer to the text, until finally you are able to paraphrase line by line. Now start your improvisation again and at some point, not determined in advance, shift into whatever part of the text you've reached by then. Use the actual words for a time, and if you find yourself speaking mechanically shift back to the paraphrase. Then surprise yourself again and shift back to the text. Keep alternating between the two until you feel you can do the text as spontaneously as the improv. Even when you do the text word for word, as of course you eventually must, *pretend* that you are free to paraphrase at any point. Or maybe tell yourself you are now going to "improvise the text."

Going back and forth between improvisation and text will make you immediately aware of any difference in quality between the two. It is truly amazing to me how seldom we realize, when we speak memorized words, that we are speaking mechanically, and how easily fooled we are by acting that gives only the impression of spontaneity. And yet if you place the genuine article right next to the fake, the differences between the two become obvious. I remember once I flipped on the TV set at random and watched a courtroom scene in which every actor seemed incredibly alive, present, open to the moment. Who *are* these incredibly gifted actors, I wondered? Why have I never seen them before? Then I started paying attention to the dialogue. It was pretty awful—it had no form, no shape, no color. Why would anybody write such crap? Finally, of course, it dawned on me that the actors were improvising. Switching to another channel, I watched some well-known actors skillfully plying their trade in a well-crafted situation comedy, repeating their familiar routines as if stuck in well-worn grooves, and I turned the set off. Not much choice between the two.

I want it both ways. To hear an actor expressing, in words far more eloquent than any I could ever devise, thoughts and feelings that I come to recognize as my own, though perhaps I'd never found a way to articulate them before, or even dared to admit to them, and to feel that these wonderful words are being newly minted on the spot—that is what astonishes and delights me in the theater. An actor who can do that is one I truly envy. I want to know his secret, just as I wanted to know the magician's secret when I was a boy. I suppose that's why, in addition to doing my own magic act as well as I can, I like to teach and write about magic. Of course magicians aren't supposed to reveal their secrets, that spoils everything. But never fear, the real secret will always be well kept. We may catch a glimpse of it from time to time, but when we come away we have no words to say what it is.

11

Connecting with a Partner—
Real or Imagined

Nothing is more crucial in acting than our connection with another human being. I have stressed the importance of knowing what we want to say, but if there's nobody on the receiving end, acting becomes a form of exhibitionism. It's the presence of the other person, in our mind's eye at least, that prompts us to speak, and it's the nature of our connection with that person that determines how we speak. When we have something particular to say, we seek out the person we most want to hear it.

But we don't always have to have our ideal listener literally in front of us. There's a story by Chekhov about a cabdriver whose son has died and who tries repeatedly to talk with his passengers about what happened. Nobody listens, and so at the end of the day the old man goes out to the stable and tells the whole story to his little mare, who "munches and listens and breathes on her master's hands." When the need is strong enough, we will talk to anybody or anything.

We have even been known to talk to ourselves. We frequently rehearse subvocally scenes we would like to play with others, and occasionally we break into speech. One common form of monologue, technically called a "soliloquy," is simply a stage convention that allows us to extend this habit of "thinking out loud." Some purists insist that this is the only "true" monologue, and some acting teachers won't allow you to do any other kind if you're working alone. Of course a soliloquy is easier to do for a class or an audition than a piece that requires you to relate to an absent partner. But even when we "talk to ourselves" I feel that we have in mind, perhaps dimly, the kind of listener we would *like* to address: maybe a boss we want to tell off, maybe an aspect of ourselves we are disgusted with, maybe an audience we want to entertain. Most of the time we talk to a kind of sympathetic, understanding presence who already knows everything about us and will readily appreciate what we are going through. I have a name for this presence: The One Who Knows What It's Like.

When you're doing a soliloquy you can either have in mind a particular listener (for some actors just imagining that they are talking to their therapist works wonders!) or just feel the undefined presence of a sympathetic ear, taking in everything you say. It's possible to feel as firmly in touch with your listener as if they were palpably before you. The only difference is that you don't have eye contact. Usually when we talk to ourselves we are engaged in some physical activity, and we carry our assumed listener around with us, rather than planting them in a particular spot and focusing on them. We don't really talk to empty chairs. Nor do we look up at the ceiling when we pray—as if God sat there like a fly.

• • •

In contemporary theater the soliloquy has been largely supplanted by another convention: the telephone conversation. For practical purposes, about the only difference is that on the phone you may have to react to specific things your imagined partner supposedly says from time to time. That should be no problem—you probably learned to "listen" on the phone in your beginning acting class, and you may need only to remind yourself to take the time to do so. As with the soliloquy, you can just let your eyes wander, perhaps to imaginary objects on a "fourth wall" or to an imaginary horizon with clouds above it at the back of the theater.

• • •

A third type of monologue, probably older even than the soliloquy, is a direct address to the audience. In the ancient Greek theater, when Oedipus speaks to the "citizens of Thebes," the actor no doubt addressed not only the chorus, but also the actual citizens of Athens sitting in the theater. Even the night watchman at the beginning of the *Oresteia*, who is supposedly alone, must have spoken to the audience—it would be pretty hard to give the impression that you are "talking to yourself" while wearing a mask and performing in the open air before 17,000 people. There are also good reasons for believing that many of the speeches in Shakespeare that we think of as soliloquies were originally addressed to the audience—and can certainly be done effectively that way today. Hamlet may seem to be talking to himself, but I have the feeling that Shakespeare's villains and clowns (Iago, for example) are taking the audience into their confidence. Remember, too, that Elizabethan actors played on the open stage in close proximity to the audience (some of whom actually sat on the edge of the stage)—and in broad daylight. There was nothing to separate the actors from the audience.

There's even a possibility, though I can't prove it, that the convention of "talking to oneself" on stage became common only after the actors retreated behind the proscenium arch and the houselights were turned out, thus isolating the actors in a pool of light behind a "fourth wall." Chekhov's plays, for example, are full of speeches in which the character seems to be talking to himself. Perhaps they were written this way because it was no longer "natural" to talk to the audience.

In contemporary theater, however, the trend has gone back the other way. Soliloquies are somewhat uncommon, although you can find a few examples, such as Martha's monologue in Act Three of *Who's Afraid of Virginia Woolf?* Instead of talking to themselves, characters are more likely to pick up the phone, as I suggested, and confide in a friend. But they are also, in increasing numbers, daring to step forward to speak directly to the audience, even in otherwise quite realistic plays. I happen to like this particular convention, and one reason I have been arguing for its historical legitimacy is that I want to encourage you to use it boldly and freely.

It's easier to talk to the audience than to yourself, and it frequently results in livelier behavior. There they are, right in front of you, there's nothing for you to imagine. Besides, unlike a scene partner, they haven't heard all this stuff over and over before. You don't have to create the "illusion of the first time," with each audience it *is* the first time. Naturally you will look at your audience, but you don't need to depend on them to give you cues or even particular reactions. In a theater you usually can't pick out individuals anyway because of the lights. In an audition I suggest making your actual auditors part of a larger imaginary audience sitting in between and around them. That way you can include them in your glance from time to time without lingering on them in a way that might make them uncomfortable.

• • •

You are the one who determines what your relationship with the audience is, and most of the time they will go along with whatever you assume. Quite often it's helpful just to realize that they have been sitting here watching the play and may have some feelings about what just happened or, if it's the opening monologue, some curiosity about what is going to take place. For example, if you're doing the Petruchio speech from *Taming of the Shrew* that we worked on earlier, remember that the audience has just seen Kate in action a few minutes ago, and they may relish the prospect of her comeuppance as much as you do.

The audience is almost always on your side. Even when they are not actually on your side, you can assume that they are, as Iago certainly does. The audience is The One Who Knows What It's Like multiplied by hundreds or thousands. It may help you to think of them as close friends or some kind of "support group" who have gone through exactly the same kinds of experiences you're talking about. They will cheer your political views, understand immediately the "in" jokes you tell, appreciate the irony in your plight. (No actors I have ever seen are better at establishing this intimacy than those of Brecht's Berliner Ensemble. Brecht was trying, as he explains in his theoretical writings, to get people to see what they never saw before, but the way his actors go about that is surprising: instead of haranguing us, as American actors tend to do when they play Brecht, they look at us with knowing eyes and hint at secrets to which they assume we are already privy. "This is how the world goes," they seem to suggest, "and don't you and I know it!")

No matter what kind of analogy you use to establish the necessary intimacy, you always need to take into account the actual human beings sitting here in front of you. You run the risk, of course, of their not responding the way you expected, and that risk is rather high when there are only a handful of people sitting there at an audition. But remember that what counts is not so much their actual reaction after you have spoken but the reaction you assume you are going to get before you speak.

In life we base what we do to others on assumptions about how they will react, and sometimes the assumption is so strong that we don't even notice the actual reaction. If we firmly believe that what we have to say is fascinating, we can go right on talking animatedly in the face of stifled yawns and restless eyes. More often, however, just assuming a certain reaction will in itself bring it about. If we are delighted to share good news, others usually become delighted with us. If we go to a friend with a tale of woe, the friend is likely to begin commiserating even before we open our mouths. If we go into a strange bank expecting not to be trusted, we will get a fishy look from the teller, whereas the professional con man will walk away with a million. Even in love, expecting rejection may bring it about, while just assuming that the other person finds one attractive can make even the most unlikely lover irresistible. (I think that's Richard's secret with Lady Anne in

Richard III: actresses sometimes find it hard to understand why she gives in to this misshapen toad who killed her husband and is now wooing her at the funeral of her father-in-law, whom he also killed, but I think it's precisely because Richard has the audacity to assume that she has a secret yen for him.)

• • •

So far I've talked about three kinds of monologues and, despite some differences, your task is the same in all three: you need to feel the presence of a particular kind of listener. It's the same with the fourth, and by far the most common type of monologue, when your listener resides not inside your head, not on the other end of the phone, not out there in the house, but right here on stage with you. Even in a scene, when you have a living, breathing person in front of you, reacting to every word you say, you still need to discover who that person is to you, what it is about them that provokes you to treat them the way you do. In other words, you need to make exactly the same kinds of assumptions that you make when doing a soliloquy, a telephone call, or a direct address to the audience.

This kind of speech may be harder for you to do at an audition, when you must either talk to an imaginary partner or focus on your auditors in a way that might make them uncomfortable. In Part Three I'll deal in some detail with that perennial question, "Where should I look when I'm auditioning?", and I'll suggest some conditions under which it would be appropriate for you to ask your auditors whether they would mind being "used," but for now let's assume that you choose to imagine the presence of your partner. That may not be as hard as you might think. If you can picture a listener in your mind's eye during a soliloquy, or at the other end of a prop telephone, it may not be too huge a step to imagine one across the room from you.

What matters is that you feel a special kind of connection with your listener, whether real or imaginary. I pointed out how frequently soliloquies and speeches to the audience are directed towards The One Who Knows What It's Like, and that's often the case too with monologues intended for a stage partner. The monologue is commonly a way of opening our hearts, and we don't open our hearts to somebody we feel will not understand. (Of course we can assume that a stranger, or even a horse, will understand.) When I coach actors I frequently ask them to take a monologue out of context and ask themselves, if this were something they wanted to say, who would they pick to say it to? Almost always I get such answers as "my best friend," "my husband" (seldom "my wife," curiously), and, of course, "my therapist."

Even when the relationship is more adversarial than supportive, we tend to speak to something within the adversary that at least *ought* to understand. The woman in *A . . . My Name Is Alice* who tells her husband off must assume that he is somehow capable of seeing how idiotic his position is, or she wouldn't go to such lengths to make that clear. When George accuses Martha of having "moved bag and baggage into your own fantasy world," he must assume that she is still sufficiently in touch with reality to appreciate how unreasonably she has been behaving. In a sense we always speak to The One Who Know What It's Like because we hope at least, often in the face of compelling evidence to the contrary, that even the most obdurate antagonist has some capacity for understanding.

Sometimes we say, "You couldn't possibly understand this," or "You have no idea what it's like," and then go right on talking as if the person is perfectly capable of understanding and already knows exactly what it's like. Actors who take such expressions literally tend to work too hard to "get through" to the listener, thus making the issue not what they have to say but whether the listener will accept it. If you want to convey how exciting or horrible or absurd an experience was, you need to focus on the experience itself, not on overcoming any difficulty your listener might have in understanding you. If you want to express how you feel about something, you have to assume that your listener is receptive.

• • •

You may, as I've said, be mistaken in your assumption. I am sometimes astonished at how readily we endow others with a greater capacity for empathy than they actually exhibit, and how long we can persist in our error. There's a monologue in Neil Simon's *Brighton Beach Memoirs* that illustrates this point nicely. Nora comes home with news that she feels will thrill her family as much as it does her:

NORA: (*A little breathless.*) **Okay! Here goes!** . . . **I'm going to be in a Broadway show!** (*They look at her in a stunned silence.*) **It's a musical called *Abracadabra*. This man, Mr. Beckman, he's a producer, came to our dancing class this afternoon and he picked out three girls. We have to be at the Hudson Theater on Monday morning at ten o'clock to audition for the dance director. But on the way out he took me aside and said the job was as good as mine. I have to call him tomorrow. I may have to go into town to talk to him about it. They start rehearsing a week from Monday and then it goes to Philadelphia, Wilmington, and Washington** . . . **and then it comes to New York the second week in December. There are nine big musical numbers and there's going to be a big tank on the stage that you can see through and the big finale all takes place with the entire cast all under water.** . . . **I mean, can you believe it? I'm going to be in a Broadway show, Momma!** (*They are all still stunned.*)

Now here's a situation that should be easy enough for you to connect with. What if you got a lead role in a Broadway play or a major film, or a contract role on television? To whom would you rush to tell the good news? Probably somebody who has been supporting you for a long time and has dreamed of this very thing for you and knows how much it means to you. That's exactly how you should think of the people you address in the play, particularly your mother. The curious thing here, however, is that Nora's family is not delighted for her; on the contrary, they are horrified. They look at her, as Simon says in his stage direction, "in stunned silence."

But Nora doesn't even seem to notice. And it takes quite a while for her to realize that they're not really thrilled for her. In fact, this monologue is followed by fifteen lines of dialogue, mostly questions from Nora's sister and mother and her responses, before she finally says, "My God, isn't anybody excited?" If you become aware too soon of what they're really thinking, your passion to share your joy will dry up in the middle of the monologue. But if you start out absolutely certain of an enthusiastic response and allow yourself to be carried away with the wonderful thing that has happened, you may not even notice their stone faces, or if you do, you can just assume that they are stunned with joy. Then, if you're doing the whole scene, the truth will dawn on you gradually, bit by bit, during the dialogue that follows.

With speeches that are addressed to a reluctant listener, it's sometimes helpful to take them out of context, as an exercise at least, and try saying them to a kind of ideal listener. You may find that it makes sense to do the speech that way to your actual listener. That kind of adjustment may also work when playing with a scene partner who does not give you what you feel you need or for an audience who is less than enthusiastic about the show.

• • •

The closest I've ever come to devising a "formula" for acting is this: get in touch with your partner, discover what it is about that person that prompts you to communicate the particular thing that the character wishes to convey, and then convey it. "To what in you do I direct these words?" is for me a key question. You may be surprised to find how readily you can discover (or elicit) exactly the right quality in the actual actor you're playing with. But it is also possible to "endow" your partner—or even a spot on a wall—with some quality that drives you nuts with rage or wild with lust or perhaps makes you melt with compassion.

You may find it helpful to "substitute" somebody you

know in your own life for your partner or to imagine that person across the room from you if you're working alone. Some actors use substitutions a lot (I'm one of them), while others prefer not to make conscious use of their own experience. If you do substitute somebody from real life, it's important to use that person only in order to discover the *nature* of the connection. The actual connection must be with what is right in front of you, here and now. You can't paste somebody else's face over your stage partner's, nor can you ignore the fact that you are looking at a spot on the wall. But you can recall how you relate to a real person at certain times and then relate that way to the partner or the spot. I find that I can use the same person from my own life to discover many different kinds of connections. The important thing is to feel strongly connected, to sense that everything you do is being elicited, in a sense, by the presence of another, and is having a particular kind of effect on that presence.

The nature of the connection may of course change. Sometimes such a change marks a dramatic turning point in a scene or monologue. Here is a monologue in which the way the speaker relates to the listener changes several times. It's from the film *Paper Moon*, screenplay by Alvin Sargent, based on a novel by Joe David Brown. Trixie is trying to coach Addie, the ten-year-old daughter of her boy friend, back into the car.

TRIXIE: **Hey, what's up, kiddo? Daddy says you're wearin' a sad face. Ain't good to have a sad face. Hey! Hey, how would you like a colorin' book? Would you like that? You like Mickey the Mouse?** (*Little girl kicks her.*) **Ohhh—son-of-a-bitch! Woo . . . Ah, now come on down to the car and let's all be friends. You see me smile? Come on, let's see you smile like Aunt Trixie. Now, come on, come on down to the car with Mademoiselle.** (*Pause.*) **Kiddo, I understand how you feel, but you don't have to worry. One of these days you're gonna be just as pretty as Mademoiselle, maybe prettier. You already got bone structure. When I was your age, I** didn't have no bone structure. Took me years to get bone structure. And don't think bone structure's not important. Nobody started to call me Mademoiselle until I was seventeen and gettin' a little bone structure. When I was your age, I was skinnier than a pole. I never thought I'd have nothin' up here. It's gonna happen up there, too. (*Pause.*) Look, I'll tell you what—want me to show you how to use cosmetics? Look, I'll let you put on my earrings—you're gonna see how pretty you're gonna be. And I'll show you how to make up your eyes, and your lips. And I'll see to it you get a little bra or somethin'. But right now you're gonna pick your little ass up, you're gonna drop it in the back seat, and you're gonna cut out the crap, you understand? (*Pause.*) You're gonna ruin it, ain't ya? Look, I don't wanna wipe you out, and I don't want you wipin' me out, ya know? So I'm gonna level with ya, okay? Now, you see, with me it's just a matter of time. I don't know why, but somehow I just don't manage to hold on real long. So, if you wait it out a little it'll be over, ya know? Even if I want a fellow, somehow I always manage to get it screwed up. Maybe I'll get a new pair of shoes, a nice dress, a few laughs . . . Times are hard . . . Now, if you fool around on the hill up here, then you don't get nothin', I don't get nothin', he don't get nothin'. So, how about it, honey? Just for a little while. Let old Trixie sit up front with her big tits.

Trixie adopts a number of different "roles" in relationship to Addie in this monologue, but you don't have to think of her as being insincere. It's pretty clear that she hasn't had much experience dealing with kids, and so she tries various ways of reaching Addie. Of course her goal is to get the kid into the car, but it's quite possible that she could be genuinely warm and supportive to a young girl who is troubled even if she didn't also happen to want something from her.

In any event, Trixie clearly starts out by assuming the role of the jolly adult, trying to cheer up the child who is bothered by some trifle. We all play that role at times, but we tend to assume it with children much younger than Addie. I suggest talking to Addie exactly as you might to an adorable two-year-old who looks terribly sad but can easily be persuaded to give you a little smile.

Doing that to a ten-year-old is of course the worst kind of insult, and Trixie certainly deserves the kick she gets. Now she must try a different tactic. The assumption now is that she and Addie are great pals and will have a terrific time together. I would make the smile as genuinely warm and enthusiastic as you possibly can.

When that doesn't work either, Trixie next tries to show that she understands what is really bothering Addie. She is now dealing with her in a way more appropriate to her actual age. I would suggest here talking to The One Who Knows What It's Like in Addie. That is, assume that Addie will readily accept that you understand her and knows already that she will eventually turn into a beauty—all you have to do is remind her of what is obvious. If you tried instead to get her to accept something she is reluctant to believe, you would revert to treating her at the younger level—and you'd also be less likely to get her into the car.

But even this approach doesn't work. Trixie next adopts the role of the fair-minded parent who tries to make a deal with the child. We parents have all tried making that kind of "bargain" with our kids. "Look," we say when all else has failed, "tomorrow we'll come back to the fair, and we'll go on all the rides, and I'll buy you some cotton candy, but right now we are going straight home and you are going to march right into that bed."

Clearly Addie remains unmoved either by the prospect of a lesson in makeup or the direct order to get into the car. At this point Trixie makes a startling shift. She drops all pretense of a mother-daughter relationship and begins to address Addie woman to woman, as if she were her own age. She talks to her as she might to an adult rival, on equal terms. To capture that connection through a parallel improv, you might try talking to an understudy who plans to quit the company because she never gets to play your role. If she persists in making a fuss, the company will be disrupted and neither one of you will get what you want, but if she holds out just a little longer she will certainly take over the role because to tell the truth you're not such a good actress and you always screw up every acting job you get anyway.

I find Trixie's honesty quite touching here. Also her self-deprecating humor. She's not really saying how painful her life is (though there may be considerable pain under the surface), she's talking about how ridiculous it is that she could ever be a threat to another woman. Deep down she may still long for more than a passing relationship, but she knows there's not a hope in hell of that, and she's perfectly content to stick it out long enough for "a new pair of shoes" and "a few laughs."

At the end of the speech Trixie asks directly for what she wants: "How about it honey? . . . Let Trixie sit up front with her big tits." This direct approach is quite a change from the manipulative tactics she employed earlier. And it seems to work a lot better, too.

• • •

What makes this speech unusual is the number of different ways that Trixie finds to connect with Addie: she begins treating her as a two-year-old and ends treating her as an adult. The speech is unusual in another way. In most of the monologues we've examined so far, you can simply assume that you are getting exactly the kind of feedback you expect. In this case you need to react several times to unexpected feedback. For that reason you might think that this speech would be harder to do for an audition, where you would not have an Addie there to supply you with cues. But actresses who have worked on this monologue tell me that they actually find it easier. Perhaps that's because Addie's reactions are so specific and so clear. At any rate, this is another example of the surprising capacity of human beings to create their own reality, in defiance of the laws of physics. Whatever we assume to exist has a way of coming into being.

I'm not saying that connecting with an imagined partner is easy. It is one of the two most difficult problems in doing monologues for auditions. (The other, getting started out of context, we'll take a look at in the following chapter.) But understanding the power of assumptions can make it less formidable. Also, there are ways of compensating. The most useful is to at least rehearse your monologue with another actor, and I recommend that strongly if it's at all possible. Once you discover how the presence of a real listener affects you, you can sometimes remove the person without too much damage. In my monologue workshops I frequently ask actors to address their monologue to another actor or to the group as a whole. They usually find it easy to assume that a whole intimate history exists with people they may have met only an hour ago, and the monologue almost always becomes more spontaneous and believable.

Even when I coach privately, I often ask an actor just to "talk to me," and I try to give the kind of feedback that seems appropriate. Again the results are frequently astonishing: the monologue becomes so "real." Sometimes it's hard for me to convince people it's because of what *they* did, not because of what I did. They got their attention outside of themselves, they stopped listening to themselves and trying to get it "right." Instead they concentrated on conveying thoughts and feelings that really mattered to somebody who was really there.

• • •

If they can do that talking to me, it may not be too big a step to do that talking to a spot on the wall. Actors sometimes make that problem more difficult than it need be by questioning whether they "really" see the person there (or course they don't!) or by assuming that they must look constantly at the spot, as if the listener is created by their staring and might disappear the instant they avert their eyes. I find it helpful to say that we "accept" the presence of another person rather than "believe" it. We actors don't really create our imaginary world, we assume that it already exists. When God created the world, all he had to say was "Let there be . . ." If he'd had to work any harder at it, he never would have succeeded.

Dealing with an absent partner is not just a necessary evil at an audition. It can also be a fine art. Nobody I've seen is better at it than Eric Bogosian. He somehow establishes, with no apparent effort, the presence of a particular kind of listener in a particular location at the beginning of each of his monologues. He seldom looks directly at his listener for any length of time, in fact he may only glance three or four times in a whole monologue, but the listener is always there. You can feel the words going out towards their target, even though the eyes may be occupied elsewhere.

What counts is being connected, and you can feel perfectly connected without looking at all, as often happens when we carry on a conversation sitting side by side on a park bench or in a car. And you can stare at somebody all day long and not be connected for one instant.

If you observe people talking in life, you will find that they look at each other far less than most actors do on stage or in film or television. In fact, staring deeply into each other's eyes is another one of those cliches of modern acting, like reliving the past, that will probably look absurd to some future audience. It's accepted now because audiences are used to it. But already it's done far less than it used to be. If you look at some of the films of the 1930s, for instance, you see a close-up of the hero staring at the heroine, interminably, cut to the heroine staring back, also for quite a spell, cut to a two-shot of them drawing closer together, ever so slowly; they almost kiss, but not quite, and then finally they look away, understandably embarrassed. It looks pretty silly now, but I think a lot of what still goes on will look silly to the next generation.

It's true that in life, when we listen to others, we look at them more often than not—after all, that's only polite. Some experiments by psychologists have shown, however, that the degree to which the listener looks at the speaker depends to some extent on their relative status: a boss listening to an employee tends to look less steadily than the employee listening to the boss.

When we are speaking, whether we look or not, and *how* we look, depends a great deal on what we intend to communicate. Take the sentence, "What am I going to do?" If you know that you are in a hopeless situation and that there is nothing to be done, you might not look at your listener at all, or if you do look, your glance will probably soon drift away. Only if you expect the other person to supply you with an answer would you keep your eyes fixed on your listener. The first kind of communication is rather common in life, but actors tend to get locked into the second. To some extent they may have been taught to do that. Perhaps they have been told that they must always go "after" something from their scene partner. (That particular theory causes a number of other difficulties that I'll take up in a later chapter.) Or they may have been taught that they must always "relate," but they haven't learned yet how to relate without staring. Curiously, I sometimes find it helpful to say to an actor, "See what happens if you look away while you're saying that." That in itself may be enough to induce the actor to try a more interesting choice.

Where do we look when we don't have eye contact? Again you can find out easily enough by observing yourself and others in conversation. If we are engaged in an activity we might focus on an object in our hands. If not, we usually let our glance wander off to either side of the listener, but if we want to indicate that we wish to continue the conversation, we keep our body turned more or less in the general direction of the listener. It's quite awkward to keep looking away and then back at a very wide angle. That's why, when we're seated side by side on a bench or in a car, as I pointed out, we tend not to look very much, and we have a kind of "permission" not to do so because we are presumably looking at the scenery or the road ahead. But sometimes a side-by-side conversation takes a different turn, and one or both people feel a stronger need to make eye contact; in such cases they usually turn their whole body in the direction of the other and keep it that way for some time.

• • •

Monologues, by their very nature, consist mainly of communications that do not require immediate responses. We may appreciate it if our listener gives us supportive nonverbal feedback: nods of understanding, expressions of concern, smiles of delight, looks of amazement. But we do not have to wait for such responses from the listener. If we feel that we must have a particular response before we can go on, we stop of course, and then we become engaged in dialogue.

If we get negative feedback, looks of disapproval or impatience at the amount of time we are using up, we can choose to go on anyway or to stop and deal with the resistance. Again, if we stop, the monologue becomes a dialogue. I pointed out earlier that certain dialogues are actually interrupted monologues because the speaker could continue on the same track even if the listener's lines were cut. In the same way, certain monologues are more like dialogues because the speaker continually reacts to what the listener does nonverbally. Trixie's monologue in *Paper Moon* is a good example.

With most monologues we go on talking until we have made our point, and even then we have a choice: we can look in a way that invites a response or we can let our eyes drift away, continuing to express nonverbally whatever we were expressing in the last sentence. We might or might not start up again—we are at what I called earlier a "full rest." If we feel finished we are at what I called a "silence." We might then turn our full attention to some physical activity or just sit there or maybe even get up and leave the room. Of course something might happen to set us going again. If you understand the range of possibilities, you may not feel so dependent on getting stimuli from an absent person when you are working alone.

• • •

It's a curious paradox: we need to feel constantly that we are in close connection with a partner, we need to be keenly aware of our partner's reaction, but we do not always depend on those reactions for what we do. Often what matters more than the actual reaction is our sensitivity, even before we open our mouths, to the potential effect of what we are *about* to do.

A number of acting exercises are designed to encourage actors to become sensitive to whatever the partner does, and I feel they can be very helpful. When I used to teach beginning acting, I often had two actors talk to each other using the alphabet, the first actor saying "A" and the second "B" and so on, and letting the sense of the dialogue be determined entirely by what each intuitively feels to be going on. (The exercise is somewhat similar, as I found out later, to the "repetition" exercise in the Meisner technique, in which actors simply repeat the same words back and forth to each other, again allowing for spontaneous interchanges.) Now that I do mainly monologue work, however, I find myself reminding actors that what they do is not always determined by what their partner does.

The alphabet exercise, I now find, can work even with an imagined partner. When an actor seems to be self-absorbed in doing a monologue, I sometimes suggest he or she picture a close friend across the room, "hear" the friend say "A," respond with "B," then hear "C," and so on, again of course operating intuitively and with no preconceptions. At some point in the middle of the exercise, the actor breaks into the first line of the monologue. During the monologue the actor keeps picturing the kind of supportive feedback that I described earlier, the particular facial expressions, gestures, or remarks that the friend might make at a particular moment. The results are very similar to what happens when I ask the actor to talk to me personally. In both cases all it really takes is for the actor to accept the presence of another human being.

You might also try talking to inanimate objects. It is really possible, for example, to talk to a doorknob. You can treat the doorknob as a dear friend or a vicious enemy. You can notice that it doesn't seem to be feeling very well today, and you can express your concern. Or you can listen incredulously as it expounds some preposterous theory and then proceed to set it straight.

Even in an audition you might find it easier to address a real object on the back wall than an imaginary person. (Try both ways and see which works better for you.) If you do picture a person in front of you, don't try to see the person down to the last detail—a vague impression of the face is often enough. I myself prefer not to set up an empty chair—it just reminds me that nobody is sitting in it. I like to work either with a real object or an imaginary person, I don't like to mix them up.

• • •

We can compensate a lot for the absence of a human partner, but it's never really quite the same. A doorknob, we must admit, has only a limited capacity to surprise us. Put it up against a human being in that department and it is at a clear disadvantage. In acting we must always allow ourselves to be open to the unexpected, to be caught off guard. No matter how specific our choices are, no matter how confident we feel about them (and I like to be very specific and very confident), we must always allow what actually happens from moment to moment in a performance to register on us and perhaps bring about at least subtle modifications in what we do. Working alone, we are deprived of our chief source of surprise, and so we have to be more attentive to other sources, slight changes in the ambience of the room or in our digestive organs— anything that will keep us rooted in the here and now.

We don't necessarily have to respond to every stimulus— for example, if our auditors are clearly restless we don't have to "use" that, but we do need to accept it as part of our mixed fiction-and-reality world. We don't need to shut out distractions, they can just be there and not matter. What matters is that compelling presence, real or imagined, that draws our attention like some giant magnet, so that we feel almost that we are taken out of ourselves into somebody else. To be strongly connected is almost like occupying somebody's else's space.

12

Getting Started Out of Context, Staying Alive in the Pauses

Next to relating to an absent partner, the most difficult problem in doing monologues for auditions is getting started out of context. In life (and in the theater when we do the whole play) events propel us into speech. Things happen over time, tensions accumulate, and by the time our cue arrives we can hold back no longer, there's something we absolutely have to say. In an audition, however, we may not feel like saying a thing. The auditors, having looked over our picture and resume and perhaps offered a few friendly words, look at us expectantly, and we know it is time to begin. How do we get ourselves started?

The problem exists not only in auditions. Film is notorious for requiring us to work out of context. And even in theater, whenever the lights come up on a new scene and whenever we make an entrance, we need to feel not that we are beginning, but continuing. Here I will focus on the problem as it exists in auditions, but the same techniques may be useful in other situations.

• • •

Naturally you'll want to become familiar with the events that led the character to this particular point in the play—the "previous circumstances" as they are called in many acting classes. But you don't need to take upon yourself the burden of making all this history clear to your auditors—after all, you're only doing three minutes, you're not responsible for the whole play. If the character happens to have a cold, for example, that may or may not be important in the particular segment you've chosen.

You don't even have to use the actual circumstances at all. For an audition it may be simpler for you to invent a parallel context of your own. You can assume you are delivering the speech to somebody from your own life, you can pick any place where you might happen to be with this person, and you can then ask yourself what might have happened between you that would lead you to want to say what the character says. In my monologue workshops I often find it useful to have an actor improvise a brief dialogue with a partner, setting up the circumstances in such a way that the actor is led into the first line of the text without a break; at that point the partner stops talking but continues to offer nonverbal feedback.

You may want to invent a considerable amount of background detail—some actors even like to write out a kind of "autobiography" of the character. But all this is homework. You don't have to review all the previous circumstances in your head each time before you do the speech. What you need is one simple event, something that happens just before your break into speech—a kind of "springboard" that will launch you into the text.

You can supply yourself with a "cue" of this kind in several different ways: 1) you can "listen" to something your imagined partner says, 2) you can say something silently yourself before you speak the first line of the text, 3) you can react to an imagined sensory stimulus, or 4) you can do a simple physical activity.

• • •

Let's use as an example of the first technique a speech from Noel Coward's *Fumed Oak*, one of the plays in *Tonight at 8:30*. Henry Gow has patiently endured a nagging wife for fifteen years, all the while secretly saving up for the day when he can finally tell her what he thinks of her and run off to begin a new life. The day of liberation has at last arrived. Henry comes home, having fortified himself with a few drinks; his wife Doris tells him to go to bed, and he turns on her and says,

---

Stop ordering me about, see. What right have you got to nag at me and boss me? No right at all. I'm the one that pays the rent and works for you and keeps you. What do you give me in return, I'd like to know? Nothing. (*He bangs the table.*) I sit through breakfast while you and Mother wrangle. You're too busy being snappy and bad-tempered even to say good morning. I come home tired after working all day and ten to one there isn't even a hot dinner for me; here, see this ham? That's what I think of the ham. (*He throws it at her feet.*) And the tomatoes and the A-1 bloody sauce! (*He throws them, too.*)

If you are doing the whole play, you would already have gone through the humiliations your wife inflicts on you in the earlier scenes, and you would have played the first part of this scene, in which you are just looking for an opportunity to put her in her place, so that by the time she says "Go to bed" you are eager to stand up to her.

But working out of context, you may feel that you need a more provocative cue. If so, try asking what this situation is like. Maybe you're more fortunate than poor Henry and have never been married to anybody who bosses you around. Still you probably know what it's like when somebody tries to take control of your life, telling you to do this and do that, making decisions for you, assuming all the time that they have a perfect right to do so when in fact they have no right at all. You may recall that your mother or father once treated you that way. Or you may remember an older co-worker on your first job who treated you as if she were your supervisor.

Now assume that you have gone along for a time in a submissive role but are now eager to declare your liberation. You are just waiting for the right cue, and finally this person makes a particularly outrageous demand. It doesn't have to be something she actually said, you can make it up. Your co-worker may never have gone so far as to send you out for coffee, but what if she did . . . ?

Imagine anything you like that would make you want to respond with "Stop ordering me about!" Then all you have to do is "listen" to your "cue" and react. Don't worry if, when you say "I'm the one that pays the rent," it suddenly occurs to you that you don't really pay the rent for your co-worker; if you've already imagined that she tried to send you out for coffee, you can just easily imagine that you pay her rent—and what's more she and her mother wrangle over breakfast every morning. Or you might want to shift substitutions in midstream and picture somebody else on the receiving end. Or you could even talk, as I've suggested, to an inanimate object.

What matters is not so much *who* you are talking to but *what* you address in your partner at the moment. Somehow the object—or the actress you're playing with—*becomes* Doris. That's true in life, too, isn't it? When we think we are talking to one person we may at the same time be talking unawares to the ghost of somebody else—a parent or a dead friend or perhaps a half-forgotten love. In the theater we can treat anybody or anything any way we like. We have the extraordinary privilege of mixing up different experiences from our lives, stirring in a dash of fantasy, and coming up with our own unique brew. After all, this is a game we're playing here, we do it for fun, there's no need to get *literal* about it.

• • •

The second way of getting yourself going is to improvise something that will lead you into the first line of the text, first aloud in rehearsal and then silently in performance. The "alphabet" exercise described in the last chapter might work fine. Or you could, as I've suggested, simply repeat your one-sentence summary of the main point: that would not only get you started, it would also help you focus on where you're headed. Another approach would be to improvise a brief "preface" to the text. If you are doing the Colonel's speech from *Look Back in Anger*, for example, you could picture your daughter across the room, say silently, "I'm absolutely baffled, I have no idea what you ever saw in such a . . ." and then interrupt yourself, so to speak, with the first line of the text, "No. Perhaps Jimmy is right." If you're doing Petruchio's speech from *Taming of the Shrew*, you might look at the audience slyly, as if to say, "OK, now that you and I are alone here, I'm going to let you in on a secret," and then add, out loud, "I will attend her here, and woo her with some spirit when she comes."

The silent introduction gets you started acting *before* you speak. It helps you connect with your partner and bring your thoughts into focus. It will also draw your auditors out of their world and into yours, for they will see that already you are occupied with something, and they will wonder what it is. Some actors turn their back to their auditors while they do an emotional "preparation," but if you work the way I'm suggesting here you won't need a lengthy preparation, and you can usually do it facing the auditors and in connection with your listener.

• • •

The third way of launching yourself into a monologue is to react to imaginary sensory stimuli. We've already had a good example in Olga's speech from *Three Sisters*; before you begin you might look out the "window," notice the sunshine and the buds on the trees and the warm air brushing against your face, and then let yourself be struck by how different it was a year ago. You could also combine the sensory stimuli with silent speaking. While noticing the signs of spring, you could say to yourself, "I can't believe it, life is stirring again," and then go into the first line of the text. When I directed this play once, the actress had difficulty getting started. She solved the problem by improvising a long inner monologue, which she kept paring down until eventually it became one word: "Strange!"

• • •

The fourth technique is to do a physical action. I used to use this in the monologue from Gurney's *Scenes from American Life*, quoted earlier. When I first started doing the piece I would begin by opening the letter from Brad and reading it silently, then crumpling it in my hand. After a time I found I didn't really need to read the letter, I could just think about what it said and crumple it. Still later I stopped bothering with a real piece of paper, it was enough just to think of what was being asked of me in that letter.

• • •

The same techniques that help you get started on a speech may also help you stay alive during whatever pauses you take in the middle of the speech. I described earlier several different kinds of pauses: those that you take while on your way towards completing a thought; "full rests," which you take after you have completed the thought, at which point you may or may not start up again; and "silences," which you take when you have no intention of going on. At any one of these points you can "listen" to responses coming from your partner or picture nonverbal feedback. With some monologues it's especially helpful to imagine the kind of supportive feedback described in the last chapter. It can also be helpful to be aware of sensory stimuli or to remain engaged in a physical activity while you are speaking. Any of these techniques may help to relax you, increase your involvement in the situation, and above all, take you mind off the words.

But the most useful technique for staying alive in the pauses is to insert brief improvised comments between the lines. Again you can do this aloud in rehearsal and then silently in performance. Let's take a look at how this technique might work with the monologue from Pinter's *Request Stop* that we examined earlier. This speech almost demands that you start by responding to an imagined cue; you could "listen" to anything you like that is sufficiently insulting. But then you could also add, both at the beginning of the speech and during the pauses, the kinds of improvised comments that I have suggested in brackets below.

WOMAN: [I can't believe my ears!!!!!!] **I beg your pardon, what did you say?**
(*Pause.*) [The nerve!!!]
All I asked you was if I could get a bus from here to Shepherds Bush.
(*Pause.*) [A perfectly innocent question.]
Nobody asked you to start making insinuations.
(*Pause.*) [You have no right. No right at all.]
Who do you think you are?
(*Pause.*) [I mean really!]
Huh. I know your sort. I know your type. Don't worry. I know all about people like you.
(*Pause.*) [You don't fool me for one second.]
We can all tell where you come from. They're putting your sort inside every day of the week.
(*Pause.*) [The jails are full of your kind.]
All I've got to do is report you, and you'd be standing in the dock in next to no time. One of my best friends is a plain clothes detective.
(*Pause.*) [Just you wait, my boyo, you'll see.]
I know all about it. [I see right through you.] **Standing there as if butter wouldn't melt in your mouth.** [Mr. Innocence!] **Meet you in a dark alley it'd be . . .** [a brutal, filthy rape] **. . . another story.**

Notice that the silent insertions simply repeat the present thought in different words. They do *not* look forward to the coming thought. That's important because the insertions are simply one way of doing something I've recommended several times in these pages: always stay with the existing thought, "dwell" on it, so to speak, keep expressing it nonverbally until such time as the next impulse arrives. That impulse may be to express the same thought again in different words, or it may be to express a new thought.

This technique is especially helpful when a totally unexpected new idea dawns in the middle of a speech. Some actors feel that during the pause before such a transition they must try to "think" the new thought. I recommend doing just the opposite: keep dwelling on the present thought and let the new thought arrive in its own time and catch you by surprise. If you go looking for it, how can it surprise you?

Notice also that, with the exception of the comment about what might happen in the dark alley, all the silent insertions are things that you would be perfectly willing to say out loud. The exercise is intended to help you keep expressing what you want your partner to receive. If there's something you do *not* want your partner to get, it's usually better not to verbalize it, even silently. Just let it simmer below the surface; any effect it has on your behavior should be inadvertent. The exception here is interesting: the woman's subconscious fascination with being raped comes very close to the surface. It wants to pop out, but she quickly shoves it back under. Letting something slip can be quite effective once in a while, and Pinter certainly gives you a clue with his use of three dots here, but if you give everything away all the time there will be nothing left to hide.

• • •

Silent insertions are also useful for freshening up a speech that has become stale. Often we find exactly how to do a speech in a way that works, but then simply because it works so well for us we begin, after a time, to repeat the intonations and gestures without the substance. We get on a kind of programmed track. Improvising silent comments will throw you off the track and force you to think about *what* you are saying rather than *how* you are saying it.

I suggest that you improvise slightly different silent comments, both before and in the middle of the speech, each time you do it. That will give you the feeling that you are making it all up, and it will allow the next line of the text to occur freshly to you. If the speech is not a classic or one that your auditors might know by heart, you might even allow yourself the freedom to improvise an insertion or two out loud, or to paraphrase slightly. I would never suggest changing a syllable of the text if you are actually doing the play. But the audition situation imposes so many artificial restraints on you anyway that I recommend cheating whenever it helps you get around them.

• • •

You may want to experiment to find out which, if any, of the above techniques work for you. One may work for one monologue and not another, or you could combine techniques or try different ones at different rehearsals. In performance, forget about technique altogether and trust that the discoveries you made in rehearsal are now a part of you. Above all, don't feel that these are techniques that you *have* to use. Acting is not a matter of fulfilling obligations set by others.

All the techniques described in this chapter are simply artificial devices to help you do what good actors do all the time, often without special effort: they are in continuous communication, they never stop. They begin to express a thought well before the words, and they continue to express it nonverbally after the words, until such time as they begin to express something new. The flow of communication continues even while they are silent or listening to others.

It's the same for both monologues and dialogues. It doesn't really matter whether your line is followed by a line of your partner's or by another one of your own or by silence: in every case you just keep communicating the same thing nonverbally. Suppose your line is "I have no idea where I'm going to sleep tonight." If you make those words real to you, you will probably begin to convey, with your face and body, some sense of being at a loss before you speak, and your listeners may sense already what you are about to say. If you continue to do the same thing after the words, your listeners will not be sure whether you are finished. At this point several different things could happen. You might decide to express exactly the same thing in different words: "I just don't know." Or you might embark on a new thought, "I know, I can get a room at the 'Y.'" Or your partner might come in with a line, "Why don't you get a room at the 'Y'?" If you just stay with the moment, continuing to "lament" nonverbally, the impulse to repeat the present thought or to embark on a new one will seem to come upon you quite unexpectedly. If it happens that your partner comes in with a line, you will actually hear it as if you had no idea it was coming. Many actors feel that the way to "listen" on stage is to stop what they are doing and wait upon the partner. Actually it works better the other way around: just continue whatever you are doing until such time as what your partner does registers on you.

Naturally there will be times when you try to elicit a response from your partner. You might say the sentence about not knowing where you're going to sleep in a way that hints that you'd like your friend to put you up for the night and then look to see whether your friend gets the hint. In that case you might continue the look until you either get a response or give up and try something else. But most of your partner's lines will be volunteered rather than elicited and will occur as a kind of "interruption" to what you are doing. You may be *literally* interrupted in the sense that you are not allowed to complete what you want to say. But more often your partner will break in on the continuing flow of your communication at a point at which you have completed the thought and may or may not intend to start up again.

When you have a line that seems to hang in midair, you can handle it in two different ways. Suppose, for example, that the playwright had written the line we've been working on as follows: "I have no idea where I'm going to . . . ." You might think that your partner is supposed to cut you off before you get a chance to finish. One of the first things many of us were told by our high school drama coaches was to keep talking at such points, just in case the partner doesn't come in on cue soon enough. But it is also quite possible for you to complete the thought nonverbally, perhaps by throwing up your hands, and your listeners might easily understand what was left un-spoken. There could be quite a long pause at that point before the partner picks up the cue, and the pause would hold. Some-times that kind of pause is more interesting than having the line cut off by the partner.

• • •

Being able to stay with the moment is especially difficult in monologue work. Even when we are engaged in dialogue there is much in the nature of our business that conspires to make us rush ahead mindlessly. There's the fear of forgetting our lines. There's the fear of boring people. And there's the terror that we will not be very interesting to look at if we are shorn of our words and stand there naked, so to speak. It's bad enough with scenes, but when we know that we have a page and a half to go before another actor can take over, or two more minutes before the audition mercifully ends, the tempta-tion to rattle off the whole speech and be done with it can be-come nearly irresistible. But the life of the speech is in the mo-ments. Although they may be part of a larger whole and not of equal importance, each moment is precious and must be given its due.

Again, it's possible to fall into the opposite error. Some ac-tors love to "think" on stage, and given the line we've just ex-amined, they are likely to spend an eternity ruminating on where they might possibly sleep tonight instead of knowing al-ready that they have no place and just saying so. How do you know if you are taking too much time or too little? Simple: let your thoughts take whatever time they require. Thought sometimes arrives in a series of lightning flashes: sometimes it dawns slowly. When the thought occurs to you, say it; if it hasn't occurred to you yet, don't say it. Often the thought will occur in the middle of your partner's speech, and you need only wait for the opportunity to come in. That's why the old-fashioned exercise of "picking up your cues" can sometimes be very helpful.

Your task is not to control your thoughts and feelings but

to communicate them. If you stay connected with your partner you will seldom go wrong. It's only when you start talking to yourself instead of to the partner that problems arise. Whenever you rush, it's because there's a voice telling you the audience might get bored. Whenever you dawdle, that same voice is telling you to be careful to get it right. It's the voice of warning and admonition. When it takes over, the connection with the partner is broken and nothing goes on but internal static. You can never tune that voice out entirely, nor should you try to—occasionally it has useful things to suggest. You can just let it be there in the background and at the same time keep sending your own signal out to the one you want to reach.

13

"What Am I Doing?": Making Choices

All the work we've done so far leads hopefully to the same result: you discover what your character intends to communicate at the moment, and you convey that, quite spontaneously each time, to a partner who is really present for you, at least in your mind's eye. Sometimes discoveries occur as you examine the text in private, asking yourself questions and trying to make the content vivid and real to you. Sometimes they take place in rehearsal or even in performance: you become aware of something about your partner at the moment that prompts you to make a startling new choice, or you manage to get so totally absorbed in conveying the present thought that the next one takes you by surprise and comes out in a way that you could never have anticipated.

The act of communicating one thing rather than another is what I call, following Mira Rostova, a "doing." I mean the total act, not just what you do with your voice, but with your face and body as well, with your whole being. You don't have to "tell" your voice and body how to behave. If you've lived sufficiently, and if you have an expressive, well-tuned "instrument," you already know *how* to communicate any number of things, so all you have to do is get in touch with *what* you want to convey and make it your task to convey it. It's that simple.

The problem arises when you don't really understand

what to convey or when you try to convey something that doesn't work in the context—in other words, when you make a bad choice. Very often, as I've pointed out, the best choices are arrived at by a kind of intuitive process. In fact, if you persist in your search, keep your mind open to new possibilities, and trust your gut feelings, you will seldom make a bad choice. Why then are so many bad choices made? Three reasons, I think: first, because words on paper have the peculiar power of making us believe that they can mean only one thing; second, because certain clichés of acting have become so widely accepted that naive actors imagine that that is what they are "supposed" to do; third, because some actors dutifully apply to every situation a formula that has been drilled into them by some teacher or director, often letting the formula override their own common sense.

• • •

In other words, we lose our way when we subject ourselves to the authority of the words, to the example of other actors who are themselves misguided, or to the voice of some teacher or director who takes up residence in our heads and tells us what we ought to do.

The range of choices actually open to us is much wider than we usually imagine. Take a simple sentence, "It's two flights up." On the page the words seem unequivocal: they appear to communicate the location of some apartment or office and nothing more. In other words, they convey information. That's what words are for, right? At least that's what we were taught in grammar school: a declarative sentence is a "statement of fact." Indeed that would be the case if somebody asked you where the Smith's apartment is. You might say, "It's two flights up," simply supplying the information requested. What you would be doing, in Mira Rostova's terminology, is "admitting to the fact." No more than that. But suppose that the person who asked you still looks bewildered—perhaps it's a stranger clutching a piece of paper with an address in her hand and obviously lost—and responds to your first direction by asking "Two flights?" as if she's not quite sure that's correct. In this case you might want to reassure her by repeating, "Yes, it's two flights up." Now you are no longer dealing with the fact, you are dealing with an issue of trust. You could just as easily say, "That's right, you don't have to worry," and the doing would be exactly the same. I believe Mira Rostova would call it "to convince."

Now suppose you have been arguing with your wife or husband about the location of a party you are going to. You know for sure where it is, but your spouse keeps insisting that it's on *this* floor. You might say "It's two flights up!!!!" not to supply information but to "chide" the other person for their pig-headedness. The content of the words in this case is not the fact of where the apartment is but rather the obstinacy of the other person in refusing to believe you.

Indeed, when we use words in speech we rarely use them for their factual content. Most of the time our listener is already acquainted with the facts. If a friend asks you to help him carry his grand piano up the staircase to his new apartment, you might reply, "It's two flights up!" in a way that conveys your astonishment at such an absurd idea. You are certainly not telling him where he lives. You could convey exactly the same thing by saying "Are you out of your mind?" What matters is not the words but what you intend to communicate by them. The same content can be conveyed in almost any words—*except* when you intend to convey information, and then your choice of words is narrowly limited. (In fact a good test of whether the content is factual is to ask yourself whether you could say the same thing in many different ways.) And the same words, as we've just been illustrating, can be used to execute any number of different meanings.

It all depends on the situation. If you have just offered to carry a heavy package for an old lady and she says she doesn't want to take you out of your way, you might say, "It's two flights up" in a way that dismisses the notion that it's any trouble. You might do just the opposite if a friend is helping you move to your new apartment, a sixth-floor walk-up, and as you reach the fourth floor, panting and gasping, your friend asks, "Are we there yet?" You might reply, "It's two flights up," expressing your regret (or "lamenting," to use Mira Rostova's vocabulary) for the ordeal you are putting him through.

It isn't necessary to find a name for the doing, though that might be helpful in distinguishing between two possible choices. Usually it's enough to be aware of *what* you are talking about. If you have a love nest on the third floor and you are standing on the ground floor with your beloved, you might say, "It's two flights up" as a kind of naughty suggestion. You would be talking about how much pleasure is so close at hand. If you have been searching for weeks for the address of a certain company and you suddenly discover, looking through your files, that it's two flights up in the same building where you work, you could use our stock sentence to say, in effect, "How could I have been so dumb?"

If you are having a disagreement with a customer who threatens that, unless you give in to his demands, he will march right up to the office and report you to your boss, you could say, "It's two flights up" to mean "Go right ahead, that doesn't bother me in the least." A somewhat more aggressive choice in the same situation would be to "defy" the customer to take an action that will bring on dire consequences, as if to say, "I dare you to do that, go ahead, you'll see what I'll do to you." If you have travelled thousands of miles to visit an historic site where a famous person, your idol, once lived, and you look up from the street at the rooms where he once lived and worked, you might say, "It's two flights up", conveying a sense of awe at actually being there.

• • •

When we pick words out of the air we seldom have a problem because what we want to say exists already. But when we lift words off the page we can easily be misled into taking them literally. It's a very common mistake, perhaps more common than you might realize, for an actor to appear to tell another character something that person would presumably know already. We saw how that might happen with the first sentence of *Three Sisters*, in which Olga mentions the date of her father's death. Of course the *audience* doesn't know the facts yet, and it may be important that they do, but like most good playwrights Chekhov buries his exposition in the action. We had another example in *Look Back in Anger*: the Colonel says, "It was March, 1914, when I left England," not in order to supply the date (which he might do at a job interview) but in order to remind Alison that it was a very long time ago. If he had said, "After all, I was away for quite a while," the meaning would be pretty much the same. It usually takes less effort to acknowledge existing facts than to establish new ones. If you can accept the facts as already known, then you can give your full energy to conveying how you feel about the facts.

Even when the listener does *not* know the facts, we can still convey some feeling or opinion. "I'm thirty-five years old," we may say, meaning that it's too late to start life all over, and it doesn't really matter whether we are speaking to somebody who knows our age or not. We tend to "admit to the fact" rarely, and then mainly in two kinds of situations: when we respond to a request for information and when we wish to acknowledge certain background information (whether known to the listener or not) in order to lead up to something else. For example, in Shaw's *Major Barbara*, Cusins says to Undershaft, his prospective father-in-law:

Mr. Undershaft, I am in many ways a weak, timid, ineffectual person; and my health is far from satisfactory. But whenever I feel that I must have anything, I get it, sooner or later. I feel that way about Barbara. I don't like marriage: I feel intensely afraid of it; and I don't know what I shall do with Barbara or what she will do with me. But I feel that I and nobody else must marry her. Please regard that as settled—not that I wish to be arbitrary; but why should I waste your time in discussing what is inevitable?

In speaking about his apparent weakness, Cusins is simply acknowledging what might be obvious to anybody—at first glance, anyway—in order to make the point that in certain cases he is the exact opposite. He goes on to admit to his feelings about marriage, and even though these are presumably not yet known to Undershaft, they are not important in themselves. The point is that *in spite of* these feelings he is determined to marry Barbara. The words "I feel intensely afraid of it," may seem to invite you to *act* the fear or perhaps to "lament" for your regrettable weakness. But if you simply "admit to the fact" that you are afraid, your determination will come across all the more strongly. Giving too much weight to a preliminary statement can weaken the main point.

• • •

"Admitting to the fact" may seem like a fairly prosaic thing to do, and most of the time it is. However, a great deal depends on *what* you are admitting to. In William Hanley's *Slow Dance on the Killing Ground*, Glas has hidden for many years the fact that he collaborated with the Nazis. Finally, in a long monologue he tells the story of his life, culminating in two simple sentences: "And then I was transferred to another run, to a place called Mauthausen, and the freight was people. . . . Three trips I made in two months and I carried hundreds and hundreds of people, Jews, to the concentration camp at Mauthausen." Suppose you had really done that! You would probably experience enormous difficulty in admitting to *that* fact. And yet I think that that is the best choice here: to admit to what you did. If you tried to "lament" for what you did, you would give the impression that you are apologizing and seeking forgiveness. How could you ever be forgiven for a thing like that? You just have to accept what you did, and accept what kind of man that makes you. If you are really in touch with the fact, the feeling will take care of itself. Although we used the same term, "to admit to the fact," to describe both what Cusins does and what Glas does, there would be an enormous difference between the two doings because of the difference in content.

No two doings are ever exactly alike. You can't arrive at a doing by deciding what the right name is and then trying to execute that particular doing—as if all the doings had been programmed into your psychic computer and all you had to do was push the right button. I suppose acting would be a lot easier if you could do that, but unfortunately, or perhaps fortunately, it doesn't work that way. You arrive at your choices by immersing yourself in the situation, becoming clear about the content, perhaps trying a parallel improv or taking a different adjustment to the partner. *After* you've discovered what to do, giving a name to it may be helpful as a way of distinguishing it from another possible choice with the same words. I find also that it is very helpful to become aware of certain *patterns* of choices, sets of alternatives that you will encounter in many different situations, such as the choice between conveying facts or your feeling about the facts. The rest of this chapter will point out other common sets of alternatives. The more aware you can become of the different paths that lie before you, and what they lead to, the freer you will be to choose wisely.

• • •

It's bad enough that the words on the page seduce the poor actor into telling other people what they already know. The problem is compounded by that voice inside the actor's head (probably planted there years ago by some intimidating teacher or director) that demands more "conflict" in the scene, thus encouraging the actor to spend enormous energy trying to overcome the supposed "resistance" of the listener to an idea that would in fact be obvious to anybody. Now sometimes there is conflict between people in plays and sometimes there isn't. (I'll have more to say on that question in the following chapter.) And even when two people disagree about something it's not necessary to treat the other person like a nincompoop.

In life when we set out to change somebody's mind we

usually start by assuming that we are talking to an intelligent, knowledgeable person who will readily agree with us once we remind them of what is evident. But on stage we tend to assume that we must work hard to get our partner to believe every word we say. That's usually how actresses approach Trixie's monologue from *Paper Moon*, quoted earlier. Let's take a closer look at one passage:

Look, I don't wanna wipe you out, and I don't want you wipin' me out, ya know? So I'm gonna level with ya, okay? Now, you see, with me it's just a matter of time. I don't know why, but somehow I just don't manage to hold on real long. So, if you wait it out a little it'll be over, ya know? Even if I want a fellow, somehow I always manage to get it screwed up. Maybe I'll get a new pair of shoes, a nice dress, a few laughs. . . . Times are hard. . . . Now, if you fool around on the hill up here, then you don't get nothin', I don't get nothin', he don't get nothin'. So, how about it, honey? Just for a little while. Let old Trixie sit up front with her big tits.

Try doing this passage two ways and see how it feels. First, assume that Addie will have difficulty accepting what you have to say. After all, she *is* a child, and she is resisting your efforts to get her into the car. So spell everything out for her, make sure she understands. Then try the passage assuming that Addie is a savvy kid who *already* recognizes that you're not trying to wipe her out and will immediately see the wisdom of cooperating. In the first case the issue becomes whether she will believe you or not and you will probably find yourself doing what I have called "to convince" with every sentence. In the second you will be free to share different feelings and opinions: you can make light of the notion that a woman like you could be a threat to anybody, you can express your regret that times are hard and that, if she continues to hold out, all three of you will come up empty-handed. The only place where you might choose "to convince" is the last bit when you ask to sit up front, but it's the kind of convincing we do when we assume the listener is already eager to oblige, as when we say to a guest, "Come on, have another piece of cake."

Once you examine both sets of choices, the second might seem to establish a better rapport with Addie and be more effective in accomplishing your goal. But you might be surprised at how many actors get stuck in the first pattern without even being aware of other possibilities. Only if you are able to execute both sets of choices are you really free to choose between them.

You will encounter a similar set of alternatives in a great many monologues, and in dialogues too. Usually the choice is between "convincing" and several other possibilities. Take the sentence, "Believe me, you have nothing to worry about." If you are talking to a fellow student about an examination you found laughably easy, you would probably make light of the idea that your friend would have trouble passing. But if you are trying to calm an hysterical mother whose child has been missing but has just been found, you might try very gently to "convince" her to believe the good news. If you did that to your fellow student you would seem very condescending. Or take the sentence, "There just aren't any jobs out there." If you are talking to fellow actors you might "lament" your common plight, probably with a touch of humor. But an anxious father talking to a teenage daughter intent on a career in theater and oblivious to the difficulty might try to "convince" her. If she stubbornly persisted in denying any difficulty, he might soon shift to "chiding": "I'm telling you, there are no jobs out there, can't you understand that!" But if he knew how to talk to kids he would probably "lament" in the first place.

You need to be guided by the situation. You need to know who you are talking with, how much of what you say is obvious already, and above all how you want to treat your listener. Under most circumstances people get insulted when we try to "convince" them and angry when we "chide," although there are times when we can do both in a friendly way, as when we say to an apologetic visitor, "Take off your coat and stay a while. What's the matter with you!" In life we often inhibit an impulse to do something that might offend others because we don't want to risk a confrontation. But on stage that sensitivity to the potential effect of what we are about to do often disappears: after all, it's only another actor there, not a human being, and there are no real consequences to face. We need to become aware, as Mira Rostova says, of what we are "inflicting" on others.

• • •

There is yet another difficulty that arises from the literal quality that seems to adhere to words once they are written down. It's quite easy to be misled into speaking specifically when the content is really general. Let me illustrate the difference. If you're going to the supermarket and you ask me what kind of fruit I want you to get, I might say, "Apples, oranges, and bananas," indicating the three specific items I would like you to include on your grocery list. But if you ask me whether I like fruit, I might reply, "I love it: apples, oranges, bananas, peaches, pears, kumquats . . . you name it!" I would then be talking not about a limited number of specific items but about fruit in general. I could give two examples or a dozen, it doesn't really matter. And I could leave out apples, oranges, and bananas, they are not important. What is important is my feeling for fruit.

A series of items, once it is written down, tends to look as if it can only be specific. In *The Glass Menagerie*, for instance, Tom says in his final monologue: "I reach for a cigarette, I cross the street, I run into a movie or a bar, I buy a drink, I speak to the nearest stranger—anything that can blow your candles out!" When you read the items on the page in sequence, each one may seem important, as if the listener needed to know the particular things you do. But the point here is that *nothing* you do can erase the memory of the crippled sister you abandoned. First you have to get in touch with that feeling of being unable to forget, no matter what you do, and then you can almost "invent," on the spot, some examples of the *kinds* of things you do to try to forget. You need to "fish" for the examples, in a sense, and you don't know ahead of time whether you will give two or twenty. But if somebody asked you what your daily schedule is, you would know exactly: "I work from ten to two, I make rounds in the afternoon, then I go to dance class." The two ways of speaking are strikingly different: one conveys information and the other feeling. Usually one goes fast and the other slow. Try both and see for yourself.

Learning to distinguish between a specific list and a series of examples is essential when language is used metaphorically. If I am describing three specific symptoms to a doctor, I might say, "My heart skipped a beat, I couldn't catch my breath, and I felt a chill down my back." Three items, no more, no less. But if I am trying to convey how stunned I was by my first sight of the Parthenon, I might say, "I stood there transfixed: my heart skipped a beat, I couldn't catch my breath, a chill ran down my back, I felt my whole body slowly rising from the earth!" Again I could go on and on. Of course I didn't really levitate; it's just that the experience was so indescribable that I need to stretch the boundaries of language to give you at least an approximation of what it was.

That's exactly what happens in a famous monologue from O'Neill's *Long Day's Journey into Night*. I'll quote just a few lines from it here. Edmund, in a rare moment of closeness with his father, tries to describe an almost mystical experience of being at one with nature:

. . . I lay on the bowsprit, facing astern, with the water foaming into spume under me, the masts with every sail white in the moonlight, towering high above me. I became drunk with the beauty and singing rhythm of it, and for a moment I lost myself—actually lost my life. I was set free! I dissolved in the sea, became white sails and flying spray, became beauty and rhythm, became moonlight and the ship and high dim-starred sky!

Of course Edmund didn't literally fall overboard and dissolve like a tablet of Alka Seltzer. Why then does he say that he did? If you've ever had anything like the kind of experience he describes, what is most striking about it is that it is not accessible to words. I remember once looking across an empty snowfield in a remote Vermont wood, seeing the trees standing there so quietly, so calmly, and being overcome by a feeling of stillness and wholeness. I know that no words can describe that feeling, but I can't help trying, and so I might improvise something like, "I felt that *I* was a tree, my feet had roots reaching deep under the frozen ground, I felt the cold wind brushing against the bark of my skin, the powdered snow blowing through the needles of my hair. I felt I would stand there in silence for another century." Now of course I *know* what I am saying is absurd, but I deliberately seek out extravagant language because ordinary language just won't do.

Shakespeare is full of extravagant language, not because the Elizabethans talked so differently than we do, but because the feeling is extravagant. Listen to Juliet, impatient for Romeo to arrive:

Come, gentle night: come, loving, black-brow'd night,
Give me my Romeo: and when he shall die,
Take him and cut him out in little stars,
And he will make the face of heaven so fine
That all the world will be in love with night,
And pay no worship to the garish sun.

The whole speech is full of the most luxuriant sexual imagery ("to die" was at that time a synonym for having an orgasm). There's a kind of wild abandon in Juliet that allows her to improvise these extraordinary metaphors.

And she does *improvise* them in a sense. All she knows ahead of time is the force of her passion, and she keeps "making up" more and more extravagant ways of expressing it. I have been saying all along that you have to have the feeling first and then the words. I would now add that the more extravagant the language, the more you have to "reach" in a way for some simile or metaphor, no matter how far-fetched, that will at last do justice to the feeling. Sometimes actors are intimidated or embarrassed by such language. They approach speeches like this seriously, even reverentially—after all, this is SHAKESPEARE! But they fail to realize that the language is not *meant* to be taken seriously. When you say something absurd you have to know that it is absurd. You have to choose to say something ridiculous. In other words, you have to play with language.

• • •

I don't trust words. They look so innocent lying there on the page, those little black squiggles. "Who, me? I only mean what I say I mean." Sometimes, in fact, they do, but we can't always be sure what may lurk beneath their literal surface. We've just seen how many mundane choices arise from the regrettable tendency to take them at their face value. There is yet another way in which they mislead us: they appear to be utterly serious, when in fact there is often at least a glint of humor hiding behind their poker faces. Missing the humor in a speech is responsible for at least as many bad choices, in my experience, as taking the words literally. Both tendencies are reinforced, as I have said, by naive notions of how you're "supposed" to act derived either from poor role models or misguided teaching.

When we play comedy we usually know enough to look for the humor in the writing. But even in comedy, if the character is in a difficult or painful situation, we may miss the irony. Viola's famous "ring" speech in *Twelfth Night*, for example, is often done in dead earnest. But surely Viola must be aware of how ridiculous it is that Olivia, having seen her dressed as a boy, has fallen madly in love with her. Imagine that really happened—to you! Would you say the line "Poor lady, she had better love a dream," as if you were seriously concerned about Olivia? Or would you make it a wry comment on her chances of being loved in return? There are multiple ironies to be found here:

> My master loves her dearly;
> And I (poor monster) fond as much on him;
> And she (mistaken) seems to dote on me.
> What will become of this? As I am man,
> My state is desperate for my master's love,
> As I am woman (now alas the day!)
> What thriftless sighs shall poor Olivia breathe!

Now that is quite a pickle! If you see the absurdity in it, you can still convey that it's a very real problem. But if you go for the pathos, you will make Viola appear to be rather self-indulgent—and not very bright!

The tendency to miss the irony is even more pronounced when we play material that we think of as "dramatic." We may forget that most of us, when speaking about even very painful troubles, take care to lighten them with humor. In Lillian Hellman's *The Children's Hour*, Martha must feel devastated now that the parents have pulled the children out of her school and accused her and her partner Karen of being lovers—a charge that at the time of the play would be the equivalent of what we call "child-abuse" today. And yet listen to the way she talks:

> There'll never be any place for us to go. We're bad people. We'll sit. We'll be sitting here the rest of our lives wondering what's happened to us. You think this scene is strange? Well, get used to it; we'll be here a long time.

Now I don't mean to suggest that this speech is hysterically funny, but surely there's irony here: that's kind of how life goes, the good people end up losing. When we find ourselves in a hopeless situation we often take what comfort we can in the realization that we are part of some kind of cosmic joke. At least we are not alone.

Or listen to Sorin in Chekhov's *The Sea Gull*, looking back on what appears to him a wasted life:

> When I was young I wanted to be a writer, and I never did. I wanted to speak well, and I spoke abominably: (*mimicking himself*) "And so on and so forth, on the one hand this and on the other hand that." I wanted to get married, I didn't get married. I wanted always to live in the city—and here I am ending my days in the country.

Again you might try this speech two ways. First, go for the pain. Feel the disappointment as deeply as you can. If you can work up a few tears, so much the better. The second time, focus more on how ironic you find the story of your life: it's almost as if somebody up there pulled just the right strings to make sure that you always got exactly the opposite of what you wanted. Be aware, too, that you are not the only one ever to have been made the butt of that particular joke.

You may well find that if you try to convey the irony, some of the pain will come across too. But if you try to convey the pain, the irony will be lost. Besides, if you go for the pain, you will necessarily inflict that pain on your listeners. You will make yourself a burden around their necks. We all know people who do just that to us: another Chekhov character, the widow in *The Boor*, makes a spectacle of how much she is suffering because in her mind that makes her quite romantic. But most of us, when we talk about our troubles, try not to be a burden to our listeners. We use irony as a way of lightening our suffering, seeing it in perspective as a part of the general lot of mankind, including that of our listeners.

Leaving out the irony also creates a burden for the audience. That may be why Chekhov's characters are sometimes described as "whiners" and "complainers" and why some people are turned off by them. But even Uncle Vanya, who is surely one of the most disgruntled characters in the history of dramatic literature, is aware of the irony in his having sacrificed his life for no good reason at all, out of sheer stupidity: he can't stop talking about it, in monologue after monologue. He may not be able to accept his fate with the philosophical good humor that Sorin exhibits, or his friend Astrov in his own play: for them irony is a refuge, for Vanya it is a torment. But there's something very funny in the way he cries out against the waste of his talents: "I could have been a Schopenhauer, a Dostoevsky!" Chekhov called most of his plays "comedies," and some directors try to superimpose humor by adding farcical business, but the jokes are written right in, and the main joke is the one that life plays on us all.

Whether we accept our fate, like Sorin, or rage against it, like Vanya, we are almost always aware of the irony in it. In the terminology I have been using here, we "lament with humor." There is one notable exception: when we lament for the sufferings of others we tend not to include humor. When we want to console somebody for a great loss, irony is not much use.

All of this may be obvious, and yet I see actors missing the point time and time again. Why? I think it's because they have been taught, either by example or by word, that their job is always to play the deepest feeling possible. If what the character feels is pain, what you express is pain. But that equation simply does not hold in life. There is an enormous difference between what we do at the moment the pain is first inflicted and what we do later, sometimes a few seconds later, sometimes years later, when we are able to *talk about* the pain. You know what we almost always say at the moment the pain strikes? Nothing. Or we might say "ouch" or groan or cry out "No" in helpless agony. There are times in plays in which the character reacts directly to the pain: Olivier's offstage scream in *Oedipus* is a famous example. But most monologues, and dialogues too, are not direct expressions of raw feeling, they are attempts to share the feeling.

• • •

Besides lightening our troubles, humor often serves another function: it allows us to acknowledge our faults and foibles without feeling guilty. If I stumble while making a simple cross in rehearsal I might say, "There goes old twinkle-toes," thus relieving somewhat my own embarrassment and that of the other actors for me. (I'm not quite sure what I would do if that happened in performance.) That's the same kind of self-deprecating humor that Michelle-Marie uses in her opening monologue in Michael Weller's *Ghost on Fire*, in which she comments to the audience, while smoking a joint, "Even at the very best of times I'm not what you would call heavily into reality." If you have trouble capturing the self-mockery in a line like that, try changing the "I" to "she," as if you were gossiping about somebody else, and it may become readily apparent.

When we talk about our daydreams, we often use humor as a way of letting others know that we are aware of how grandiose they might seem. In David Mamet's *Lakeboat*, for example, a seaman confesses to a youthful dream of becoming a ballet dancer:

JOE: You get paid for doing a job. You trade the work for money, am I right? Why is it any fucking less good than being a doctor, for example? That's one thing I never wanted to be, a doctor. I used to want to be lots of things when I was little. You know, like a kid. I wanted to be a ballplayer like everyone. And I wanted to be a cop, what does a kid know, right? And can I tell you something that I wanted to be? I know this is going to sound peculiar, but it was a pure desire on my part. One thing I wanted to be when I was little (I don't mean to be bragging now, or just saying it). If you were there you would have known, it was a pure desire on my part. I wanted to be a dancer. That's one thing I guard. Like you might guard the first time you got laid, or being in love with a girl. Or winning a bike at the movies . . . well, maybe not that. More like getting married, or winning a medal in the war. I wanted to be a dancer. Not tap, I mean a real ballet dancer. I know they're all fags, but I didn't think about it. I didn't *not* think about it. That is, I didn't say, "I want to be a dancer but I do *not* want to be a fag." It just wasn't important. I saw myself arriving at the theater late doing Swan Lake at the Lyric Opera. With a coat with one of those old-time collars. (It was winter.) And on stage

with a purple shirt and white tights catching these girls
. . . beautiful light girls. Sweating. All my muscles are
covered in sweat. You know? But it's clean. And my
muscles all feel tight. Every fucking muscle in my body.
Hundreds of them. Tight and working. And I'm standing up straight on stage with this kind of expression on
my face waiting to catch this girl. I was about fifteen. It
takes a hell of a lot of work to be a dancer. But a dancer
doesn't even fucking care if he is somebody. He *is*
somebody so much so it's not important. You know
what I mean? . . .

An actor I worked with on this speech caught the humor
in the early part, but when he got to the description of himself
in *Swan Lake* he began to adopt a dreamy and romantic tone.
He spoke quite seriously, for example, about wearing a coat
"with one of those old-time collars" and appearing on stage
with a "purple shirt and white tights," without seeming to
recognize that these were rather silly boyish fantasies. I asked
him if he'd ever had any foolish ambitions when he was young,
and when he confessed to having dreamed of playing center-
field for the Boston Red Sox, I suggested that he improvise a
story of his catching an impossibly difficult fly ball with incredible grace on an idyllic afternoon at Fenway Park. The
more sublime he made the description the funnier he found it.
I asked him to use some of the lines from the text about "clean
sweat" and "tight muscles," and in the context of his own day-
dream he did not romanticize them, he treated them almost as
if he were embarrassed to employ such silly cliches. In other
words, he belittled his dream instead of magnifying it. Oddly
enough, adding the humor did not make the dream any less
beautiful, it just made it more touching: he knows now that he
can never attain his dream. It was different when he was a boy.

There's a similar speech in William Saroyan's *The Time of
Your Life*. Kitty Duval, a prostitute working out of a bar, is
asked by a kind stranger what she is daydreaming about. She
replies,

I dream of home. Christ, I always dream of home. I've no *home*. I've no place. But I always dream of all of us together again. We had a farm in Ohio. There was nothing good about it. It was always sad. There was always trouble. But I always dream about it as if I could go back and Papa would be there and Mamma and Louie and my little brother Stephen and my sister Mary. I'm Polish. Duval! My name isn't Duval, it's Koranovsky, Katerina Koranovsky.

The words here practically beg you to milk every bit of pathos out of them. But you may discover that the speech becomes more moving if you find it stupid that you can't help dreaming about a worthless old farm and a family life that you never really had in the first place. Kitty knows her childhood was not really idyllic, and she is confessing here to being a sap for romanticizing it, just as she romanticized her name.

• • •

So far I've described the difference between speaking literally or feelingly, specifically or generally, solemnly or ironically. I'm sure that my bias towards one choice in each pair comes through. But I want to remind you that I'm not telling you always to do this and never that. I'm simply saying you don't *have* to do this, you have the option of doing that. And of course you have more than two options. I have been describing some common choices that I believe to be misguided, but I'm not at all sure that the alternative I suggest will be clear—perhaps you will follow my directions diligently and end up doing something that doesn't work at all. And even if you understand exactly what I mean, you may find a third choice that is even better. All I can do is repeat that you need to remain open to all possible choices until you find what works best, and even in performance you may continue to make discoveries. You'll be lucky if after a run of a year or more you find the best possible choices in eighty or ninety percent of a role.

• • •

Before ending this chapter I want to suggest one other set of alternatives. When you have been injured by somebody you have the choice of inflicting punishment on the offender or conveying how hurt or disappointed you are by what that person has done. Take the line, "You're not the kind of man to teach me how to be a wife." Out of context the words may invite you to berate your husband for being such an insufferable prig. But there's another possibility here. The line is one of many hard truths that Nora confronts her husband Torvald with in a lengthy monologue, occasionally interrupted by him, that she delivers at the end of Ibsen's *A Doll's House* before walking out the door. Some actresses use this speech as an occasion to vent their resentments against the men in their lives. But Nora has more cause to feel disillusioned than resentful. She has always, for reasons that may not be clear to an objective observer, adored Torvald. She had fantasized over and over again that when he found out she was being blackmailed he would try to sacrifice himself for her. Up until a few minutes ago she was so certain of this that she was prepared to kill herself rather than let him take the blame for her. But when the moment comes, he suddenly turns on her and thinks only of saving himself. How could she ever have loved such a man? In a single moment the fantasy by which she had lived for years is shattered. She must accept that she was just as responsible as Torvald for indulging in that fantasy. But now the painful truth must be spoken. When she tells him he's not the man she thought he was, you have a choice between "chiding" him and "lamenting" about the painful gap between what he once was to you and what he is now. Again, different choices have different consequences: one will just make him angry, the other will leave him devastated. One might arouse ire in the audience; the other, tears.

• • •

Actors love to play resentment. It's readily accessible for most of us, whereas pain sometimes resides at a deeper level. We often find it easier to yell at somebody than to acknowledge the hurt that person has inflicted. Besides, there's no easier way to add "conflict" to a scene than to start castigating your partner. If you do that you may score a lot of points for dramatic intensity. But if you lament the loss of love, your work can be both dramatic and moving. Nobody is ever deeply touched by hearing somebody air their grievances. In fact, they often find it irritating to listen to. That's frequently my response as an audience. And casting people sometimes warn actors to stay away from "angry" monologues for the same reason, I suspect. But the mistake lies not in the choice of material but in the execution.

We tend to think of anger as a single emotion, but actually there are several different kinds of anger. There's the joyous and liberating self-assertion that we found when the wife tells the husband off in *A . . . My Name Is Alice* and again when the husband tells the wife off in *Fumed Oak*. That can be exhilarating to witness. Then there's an all-out temper tantrum. Irritating as that can be in a serious speech, it can sometimes be quite funny, as we saw with Pinter's lady in *Request Stop*. We recognize that the injury is to the pride, not the heart.

Then there's the kind of "righteous anger" that focuses on the enormous injustice that has been done rather than on the malicious person who has done it. Shaw's St. Joan, for example, has as much reason to feel abused as anybody in history: to be branded as a traitor, a witch, and a heretic, when all she was doing was following God's orders, and then to be condemned to life imprisonment even after she has confessed—that seems pretty unfair. When Joan says to her judges, "You promised me my life, but you lied," I feel she is expressing not resentment against them but her shock and dismay. She can hardly believe that holy men of God could do such a dreadful thing. She goes on to describe how intolerable a lifetime in prison would be:

To shut me from the light of the sky and the sight of the fields and flowers; to chain my feet so that I can never ride with the soldiers nor climb the hills; to make me breathe foul damp darkness and keep from me everything that brings me back to the love of God when your wickedness and foolishness tempt me to hate Him; all this is worse than the furnace in the Bible that was heated seven times.

I suppose you might call this an "angry" speech, but it is certainly not the kind of anger you might express to somebody who once again leaves a mess in the kitchen. One kind assumes that people are basically good and finds it appalling that human beings could inflict such suffering on a fellow creature. The other assumes that people are out to get you.

You don't have to be a saint to focus more on the sin than the sinner. In August Wilson's *Fences*, Rose has just learned that her husband Troy is going to father a child by another woman. Troy tries to explain that he needed to have an affair because he felt he had been "standing in the same place for eighteen years." Rose replies,

I been standing with you! I been right here with you, Troy. I got a life, too. I gave eighteen years of my life to stand in the same spot with you. Don't you think I ever wanted other things? Don't you think I had dreams and hopes? What about my life? What about me? Don't you think it ever crossed my mind to want to know other men? That I wanted to lay up somewhere and forget about my responsibilities? That I wanted someone to make me laugh so I could feel good? You not the only one who's got wants and needs. But I held on to you, Troy. I took all my feelings, my wants and needs, my dreams . . . and I buried them inside you. I planted a seed and watched and prayed over it. I planted myself inside you and waited to bloom. And it didn't take me no eighteen years to find out the soil was hard and rocky and it wasn't never gonna bloom. But I held on to you, Troy. I held you tighter. You was my husband. I owed you everything I had. Every part of me I could find to give you. And upstairs in that room . . . with the darkness falling in on me . . . I gave everything I had to try and erase the doubt that you wasn't the finest man in the world. And wherever you was going . . . I wanted to be there with you. Cause you was my husband. Cause that's the only way I was gonna survive as your wife. You always talking about what you give . . . and what you don't have to give. But you take, too. You take . . . and don't even know nobody's giving!

Of course Rose is angry, but she's hurting too. What she wants to convey, I feel, is how unendurable it is that she has given eighteen years of her life to this man, burying as she says all her own wants and needs and dreams in him, only to find that he has given the best part of himself to another woman. There's an unbearable ironic gap here between what she had a right to expect and what she in fact got.

The irony here is somewhat different from the kind we talked about earlier that we use to lighten our troubles: it's a more bitter, painful irony. There is the same kind of irony in Nora's speech to Torvald and Joan's to her judges: in all three cases there is a heartrending gap between what could be and what is. One might hope that Torvald would live up to his wife's idea of him, that Joan's judges would be compassionate, that Troy might give as much to Rose as she to him. Instead, the opposite happens. There are some differences—Nora, for example, seems to accept what has happened, whereas Joan and Rose cry out against it—but all three seem to be voicing deep disappointment in others rather than inflicting punishment on them.

• • •

If you want to see an example of how moving a scene can be when the actor is aware of that painful gap, take a look, if you can arrange it, at the classic scene in the taxicab between Marlon Brando and Rod Steiger in the film *On the Waterfront*.

They are brothers, but Steiger is taking Brando to be shot, and at one point he actually pulls a gun on him in the cab. What does Brando do? Does he explode with indignation? Not at all. He just stares at the gun unbelievingly and then says, very quietly, "Charley . . . Charley." Just two words, but they break your heart. Later in the scene he points out that he could have been a great success as a boxer if his brother had not sabotaged his efforts. "It was you, Charley," he says. "You was my brother. You should of looked out for me." The way Brando does that remains in my mind as one of the most touching moments I've ever seen on film.

I doubt that Brando made a deliberate choice to "lament" rather than to "chide" here. More likely, he was simply aware that this was his *brother* holding that gun. Brothers don't do things like that; brothers love each other and take care of each other. Brando seemed to be deeply in touch with the lack of a love that an older brother should have provided but never did.

• • •

Although I don't believe in formulas, here's a rule of thumb you might find useful: always look for irony in a speech. If the character is being deliberately witty, find and appreciate what's funny. If it's a speech about your own troubles, try using irony to lighten them. If it's about your own weaknesses, including daydreaming, try a touch of self-mockery. If it's about what somebody else has done to you, ask yourself whether there's a painful, ironic gap between what could have been and what is. If there's no irony in a speech at all, or if the character seems unaware of it, try playing the speech very seriously, but don't be surprised if you get a lot of laughs: being solemn about something that other people find trivial is the main source of humor in people who are unintentionally funny.

• • •

Does it seem strange to you that this whole chapter has

been devoted entirely to making choices? Perhaps you were taught that all choices are equally valid. You make one choice and another actor another choice in the same role, and you might hesitate to say flatly that you are right and he is wrong. Instead you say, in all due modesty, "Of course that's just my interpretation." Or a director asks you to give up one choice and do something else and you go along, even though it doesn't feel right, because after all he's the boss, and anyway it doesn't make much difference, it's just a matter of choice, as they say.

I have been arguing that choices are not arbitrary; they are determined by the context, and they matter very much. I've spoken mainly about the effect they have on your stage partner and on the audience, but the main effect may be on yourself. When you are having difficulty with a moment on stage, you may feel that the problem is with your technique—you're not concentrating properly, you're not relaxed, you're rushing or not listening, and so on. There are lots of possibilities, and indeed one or more of them may in fact be the source of the problem. But very often the difficulty vanishes instantly when you try a different choice: you suddenly find yourself relaxed, your concentration improves enormously, and a flood of energy is released that carries you not only through the moment but the whole monologue or scene. That's because you finally understood what that moment was about.

Fortunately it works both ways: when you're feeling relaxed and concentrated, you are more likely to make good choices; and when you have made a good choice, it's much easier to relax and concentrate. But adhering to a bad choice can bottle you up, no matter how hard you try to free yourself. Unfortunately most acting training in America today deals mainly with what Stanislavski called "the actor's work on himself" and neglects what he called "the actor's work on the role." (Those are the literal translations of the titles of his two major works.) Many teachers don't know how to help you take a text apart and discover what you are doing from moment to moment, or they may not want to. They call that part of the teaching process "coaching" or "directing" and don't feel that it is important.

I want an actor with an exquisitely expressive instrument who *also* knows how to read a score and play the right notes. I certainly feel that emotional freedom, imagination, and sensitivity to others are essential to acting—if you haven't developed these qualities naturally or through some sort of a training program, your work will remain quite limited; and the more you continue to develop them after your formal training is complete, the richer your work will be. But I also feel that exercises in emotional freedom cannot be applied indiscriminately to any text. For example, your teacher may have you do an emotional memory exercise that happens to release a flood of tears or an outburst of rage. The teacher may then have you express that feeling in a monologue—any monologue that happens to be handy. The exercise feels wonderful, you get a lot of praise from the teacher and support from your classmates. Nobody bothers to ask whether the feeling is appropriate to the particular monologue. That's just a matter of "interpretation." If you do enough exercises like this and never learn how to examine a text closely, you will come to assume after a time that what counts in acting is the degree of emotional intensity that you bring to the stage. You begin to treat a text not as something to be explored, but as a means for you to demonstrate how freely you can express you deepest feelings. This is precisely the habit of mind that leads to "reliving the past" and failing to grasp the whole of what the character wants to communicate in the present. It is also what leads to some of the misguided choices described in this chapter, particularly leaving out the irony and playing resentment where regret is more appropriate.

Some teachers do go on to a second stage of training and show you how to analyze a script in terms of what you "want." But deciding what that is may be left up to your own whim or the whim of a director. You teacher may even have told you, "I don't care what your choice is here, but whatever you want, go after it strongly." Moreover, as I intend to demonstrate in the following chapter, the particular way that actors are commonly taught to "go after" what they want can, in itself, severely limit the range of choices open to them.

Some directors can help you make good choices and some can't. If you have to depend on a director to make your choices for you, you may be in for a lot of trouble. (I'm talking of course about acting choices, not blocking or "business," which you can usually rely on a director to give you or at least help you with.) What you *can* expect most directors to do is give you feedback on how your choices affect them as an audience of one. Good directors usually know when something is off, though they can't always tell you how to fix it. When a director stops you and tells you to do something different, you may realize that what you were doing was a bad choice, or that you were not really doing what you thought you were. Of course try what the director suggests, but if it doesn't feel right to you, you may be able to demonstrate a third choice—you have to show what you mean, it's no good just talking about it—and the director may accept that. Oddly it may turn out to be exactly what the director had in mind in the first place but was unable to communicate to you. If both you and the director are openminded, you may be able to experiment together until you find what works best. Unfortunately there may be times when a director insists that you do something you find utterly repugnant. In such cases you have three options, none of them pleasant: you can quit the show, you can grit your teeth and do what the director wants, or you can pretend to understand and agree completely and go right on doing what you feel works for you.

Of course when you're doing a monologue for an audition you won't have a director, and you do need to get feedback from somebody. You may be able to find an acting coach you trust, or you might ask a director you know to work with you. You could also try your monologue out with friends or family, but try to get them to tell you how they *react* as an audience rather than telling you what you ought to do. In some cases it's appropriate to ask for feedback from agents and casting directors. Many are eager to give it, but remember that the fact that they are in a position to get you work doesn't necessarily mean that they are experts on acting. Be sure to get feedback from more than one person, and never change what feels right to you simply because somebody tells you it's all wrong, no matter how authoritative this person may sound. You will certainly get conflicting advice from different people, and in the end only you can decide what works best for you.

14

"Why Am I Doing It?": Discovering the Need

An actor came to me once terribly confused and frustrated. He had always been taught that the essential thing in acting was to decide what he wanted to "get" from his partner and then to "go after" that as vigorously as possible. He had been working on a monologue, and he couldn't for the life of him figure out what the speaker wanted from the listener. He felt there must be something wrong with him.

The monologue was the same one I quoted on the cover and mentioned briefly in the chapter on finding the structure of a speech. Let's take a closer look at it here. It's from Horton Foote's *Valentine's Day*, one of nine plays in *The Orphan's Home Cycle*. Horace is talking to his young wife Elizabeth, who is expecting their first child. It's their first Christmas morning together, and they have just been visited by her wealthy father, who was outraged when she ran off to marry him but has now come to make up and lavish expensive gifts on them.

HORACE: **When I was nine I had some chickens that I raised as pets. They were the only pets I'd ever had and I loved them. They would eat out of my hand when I fed them and would follow me around the yard like dogs do their owners. Mama had a boarding house then and on the Christmas of my ninth year, she had no** money to feed her boarders, so without telling me she went out back and killed my chickens for their Christmas dinner. (*Pause.*) When I found out I became ill. I had a raging fever for a week. They despaired for my life. Mama says the illness was never diagnosed. (*Pause.*) When I see her now she is all smiles and honey. She doesn't know the pain and the bitterness and the unhappiness she has caused me. Sometimes when I'm around her I have to walk out of the room to keep from telling her. I am no orphan, but I think of myself as an orphan, belonging to no one but you. I intend to have everything I didn't have before—a house of my own, some land, a yard, and in that yard I will plant growing things, fruitful things, fig trees, pecan trees, pear trees, peach trees . . . and I will have a garden and chickens. (*Pause.*) And I do believe I might now have these things because you married me. I said to myself before our marriage, "She'll never marry you, no matter how much she says she loves you, because her father will stop it. He's a powerful man and he will prevail as he does in all ways." But he didn't stop us; you did marry me, and I tell you I've begun to know happiness for the first time in my life. I adore you. I worship you . . . and I thank you for marrying me.

When I told the actor I didn't think Horace wanted *anything* from Elizabeth, all the anguish drained from his face. "You know," he said, breaking into a grin, "that's what *I* thought." His common sense had told him the formula did not apply, only he hadn't trusted it.

What Horace wants, we both felt, is to express to his wife his adoration for her, his gratitude for bringing him happiness for the first time in his life, and his deep conviction that he will build a whole new life for his young family. He owes everything to her, and he must feel that by marrying him she has been "deprived" in a sense, of the kind of life her father could have provided. He is not yet able, for example, to give her and the baby the kind of Christmas presents her father has just lavished on them. Rather than trying to get something *from* her,

he wants to give something *to* her: the gift of his appreciation
and love. The satisfaction in the speech arises from the very
act of expressing what he feels towards her.

• • •

If you look back at the monologues we have examined in
this book, I think you'll see that in almost every case there is a
similar kind of satisfaction to be found. Sometimes it's the
only kind. Some psychic pressure has been building up, and
the act of communication brings its own reward in release of
tension. The woman in *A . . . My Name Is Alice*, for example,
gets considerable gratification out of finally being able to express her true feelings towards her husband. That is all she
really wants.

Sometimes there is a mixture of present satisfaction in the
communication itself and a feeling of progress towards some
future goal. Louis in *Suicide in B♭* not only takes great pleasure
in articulating his brilliant theory, but he also feels he is moving towards his goals of solving the case and establishing how
wise he is.

We have had only one example of a speech in which the
satisfaction seems to depend primarily on the listener taking a
particular action in response: in *Paper Moon* Trixie wants to
get Addie into the car. But even here I think you could say that
Trixie also gets some gratification out of being able, after several false starts, to communicate with Addie woman to woman.

Even poor Alec in *Dear Janet Rosenberg*, who doesn't really
want to say anything, gets some temporary relief out of breaking the painful silence. A behavioral psychologist might call
that "negative reinforcement." Alec is rather like a rat in an experiment who has learned that whenever he presses a lever the
current supplying an electric shock will be interrupted. And so
he babbles on.

But most communication is satisfying in itself. It is what
the behaviorists call "self-reinforcing": that is, we keep doing it
because we find pleasure in the act itself, although it can also

be reinforced, as I've said, by the positive feedback that we get (or at least have been conditioned to expect) from others. Moreover, the satisfaction occurs at the moment—here and now. We do not have to depend for our motivation on the prospect of some future "reward."

• • •

All this may seem evident. But perhaps you have been taught that you must always pursue an "objective." I used to teach that too, but I don't anymore because the term "objective" suggests a goal to be attained in the future and does not seem to allow for the possibility of doing something for its own sake in the present. Moreover, I can no longer accept Stanislavski's theory that each objective leads into a larger one and all of them into a "superobjective," which he likened to the "spine" of a fish, all the little bones feeding into larger ones. That way of thinking strikes me as rather cold and calculating. I find it hard to believe that human beings organize their lives so neatly. When we are really passionate about doing something, we feel that we are *driven* by the need to do it, and sometimes we don't even know why. We don't have to keep constantly in mind the ultimate goal of our lives, dangling it in front of our noses like some giant carrot.

I prefer to speak of "needs" rather than "objectives." A need is something we experience here and now. We tend to become preoccupied with a present need until it is either satisfied or interrupted by a more pressing one, which forces its postponement. Later on, needs that have been postponed may possess us again and demand attention. But we are usually absorbed by one pressing need at a time or, at the most, torn between two conflicting needs.

Sometimes the need is to do something not very satisfying in itself in order to attain some future goal. But even at such times we tend to be conscious not so much of the future reward as of the immediate pressure to get the task out of the way, like the rat trying to disconnect the electricity. Then, once we start the task, we may find some pleasure in it after all. There may be times when we are dimly aware of a number of unmet obligations circling about in our heads like planes stacked up over La Guardia, each one waiting for clearance to come in for a landing. But we usually manage to attend to only one at a time. Or we may find a way to cut them all out of awareness by getting absorbed in something else.

● ● ●

I don't like to use the term "action" either, because it means different things to different people. Stanislavski was quite right to point out that acting is an active process—we don't try to feel things, we do things. That was one of his greatest insights. But what is it exactly that we do? Stanislavski used the Russian word *deistvie*, which suggests process or movement, and it is usually translated as "action." But many teachers use it as a synonym for "objective." To "play an action" means, as they explain it, to go after what you *want* in a scene or a "beat" (a small section of a scene). Other teachers describe an action as what you *do* in order to get what you want. But if you ask them for an example they will usually give you a physical action, such as "to slap my enemy's face." Ask them what the actor does with words, and they will describe it as a kind of substitute for physical action: you are supposed to "stroke" your partner with words, for example, or "cut her to ribbons."

Perhaps you find that approach helpful, I don't know, but I tried it for years and was totally at sea. I found all these terms very confusing. I prefer now simply to say that we *do* things in order to satisfy present *needs*. The "doing" can be either a physical action or an act of communication.

Today, for example, I am beginning to feel oppressed by the heat and noise of the city in August. I picture myself driving to the country, walking through the silent woods, slipping into the cool water. Very well, that is my need, to get to the country. But what do I do about it? I could just get into my car and go, thus satisfying the need by direct physical action. But if I need company too, I might communicate a number of different things to my wife to encourage her to join me, perhaps "lamenting" how hot it is or "conveying delight" at the prospect of a swim or even "convincing" her to forget about her work. But now suppose that circumstances prevent our going. I could still convey my feeings, not for the sake of getting anywhere, but simply to unburden myself. I might even go on at length expressing how intolerable I find the city in the summer and how much I long to be in the country. I would then be doing a monologue. Monologues, and scenes too, are often played not in order to get something, but in order to relieve our frustration at not getting it or our pain at having lost it.

• • •

If you assume that you must always strive to wrest some prize from somebody who refuses to yield it, you will find it difficult to understand those situations in which all we want from our listener is an attentive ear. We may need to pour out our troubles to a friend, but that doesn't necessarily mean that we are looking for sympathy or advice. In fact we are often embarrassed by sympathy and irritated by advice. We don't want to be pitied or told what to do, we just want to be heard. Naturally we may hope for a particular response, usually understanding. Or if our need is to share some marvelous news, we may expect to see delight on the face of our listener. Usually we get exactly the kind of response we anticipated, but that is because we picked the right person at the right time. We don't speak *for the sake* of eliciting the response, we assume ahead of time that it will be there, and sometimes, as in the case of Nora's monologue from *Brighton Beach Memoirs*, the assumption is so strong that we don't even notice that the response is missing. If we do become aware that our listener seems unexpectedly preoccupied or disinterested, we usually stop expressing the feeling we came to share and withdraw or get angry. Some teachers routinely instruct your partner to present an "obstacle" to you. That's supposed to make you work harder to "break through" the resistance, but it may just make you want to clam up.

• • •

Of course there are times when we want something more than an attentive ear. If you're doing Romeo in the balcony scene you need to be aware that he will never rest until he holds Juliet in his arms. But you don't have to remind yourself, as you climb over the wall, just what you "want" from Juliet, as a salesman might remind himself of his quota before knocking on the door. You are *driven* by the need to declare your love for this fabulous creature, you don't have to egg yourself on. Shakespeare gives you some pretty passionate things to say, and you're not just sweet-talking this girl to get her into bed. In fact you have a rather lengthy monologue (thirty-two lines of iambic pentameter) to speak before you even dare to let her know you are here. If you just wanted to overcome her resistance—which doesn't exist, by the way, though there are plenty of other obstacles to the consummation of your love—one would think you'd get right down to it. Your task as an actor is to make these words your own, to become possessed by an overpowering need to speak them. You find joy in being here at last, alone with her in the moonlight, able to feast your eyes on her and pour out your adoration. There is satisfaction to be found in the expression of your feelings, not just in the attainment of your goal.

Whether you choose to focus on what you want to *communicate* to another person or what you want to *get* from that person can make quite a difference in how you behave. One way of thinking will encourage spontaneous behavior; the other, behavior that is calculated. One will allow you to convey different things at different moments. The other may lead you to lock eyes with your partner and pursue your "goal" with every sentence, looking constantly to see whether you have achieved the desired effect. Of course you need to know what you want in a monologue or scene, but the only thing you can play is what you do. And not all doings require an immediate response.

• • •

Even when another person does present an obstacle to your goals, you can still choose to do a number of different things to break through the resistance. Many situations are confrontations between individuals with opposing needs—what the Greeks called an "agon," or kind of contest, as when Creon tries to get Antigone to give up her plan to bury her brother and Antigone defies him. Of course you need to keep after what you want in such cases, but you still have to examine the text closely to find out exactly what you do to get it. And even when you disagree with somebody your satisfaction may not depend entirely on winning the argument. There's a certain pleasure in articulating our reasons so persuasively that they can hardly be denied. There's great fun in playing Shaw, for example, because he gives such compelling arguments to both sides. His people love to engage in disputation, often on quite friendly terms, as Cusins and Undershaft do.

• • •

When we want something from somebody we can either ask for it directly or we can try to manipulate the other person to give it to us. We can say, "I need ten dollars, could you lend it to me please?", or we can embark on an elaborate campaign, demonstrating how impoverished we are, appealing to "friendship," trying to arouse guilt. We can manipulate others to attain either a material reward or some psychic gain, such as power or prestige. Much of what we do in modern life is prompted by some ulterior motive, sometimes unacknowledged even to ourselves. Perhaps we are devious more often than we are direct. But the "What-are-you-really-after?" school of acting assumes that *all* communication is manipulative—that if we pay a compliment our "action" must be "to butter her up," that if we mention an accomplishment we are proud of to a friend we must be trying "to score a point on him." No allowance is made in this particular theory of motivation for the possibility of just sharing our feeings openly and honestly.

Now it is precisely in those situations when the character *is* trying to manipulate others that the theory can cause the most problems. At such times we are seldom willing to acknowledge what we are up to, and so we disguise our communication to make it *look* as if all we want is to express our feelings. We end up doing exactly what we would do if we had no ulterior motive. But the actor intent on "pursuing my objective" or "playing my action" may give away the whole show.

Let's assume, for example, that you have a close friend who is like a younger sister to you. You sense that she is in trouble and has come to you for help, but she seems embarrassed to talk about her problem. She goes so far as to confide in you that her husband leaves her alone a lot, and you suspect that she's in love with another man. You want to encourage her to open up to you completely. "Now Terry," you say to her, "my dear Terry, I want you to tell me the whole thing, now, just the way it is."

Try the sentence with that motivation in mind. Then change your motivation entirely. Assume that you yourself are in love with the man you suspect her of being in love with and that you are deliberately pumping her to get all the information you can get out of her. Now try the same sentence again.

Did you say it any differently? If so, why? Do you really want Terry to know what you are up to? Of course not. Why not speak then just as if you were indeed her close friend? But perhaps you still carry around in your head the voice of a teacher or director who tells you, "Play your action more strongly here, raise the stakes. Show me what you're really after." A perfectly appropriate response to that might be, "I don't *want* you to see what I'm after; if I show it to you, I'll give it away to Terry too. If you want to know what my motivation is, read the play."

Actually the play is *Hedda Gabler*, and the second motivation is the correct one. All I did was change the name of Thea to Terry. I have seen this scene dozens of times and the actress playing Hedda usually has all the warmth and compassion of a cobra about to strike. Thea is not the brightest character in the history of dramatic literature anyway, but in order for her to be taken in by the way Hedda is usually played she'd have to be *really* stupid. Surely Hedda is too skillful to give herself away. If you play her just as if she were indeed the warm and concerned "big sister" that she wants to be seen as, your duplicity will be all the more striking.

• • •

Sometimes I don't understand actors. They will go to extraordinary lengths to be "believable" to their teachers, to their directors, to their audience. Then they try very hard to be insincere to their partners. I don't understand.

Let's try another example. You work for a man who also happens to be a close friend. You have reason to believe that somebody in the office is sleeping with your friend's wife, and you are troubled. On the one hand you feel you owe it to him to let him know what's going on; on the other hand you have no proof, and it's not your place to tell him. But he begins to suspect something anyway and presses you to tell him what you think. You don't want to lie to him, but you don't want to see him hurt either, and so you say,

---

Please. Even though I might make a nasty guess here—and I have to admit I have a bad habit of prying into other people's business and sometimes I'm so suspicious I imagine things that aren't really true—it wouldn't be wise for you to pay attention to anybody whose judgement may be way off, or to make a lot of trouble for yourself out of a few scattered and meaningless incidents. It wouldn't be good for your peace of mind, or for my self-respect either, if I tell you every thought that passes through my mind.

Try the speech as if you're really torn and don't know quite what to say.

And now assume that this other guy isn't really sleeping with your boss's wife at all, you planted that suspicion yourself because you actually hate your boss for promoting this other guy ahead of you and now you want to make them both suffer. Perhaps you've recognized already that all I did was paraphrase a speech of Iago's from *Othello*. Again, is there any reason why you shouldn't do the speech just as if you were Othello's loyal friend and ally? Here's the monologue I paraphrased:

        I do beseech you,
Though I perchance am vicious in my guess—
As I confess it is my nature's plague
To spy into abuses, and oft my jealousy
Shapes faults that are not—that your wisdom
From one that so imperfectly conceits,
Would take no notice; nor build yourself a trouble
Out of his scattering and unsure observance.
It were not for your quiet nor your good,
Nor for my manhood, honesty, or wisdom,
To let you know my thoughts.

• • •

The fascination in watching an Iago or a Hedda at work lies in the striking contrast between the evident sincerity of their behavior and the inner machinations that we as an audience know must be going on. Don't spoil our pleasure. Leave it to the author to let us in on the secret. Shakespeare gives Iago plenty of opportunity, when he is left alone with the audience, to share with us his delight at how swimmingly his plan is going.

The author might also set up the circumstances in such a way that any reasonable person might be suspicious of your motives. For example, Thea knows quite well that she and Hedda were not close friends in school as Hedda insists they were, but she seems half persuaded that she misremembered. Hedda even calls her "my dear Thora," at one point, and though Thea does manage to correct her, she goes right on to blurt out everything that Hedda wants to know. Maybe Thea's own need to confide in somebody is so strong that she shuts out all the danger signals.

Most of the time, when you're playing somebody who is not being sincere, you can trust that the circumstances will give you away. In life that's almost always how we get caught out. Suppose a husband says to his wife, as they are getting ready to go out, "Why don't you wear the green dress tonight?" He intends to convey his delight in the prospect of seeing her in such a lovely dress, and that is exactly what he does. The wife, however, may know from past experience that her husband is anxious about the impression she makes on his boss, with whom they are having dinner tonight, and she may suspect that he really wants to prevent her from wearing some outlandish outfit that would embarrass him. She may pick up on the unexpressed anxiety and respond angrily. She would be responding then not to what he *does*, but to what might be *inferred* from what he does. Her inference may be correct or incorrect. But the husband's motivation does not determine what he does: that is determined by what he wants her to receive. For many actors their "motivation" is all that matters, and they firmly believe that if the motivation changes, the behavior must change. This is simply not true. You can do exactly the same thing for any number of different reasons, acknowledged or concealed.

We are often unaware ourselves of the hidden meanings behind the messages we send, but we are almost always aware of what we want the other person to receive. And we are usually capable of sending just that. Most of what is popularly called "miscommunication" does not arise from any inability to send or receive clear messages. It arises either from the refusal of the sender to accept responsibility for what was actually sent— for example, we can "chide" somebody unequivocally and then deny that we did—or from the receiver's assumption, correct or incorrect, that an undelivered message lies behind the one that was sent.

• • •

Is it an ironclad rule then that you must never betray on stage any motives or feelings you don't want your partner to get? Of course not. There are times when something in our voice or face or body gives us away in spite of ourselves. A lot depends on how much practice we have had at lying. Iago and Hedda are masters at it, they've been doing it all their lives. Some of us are terrible at it: we get caught quite early in life, we find that rather painful, and we are afraid to try again. We grow up handicapped by lack of practice. But it's impossible to get through life without a certain amount of dissembling, if not downright deception. And even those of us who aren't very good at it still try to do it as well as we possibly can.

A lot depends too on how prepared we are. We may be able to deal smoothly with a challenge to our veracity that we had anticipated, but if we are confronted with something unexpected we may hesitate, fidget, perhaps even stammer or blush. Such reactions are inadvertent. We do not do them, they happen to us. I have been careful to describe a doing as what we *wish* to communicate. A lot may get communicated that we don't intend, but that is beyond our conscious control. As an actor you should always play what the character wishes to convey as well as you possibly can *under the circumstances*. If there is some danger that you will be caught out in a lie on the witness stand, just being aware of that may have some involuntary effect on your behavior, particularly if you have to field an unexpected question. Paradoxically, the more you *try* to convey only what you intend, the more susceptible you will be to letting something slip inadvertently—provided, of course, that you are really there in the moment, unprepared, and open to what actually happens.

The proviso is crucial. I have been putting all the emphasis on intentional behavior, but I take it as fundamental that the actor must maintain an exquisite sensitivity to what others on stage are doing. I would not go so far as to agree with those who say that "acting is reacting"—I think that we initiate much of what we do, and sometimes we choose *not* to react—but we must certainly allow our own behavior to be modified, sometimes profoundly changed, by what we receive. It's precisely because sudden, inadvertent betrayals of underlying feelings are so striking that you need to let them happen, not try to make them happen. (It's the same, by the way, when we are suddenly overcome by tears. In Robert Sherwood's *Abe Lincoln in Illinois*, Abe breaks down and cries when telling his neighbors of the death of his fiancée, Anne Rutledge. In playing this monologue, your best bet would be simply to make it your task to break the sad news to your neighbors and try, as much as possible, *not* to cry. As Abe says, when pressed to stay the night, "I don't want to inflict you with a corpse.")

• • •

Often when we hide what we really want from other people, we are not being deceitful, only shy. For any number of reasons we may be afraid to acknowledge our desires, and so we do nothing about them. And yet in a social situation we cannot just remain silent, and so we engage in small talk. There is a whole scene in *The Cherry Orchard* that is made up entirely of small talk, and it is one of the most dramatic scenes ever written. Lopahin and Varya have been brought together expressly so that he may propose to her. Both of them understand perfectly why they are here, and both of them want to get married—or so they have told others. But she acts as if she came into the room to look for something she had packed, and he appears to be highly interested in the weather. At one point, for example, he says, "Last year at this time we had snow already, if you remember, but now it's calm, sunny. A bit cold though. Three below zero." She replies, "I hadn't noticed." Then, after a pause, she adds, "Besides, our thermometer is broken." Neither does a thing that might lead towards a proposal, and the scene ends with his running out of the room and her dissolving in tears.

How do you "pursue an objective" when your character doesn't do a thing about it? I don't think you should try. Simply search through the luggage as if you need to find something terribly important. Express genuine fascination with the vagaries of the weather, as if you had absolutely nothing else in mind. Allow time, of course, during the frequent pauses that Chekhov indicates, to find a way to broach the subject of marriage if you can, but try to act as if you are still preoccupied with the spoken rather than the unspoken thought. Stay with the moment, not knowing yourself what you will do next, until the silence becomes unbearable, and you find yourself once again taking the safe course. You will probably want to avoid each other's eyes as much as possible—looking would only make the situation more awkward. I once saw a highly acclaimed production of this play in which Lopahin and Varya gave each other long, significant stares between each line of this scene, thus tipping off the audience to the very thing the characters are trying so desperately to hide.

• • •

In other words, don't play the "subtext." That's another one of those acting terms I have stopped using because it can be misleading. Many people mean by it the entire flow of consciousness that accompanies speech. But if you tried to include in your awareness everything that might conceivably pass through your character's mind at a given moment, you would just drive yourself crazy. It's much simpler to concentrate on what I've been calling the "content," the particular thing the speaker wishes the listener to receive at the moment.

Of course what you communicate may be only a small part of your consciousness. We are seldom willing to make public every thought that comes into our heads. We select, more or less deliberately, that part of our mental life that we want to share with others. You may be afraid, as an actor, that if you express only those wishes that the character is willing to acknowledge, your "inner life" will be empty. But unacknowledged wishes do not go away so easily. When a feeling we don't dare to voice is struggling towards the surface, the more we try to suppress it the more force it gathers. When it can be contained no longer—as often happens at the climax of a play—it will burst forth, out of control, as the expression of true passion always is. Often when it bursts, it takes the form of a monologue.

• • •

In dealing with this whole question of unacknowledged motivation I have had to use examples mainly of dialogues. That's because when we avoid the direct expression of our deepest longings, either by manipulating others or by engaging in small talk, we tend to carry on dialogues rather than deliver monologues. (That doesn't mean, of course, that all dialogues are veiled and all monologues open.) A monologue that is manipulative (like the one of Iago's I quoted) may not be very interesting out of context because the audience may not know what is going on. And monologues that consist entirely of small talk (like Alec's in *Dear Janet Rosenberg*) may be amusing but of course don't seem to "go" anywhere. That's why, if you want to find a really passionate monologue, you're better off looking toward the end of the play, where the really juicy bits are more likely to lie. (Unfortunately there's a catch here too: such monologues may be especially hard to do out of context.)

Another way of putting it: I talked earlier about needs that absorb us and those that are postponed. It's the ones that are postponed continually over a long period of time that build up the most force and bring about the most satisfying release. In the last act of *Long Day's Journey into Night* a number of postponed needs find expression in a whole series of magnificent monologues. One of Edmund's deepest needs is to be close to his father, to be able to share with him everything he is going through. And the father wants to be close to a son whom he loves dearly but doesn't really understand and has never been able to talk with, except superficially. Throughout the first three acts these two mainly snipe at each other and mock each other. Meanwhile pressure builds: Edmund's mother has once again taken up a drug habit that now appears impossible to shake, and Edmund has always felt that his father is partly responsible because he refused to pay for proper medical care. That same day Edmund learns that he has tuberculosis, and again his father plans to save money by sending him to a state sanatorium.

At the beginning of Act Four, Edmund comes home about midnight and finds his father sitting alone, drinking and playing solitaire. They fall into familiar squabbles, out of habit. But they manage to joke a bit, too, and Edmund even dares to share some of his favorite poetry. Father and son begin to drink together, they start a game of Casino. They hear the mother stirring upstairs and are terrified that she will come down in a drugged stupor. Both seem quite tense. Suddenly the dam bursts. Edmund begins to pour out years of resentment at the way his father treated his mother in a kind of interrupted monologue ending with, "Christ, is it any wonder she didn't want to be cured. Jesus, when I think of it I hate your guts!"

The father is understandably stricken. He tries to defend himself as best he can, then he is goaded into counterattacking: he reminds Edmund that it was the trauma of his birth that brought on the first use of morphine. Instantly he apologizes, and so does Edmund. Edmund even admits, "I can't help liking you, in spite of everything." And the father responds, "I might say the same of you. You're no great shakes as a son. It's a case of 'A poor thing but mine own.'" And they both laugh.

This is as close as they can come to saying they love each other. But they are on more intimate terms. Edmund has dared to speak the unspeakable, and they have survived. Equilibrium is restored. But only for the moment. There is still "unfinished business," as the gestalt psychologists call it.

They begin to talk of Edmund's illness. The father tries to reassure him, but Edmund will have none ot it. "You think I'm going to die," he says. "So why waste money? That's why you're sending me to the state farm." Again Tyrone makes a feeble effort to defend himself, but Edmund points out that on that very day his father had bought another piece of land as an investment. The father denies it, but Edmund bursts out,

Don't lie about it! (*With gathering intensity.*) God, Papa, ever since I went to sea and was on my own, and found out what hard work for little pay was, and what it felt like to be broke, and starve, and camp on park benches because I had no place to sleep, I've tried to be fair to you because I knew what you'd been up against as a kid. I've tried to make allowances. Christ, you have to make allowances in this damned family or go nuts! I have tried to make allowances for myself when I remember all the rotten stuff I've pulled! I've tried to feel like Mama that you can't help being what you are where money is concerned. But God Almighty, this last stunt of yours is too much! It makes me want to puke! Not because of the rotten way you're treating me. To hell with that! I've treated you rottenly, in my way, more than once. But to think when it's a question of your son having consumption, you can show yourself up before the whole town as such a stinking old tightwad! Don't you know Hardy will talk and the whole damned town will know! Jesus, Papa, haven't you any pride or shame? (*Bursting with rage.*) And don't think I'll let you get away with it! I won't go to any damned state farm just to save you a few lousy dollars to buy more bum property with! You stinking old miser—!

Notice that what really gets to Edmund is not "the rotten way you're treating me" but that "you can show yourself up to the whole town as a stinking old tightwad." Again there's that unbearable ironic gap—this time it's between what every son wishes his father to be and what this particular father is in fact. That pain is what fuels the entire speech.

The truth seems to hurt the father as much as it does the son. Tyrone certainly seems crushed. Almost immediately he offers to send Edmund anywhere he likes (though he later adds the qualification "within reason"). Father and son have another drink together, and they resume the card game. And then Tyrone says something utterly astonishing. One would think he might try to defend himself again or maybe even counterattack. Instead he says simply, "A stinking old miser. Well, maybe you're right." That admission is the beginning of a very long monologue, five pages in my edition, though again interrupted occasionally. Tyrone describes in vivid detail the excruciating poverty he endured as a child, and how, even after he became a successful actor, he could never shake the fear of losing everything and becoming penniless again. That's what drove him to keep acquiring land even while he was skimping on the immediate needs of his family. That's also what ruined his career. At one time Edwin Booth had said of him, "That young man is playing Othello better than I ever did"; but then he became extremely popular in a cheap melodrama (in real life that was *The Count of Monte Cristo*, which indeed made O'Neill's father rich and famous) and could never stop playing it out of fear. "On my solemn oath, Edmund," he says at the end of the monologue, "I'd gladly face not having an acre of land to call my own, not a penny in the bank—I'd be willing to have no home but the poorhouse in my old age if I could look back now on having been the fine artist I might have been."

It's an extraordinary confession. Edmund seems deeply moved by it. "I'm glad you told me this, Pop," he says. "I know you a lot better now." It's after his father has opened up to him in this way that Edmund embarks on the famous monologue about being at sea that I quoted part of earlier. (This whole act is a bit like an opera: one magnificent aria after another. And I haven't even mentioned the older brother Jamie and the mother, who have their moments later.)

Edmund's monologue begins, "You've just told me some high spots in your memories. Want to hear mine?" Clearly Edmund now feels close enough to his father to reveal things he has never told anybody. That experience of being at one with the sea was only one of several in which he felt a kind of mystical sense of peace and understanding and union with "god, if you want to call it that." He goes on to lament,

---

It was a great mistake my being born a man, I would have been much more successful as a sea gull or a fish. As it is, I will always be a stranger who never feels at home, who does not really want and is not really wanted, who can never belong, who must always be a little in love with death.

Tyrone had always mocked his son's "morbid philosophy" before, but on hearing this he "stares at him—impressed," as O'Neill's stage direction indicates, and says, "Yes, there's the making of a poet in you all right."

What more could any son wish for? To be accepted and valued by his father for what he is. And what more could any father want: to understand his son, to be understood, and to be forgiven. This scene may be realistic, but it is too perfect to be real. Just as the balcony scene in *Romeo and Juliet* is the ideal expression of romantic love, this scene strikes me as the ideal expression of filial rage and reconcilation. I imagine it's the kind of scene O'Neill himself would love to have played with his own father, and never did. The theater brings many gifts, but the greatest is the opportunity, not to relive our lives, but to rewrite them, and to play them out the way they ought to have been played in the first place.

• • •

Again the motivation is to be found not in what father and son are trying to get from each other but in what they are able to give to each other: the gift of true feeling, painful as it may be, openly and honestly expressed. Of course at first Edmund is more driven than his father to speak the truth. Not because he has set that as his "objective," but because he can't help it: the rage and the hurt have been building up for so long that he can no longer contain them. It's all right there in the text, you don't have to add a thing. Your job is to make these words your own, get in touch with the experiences that give rise to them. You may be able to do that just by a close, empathetic reading of the text, perhaps using the words and pictures technique. Or you might want to ask what it would be like for you, or find some other way to make a personal connection with Edmund's experience. If it helps you to do an emotional memory exercise, fine, but use your discretion: if you never felt anything for your own father but resentment, if you never experienced deep disappointment in his failure to show his love for you or to live up to your idea of him, then the substitution may lead you astray.

All this is "homework": you do it while sitting alone with your script or in rehearsal or just while thinking about the play. By the time you get to playing the scene or a monologue form it, everything should be already prepared—just as it is with Edmund. He doesn't have to goad himself on, as he enters the house, to go after what he wants from his father. If anything, he is probably struggling to *contain* everything that is welling up inside him. He may even experience the idea of his actually saying all this as somewhat unreal—a rather remote and terrifying possibility.

Tyrone, of course, spends a good part of the scene defending himself against Edmund's charges. It might be possible to make out a case, as did one actor I tried to coach on this scene, that his action is "to deny the truth." But I don't see what good that would do you. You can't tell yourself, as you're sitting there playing solitaire and drinking, that you are going to deny everything Edmund says—he hasn't even come in yet! And when he does, you have to be *un*prepared for what he says. If you want to give yourself a purpose, try getting as drunk as you possibly can.

If you do set out "to deny the truth," then you're going to have to change in midstream when Tyrone admits to being "a stinking old miser." But the actor I tried to work with decided, for reasons of his own, *not* to change. He argued, quite forcefully, that Tyrone is just "feeling sorry for himself" and "making excuses." He brings up the whole story of his early poverty, according to this actor, only to plead for Edmund's pity and avoid responsibility by "blaming it all on his childhood." The actor thereupon played Tyrone's whole magnificent monologue as an exercise in maudlin self-pity. Of course there are people who act that way, but I feel that this actor was so blinded by his negative feelings towards such people that he couldn't really imagine Tyrone acting any differently. It was inconceivable to him that a man could accept full responsibility for the failure of his life and want only to be understood.

When I pointed out to the actor that there was another possibility here, he listened perfunctorily and then said, "Well, I interpret it differently." End of argument. That was a long time ago, and if I had a second chance to work with this actor, instead of getting caught up in a discussion of "interpretation," I would try to get him to feel his way into Tyrone's situation, perhaps by imagining that he had destroyed his own life in some way and had nobody to blame but himself. Also I would make no attempt to get him to give up the notion that he had to get something from Edmund—at least not until he had discovered for himself that he wasn't really helpless without it. The reason actors cling to a rule of any kind—and there are lots of rules, including the refusal to mention the name *Macbeth* in a dressing room—is that it gives them a sense of security in a very uncertain profession. They never know for sure if they're going to be good that night or if they're going to be awful, and so they try to find and hold on to a magic key that will insure that they are good all the time. Try to take their key away, and they will fight you to the death. It's only when they are able to live with uncertainty that they may be able to let go a bit.

• • •

I'm not really trying to get you to substitute my magic key for yours. You may not be able to accept the particular way of thinking about motivation that I have proposed here, and it's not essential that you do. Theory, after all, is only theory. It doesn't really create anything, it only describes what already exists. And different people can describe the same thing in different terms. You don't have to have the correct theory, or even correct training, in order to act well. That has been demonstrated repeatedly. And of course you can have a perfect understanding of theory and not be able to act at all. My concern has been simply that certain theories, if applied too diligently, can cloud your judgement and lead you astray. Having an "objective" or "action" in mind may be helpful simply as a way of taking your mind off the words, but telling yourself that you must constantly think about your goal—or about your "need" or "doing" for that matter—can tie you up in knots.

Many fine actors don't know how they work, and many who do know don't like to talk about it. Perhaps it would have been better if all of us who like to talk about acting had held our tongues. Perhaps, to paraphrase Lady Bracknell in *The Importance of Being Earnest*, anybody who desires to be an actor should know either everything or nothing. As that surprisingly wise old dowager goes on to say, "I do not approve of anything that tampers with natural ignorance. Ignorance is like a delicate exotic fruit: touch it and the bloom is gone."

Many actors might be better off to be ignorant. They carry on stage with them the accumulated burden of all the instructions that have been drilled into them over the years. They are constantly admonishing themselves: "Go after your objective now, think about your relationship, remember your previous circumstances, relax now, concentrate, *con*centrate, use your subsitution for this moment, oh my God I forgot my obstacle, what's my obstacle?" All I am suggesting here is that you try to get rid of the excess baggage and reduce the whole process to the simplest possible terms. It's more important to challenge misguided ideas than to preach the "right" ones. As Sherlock Holmes was fond of remarking to Dr. Watson, "When you have excluded the impossible, whatever remains, however improbable, must be the truth." That applies to acting in the sense that the way to play a given moment is improbably simple and inevitably right. Like Dr. Watson, we should have seen it all along, but we didn't.

• • •

It's too bad that the disciples of Stanislavski have splintered into as many quarreling factions as the disciples of Freud. (Or of Jesus for that matter.) Put a dozen acting teachers into the same room and you'd be hard pressed to find any two who agree with each other about very much. And yet if you placed before them a really first-rate piece of acting, all twelve would beam and say, "Yes, that's exactly what I teach!"

There's a story—I think it's a Sufi tale—about three blind men who try to describe an elephant. One gets hold of the tail and says the elephant is like a rope; another grabs the front legs and says that an elephant is like a pair of columns; the third feels the trunk and says that an elephant is like a large snake. And they argue endlessly. I sometimes feel that we acting teachers have all got hold of different parts of the elephant.

In a sense everything that has ever been said about acting is perfectly true. It's true that when we speak about the past we relive it (but not literally). It's true that we pursue objectives (sometimes), that we encounter obstacles (but not always), that there is conflict between people, and that there is not conflict between people. It's true that we speak literally and we speak metaphorically, that we are ironic and we are humorless, that we "chide" others when they hurt us and we "lament" for them. It's true that exercises in concentration and relaxation are very helpful. It's also true that they are totally unnecessary. It's true that affective memory exercises are essential and also useless and misleading. Everything is true, so long as we recognize that it is only partly so.

Nobody has ever seen the whole elephant. If any human being could ever get far enough away from it and were granted the gift of seeing clearly with open eyes, even this godlike individual would miss the textures and smells with which we blind men are so intimately acquainted. About the best that any of us can do is cling to whatever portion of that vast flesh is accessible to us and realize, at least, that we are connected to something considerably larger.

15

Some Thoughts about Character

You won't always play people who are markedly different from yourself. Even when there are striking differences, you can usually establish them just by doing one thing rather than another. Take the words, "Did you see the fire?" If you are talking about a magnificent bonfire at the beach, the flames reaching up towards a starlit sky, you would probably convey your delight. If you were to do exactly the same thing about a fire in a hotel that forced residents to jump out windows, their clothes aflame, you would undoubtedly come across as a pyromaniac. Not because you literally *became* somebody else, but because you took a different view of the situation.

Most of the time all you have to do is put yourself into the situation *as the character sees it* and convey whatever you think the character intends. But many actors don't feel that that is enough. Instead of conveying genuine delight in the fire, an actor cast as a pyromaniac might try to demonstrate how "crazy" people are presumed to act. He would adopt a certain "quality" or "manner" that illustrates his idea of madness and spread it like so much margarine over the entire performance. He would exhibit his madness not only in talking about the fire, but at all times, even if the character is just ordering a cup of coffee. It would never occur to him that a pyromaniac, if he's clever and doesn't want to get caught, might even be able to talk about the fire in a way that conveys what appears to be sincere regret for the victims. In other words, the actor would comment on what the character *is* instead of doing what the character *does*.

• • •

Some roles invite comment more than others. One that seems positively to demand it is Arsinoé in Molière's *The Misanthrope*. Here is what she says when she comes to call on her "friend" Célimène.

ARSINOÉ:
Madam, the flame of friendship ought to burn
Brightest in matters of the most concern,
And as there's nothing which concerns us more
Than honor, I have hastened to your door
To bring you, as your friend, some information
About the status of your reputation.
I visited, last night, some virtuous folk,
And, quite by chance, it was of you they spoke;
There was, I fear, no tendency to praise
Your light behavior and your dashing ways.
The quantity of gentlemen you see
And your by now notorious coquetry
Were both so vehemently criticized
By everyone, that I was much surprised.
Of course, I needn't tell you where I stood;
I came to your defense as best I could,
 Assured them you were harmless, and declared
Your soul was absolutely unimpaired.
But there are some things, you must realize,
One can't excuse, however hard one tries,
And I was forced at last into conceding
That your behavior, Madam, is misleading,
That it makes a bad impression, giving rise
To ugly gossip and obscene surmise,
And that if you were more *overtly* good,
You wouldn't be so much misunderstood.
Not that I think you've been unchaste—no! no!
The saints preserve me from a thought so low!
But mere good conscience never did suffice:

One must avoid the outward show of vice.
Madam, you're too intelligent, I'm sure,
To think my motives anything but pure
In offering you this counsel—which I do
Out of a zealous interest in you.

[Translated by Richard Wilbur]

The temptation here is to adopt a haughty demeanor and a disapproving tone, looking down your nose at Célimène and heaping disdain on her for her loose ways. When you understand the circumstances of Arsinoé's visit you might seem to have all the more reason for behaving that way. Célimène is being pursued by Alceste, whom Arsinoé rather fancies for herself. Clearly Arsinoé uses her "piety" both as an explanation for her failure to attract a man and an excuse for tearing down women who are more successful. There is no question that this woman is prudish, hypocritical, envious, spiteful, and malicious. Nobody could possibly disagree.

Except perhaps Arsinoé. Put yourself in her place for a minute. If she were asked what she was really like, how might she respond? You might even try doing a kind of "imaginary interview" with her, something like the following:

Q. Madam, are you a prude?
A. Me? Heavens no! Whatever gave you that idea? I just refuse to do what a lot of men expect of a woman in our society. You know I've even heard that there are some women who become successful in the theater by . . . well, associating with the playwright, shall we say? Well, if I were willing to do what some of them do, I could be very famous, believe me.
Q. Do you feel any spite towards Célimène?
A. She's my best friend.
Q. Well, I mean you did come here and tear her down, so to speak.
A. What are you talking about? I came here because I heard some ugly rumors about her and wanted to warn her be-

fore it was too late.

Q. But didn't you expect her to feel insulted?

A. Well, I *thought* she'd be grateful. I expected she would realize that she does flirt a bit too much and try to change.

Q. Become more like you, you mean?

A. Well . . .

Q. Wouldn't it be a logical inference to say that, perhaps without being fully aware of your own motives, you came here to attack your rival because she uses what you consider an unfair advantage to hold on to the man you want for yourself?

A. (*After a long pause.*) I can't quite follow that.

Q. What I mean is . . .

A. What are you, a philosopher?

Q. Well, let's drop that. Tell me, what do you think of Alceste?

A. The finest man I've ever met. You know, between you and me, and I wouldn't breathe a word of this to Célimène, I don't think those two are right for each other. I love them both dearly, but he needs somebody more simple and honest, somebody to stand up with him against the hypocrisy in our society today. You just can't find anybody at court who is really *sincere* any more . . .

Instead of commenting on Arsinoé's character, try to get inside that rather peculiar head of hers and present her, as much as possible, the way she would like to be perceived. Don't make any effort to change your accustomed way of speaking and moving. Do not pose or put on airs or talk in an affected manner. Simply respond to the questions, saying of course what you imagine Arsinoé might say, but as sincerely as possible, as if you believe every word. You may well discover that you will *still* come across as hypocritical. Why? Because, as we saw with Hedda Gabler, the circumstances will give you away.

It's hard to say whether Arsinoé is deluding herself or (like

Hedda) deliberately trying to deceive others. Perhaps she really believes she is what she pretends to be. But for your practical purposes in playing the role, what matters is not what she believes but what she wants others to believe. Certainly she wants to make it appear, at least, that her behavior towards Célimène is reasonable and just, even kind and friendly. Why not, then, play her exactly as if that were the case? Suppose, for example, you had a close friend who is rapidly slipping into alcoholism. You have heard some people at work gossiping about her, and you are very much afraid she will be fired. You go to her and say, "Look, you need a friend most when things really matter, and since I know nothing matters more to you than your reputation with this company, I rushed over here to tell you, as your friend, some things I've been hearing. Last night I happened to drop into the staff cafeteria, and there were some pretty important people there. Just by chance, they started talking about you . . . " And so on, paraphrasing line for line.

If you approach the text the same way, conveying quite sincerely your concern for what might happen if Célimène continues on her self-destructive path, and assuming that she would not doubt for a moment that you spoke up for her, the contrast between what Arsinoé is and what she would like to appear to be may seem quite funny, perhaps even a bit touching. You will come across not as a stock figure but as a rather complex and fascinating human being.

But is it enough just to "be yourself" on stage? You might feel that because this is a *grande dame* in a "stylized" play, you have to imitate what you have seen other actresses do in such roles. It is true that if you have a regional speech pattern you may have to get rid of it. If you are not already comfortable speaking in rhymed couplets, you will need to practice until you can do so without being too conscious either of the rhythm or the rhyme, breaking up the regular pattern of the verse when necessary and going for the sense rather than stopping at the end of every line. You may need to discover how the clothing of the period would make you carry yourself. You may want to experiment with hair and makeup until you find something that makes you look not too attractive and perhaps a bit severe. You may even decide to model, to some extent, the way you move and speak on somebody you know in life who reminds you of Arsinoé. But all these are changes in the "language" of your role and should never be allowed to obscure the content.

Whenever you play a person whose habitual way of speaking and moving is very different from your own, you will need to learn a new "language," so to speak. If you grew up in the Midwest and are cast as a French chef, you will need to develop some new speech patterns. If you were trained as a dancer and have to play a boxer, you will need to develop a whole new way of moving. But you must learn your new language so thoroughly that you no longer have to think about it and can give you attention to *what* you are saying, which can be essentially the same in any language. It's quite possible that a Midwesterner, a French chef, a dancer, and a boxer could all bump into somebody on the street and say "I'm sorry" in a way that means pretty much the same thing. But an actor who is busy being "French" will not convey that he's sorry, only that he's from Paris.

• • •

In a sense you must always "play yourself" on stage. No matter how bizarre your point of view, no matter how alien your "language," no matter how different your choices from what *you* would do in that situation, you are the only one up there who can do what the character does. You really have to do it, not give us your impression of somebody else.

If you're having difficulty with a monologue or scene, sometimes just accepting that "I am I" and "you are you" can have a remarkable effect. In my workshops, for example, when I see an actor do a piece in what seems to be a stiff and self-conscious manner, I often suggest that the actor drop all pretense of being the character: "There you are, Elizabeth, sitting in that gray metal chair, in your blue dress, fingering that gold bracelet and over there is George in his tan shirt, and there's Sally, whom you know, smiling, and here I am, I'm Jack, you remember me. Now pick one of us to talk to, or talk to all of us if you prefer, and just speak your monologue as yourself, the real Elizabeth to the real us. In fact, whenever the text calls for you to address somebody by name, substitute one of our real names, just for now. Keep the character's point of view, but make it *your* point of view towards *us*." Almost always the actor comes alive in a unique and quite personal way. Paradoxically the character may also come across as a richer, more varied person, partaking somewhat of the actor's individuality.

Actors are sometimes reluctant to bring themselves to the stage. Perhaps they have been taught that unless they "become somebody else" they're not really acting. "Get into character" was probably the first instruction they heard from their teacher in their first school play. And when they and their cohorts were unruly, instead of telling them to settle down, the teacher would call out "Stay in character!"—as if the problem were to keep a bunch of rebellious portraits safely contained within their frames.

But there's an even more compelling reason why actors feel they must "put on a character." They are deeply convinced that if they are "just themselves" up there they could not possibly be very interesting. They are terrified to let anything of themselves come through. And yet if they only knew how fascinating they would become if they were to drop their masks and allow themselves to be spontaneous and unpredictable!

Some actors, however, are more free and expressive if they feel they are "protected" by a mask. For them it's better *not* to think of being themselves up there. I once worked with an actor who was extremely self-critical; he couldn't stop himself from judging everything he did while he was doing it. Once, when he was struggling with a monologue, he stopped and said, apparently on impulse, that he would like to try the piece with a Southern accent. I doubted that that would help much, but the dialect was appropriate to the piece, and I said fine, go ahead. The result was astonishing. He launched into the speech with a passion I'd never seen in him before, and he was incredibly spontaneous and free. I sat there open-mouthed. "What happened?" I asked when he was done. He told me it wasn't really "himself" speaking, it was a distant relative of his (Southern, of course). All he had to do, he explained, was "get out of the way" and let the character say what he was burning to say.

• • •

You can play any role, no matter how remote from yourself, provided you can put yourself into the character's place and look out at the world from their peculiar angle of vision. The only block that ever stands in your way is the inability to see as the character sees, and this very often comes of looking at the character from the outside, making judgments and forming opinions. Most people find it easy to identify with those they find sympathetic or familiar, but we actors have to identify with all kinds, with oddballs and freaks and villains, and they don't think of themselves as odd, freakish, or villainous. (Or if they do, like Iago, they take pride in their villainy.) Robert Burns prayed for the gift of seeing ourselves as others see us. The actor might well pray for the gift of seeing others as they see themselves.

The ability to identify depends to some extent on your experience of life. Young actresses are seldom able to play Amanda in Williams' *The Glass Menagerie* without commenting on how silly she is. (I suspect they are really trying to show what's wrong with their own mothers.) But older women are more likely to understand Amanda's concern, misguided though it may be, for the welfare of her children. She really believes that Tom's life will go down the drain unless he stops going to the movies so much, starts taking his job at the shoe factory more seriously, and learns to chew his food properly. She also believes (and with good reason) that Laura may never find a man to take care of her, but she can't help trying to get her to develop a little "charm."

You don't always have to find a connection with your own experience. What counts is that you *understand* the point of view, and you can do that even if it's impossible to imagine yourself ever sharing it, under any circumstances. When I played Pastor Manders in Ibsen's *Ghosts*, for example, I had to deliver what is in effect a long "interrupted" monologue in which he accuses Mrs. Alving of being responsible for her son's ruin. He says some pretty outrageous things. At one point, she says she left her husband because she was "desperately unhappy," and he responds:

> **Yes, that is the sign of the rebellious spirit, to demand happiness from this earthly life. What right have we to happiness? No, Mrs. Alving, we must do our duty! And your duty was to remain with the man you had chosen, and to whom you were bound by a sacred bond.**
>
> **[*Translation by Michael Meyer*]**

I found it quite a challenge to imagine myself ever believing that. But then I decided just to say it *as if* I believed it. And suddenly I did. What Manders says is actually true! Individual happiness is not important in life. What matters is our commitment to some higher purpose. The more I thought about it the more passionate I became in my belief. I came to see this as an *inspiring* speech and Manders almost as a charismatic figure. I understood for the first time why Mrs. Alving had fallen in love with him.

He is relentless in exposing the weakness in her character. A bit later in the same monologue he says to her,

> **All your days you have been ruled by a fatal spirit of willfulness. You have always longed for a life unconstrained by duties and principles. You have never been willing to suffer the curb of discipline. Everything that has been troublesome in your life you have cast off ruthlessly and callously, as if it were a burden which you had the right to reject. It was no longer convenient to you to be a wife, so you left your husband. You found it tiresome to be a mother, so you put your child out to live among strangers.**

This part of the speech was a bit easier for me because I know what it's like to watch somebody you love destroying their own life and the lives of others by being irresponsible. I'm also familiar with the confrontational approach that is used by some drug and alcohol counselors to get a person to face the underlying weakness that causes the addiction. It's tough, but it's done out of caring. Still, I don't think I'd ever talk to anybody the way Manders talks to Mrs. Alving here. Again it was enough just to understand the point of view. I simply assumed that Mrs. Alving is somebody I care deeply about and that unless I get her to face the painful truth about herself both she and her son will be lost. I came to understand Manders' passionate desire to save her soul. (I also sensed the power of the sexual attraction towards her that he must have worked so hard to suppress.)

• • •

Simply adopting an alien point of view can sometimes cause a surprising alteration in your habitual patterns of speech and movement. What I called earlier the "language" of a character is due only partly to the cultural and physical forces that condition a person's way of speaking and moving. To some extent it is due to habitual ways of thinking. Let's say that you are playing a husband in a French farce who has just been told that his wife is unfaithful, and you respond, "With whom?" in a way that suggests not that you are in the least perturbed, but rather that you are eager to hear the details. You may well come across as somewhat "French," even if you spoke without a French accent.

Even our impression of a person's age is not due entirely to physical conditioning. A five-year-old might walk up to a stranger and ask, quite directly, "Why do you have a beard?" If you were to do that, even in your own voice, you would suddenly appear quite child-like.

In Congreve's *The Way of the World* Millamant has a delicious monologue in which she takes a proposal from Mirabell, a man whom she presumably loves, as an occasion not for rejoicing but for stipulating exactly what rights she must have before she allows herself to "dwindle into a wife." Here's only a small part of it:

MRS. MIL: **I won't be called names after I'm married; positively I won't be called names.**
[MIR: Names!]
MRS. MIL: **Ay, as wife, spouse, my dear, joy, jewel, love, sweetheart, and the rest of that nauseous cant, in which men and their wives are so fulsomely familiar—I shall never bear that—good Mirabell, don't let us be familiar or fond, nor kiss before folks, like my Lady Fadler and Sir Francis: nor go to Hyde-park together the first Sunday in a new chariot, to provoke eyes and whispers, and then never to be seen there together again; as if we were proud of one another the first week, and ashamed of one another ever after. Let us never visit together, nor go to a play together; but let us be very strange and well bred: let us be as strange as if we had been married a great while; and as well bred as if we were not married at all.**

If you simply accept how distasteful it would be for you if your husband expressed any affection for you in public, you may already begin to seem like a creature from another century. You may also need, as I've pointed out, to work on speech and movement, but you can wear a long skirt in rehearsal for ten years and still not capture the point of view.

• • •

It works both ways: sometimes just making a physical or vocal adjustment can alter the way you think and feel. Some actors like to approach a character by copying some external detail of behavior, or perhaps modelling their movement on some animal. If that works for you, fine, but I think you have to be careful not to let your performance become so mannered that your character has, as Hamlet puts it, "neither the accent of Christians, nor the gait of Christian, pagan, nor man." Of course close observation of others is essential in acting. But you can pick up a lot more than a particular vocal quality or way of walking. You can begin to feel your way into a person and try to think and operate the way they do, not just mimic their outer behavior.

I mentioned back in Part One that some actors are better than others at what I called "impersonation," and I gave Eric Bogosian as an example. Those who are best at it make us feel not that they are giving their impression of somebody else, but that they have thrown some kind of internal switch and are now operating in a rather odd mode.

The best example I can think of is Alec Guiness. Surely he is one of the most versatile actors of our time. And yet we all have some sense of Guiness as a person, and if we look closely we can usually see him there, sometimes peeping impishly through the mask. "Is it really him?" we ask, and part of our pleasure comes from recognizing, "Of course it is, it couldn't be anybody else." I don't know how he does it. Guiness is peculiarly reticent about his way of working: he doesn't say a word in his autobiography, *Blessings in Disguise*, about how he created any of his characters. I suspect that he based them on a close observation of others but then managed somehow to infiltrate himself into the character, occupy his man, own him so to speak.

Olivier, by contrast, wrote a good deal about his way of working. If we take him at his word, his approach was entirely "external": he always looked first for the right walk or voice or bit of makeup. I get the impression, however, that he did examine the text closely and make decisions about what the character is communicating—perhaps that side of the work came so naturally to him that he thought it hardly worth mentioning. Olivier's characterizations were sometimes more daring and theatrical than Guiness's, but those that I have seen were not as consistently believable and rich. Sometimes Olivier seemed to be exhibiting a character rather than inhabiting him. I certainly admire his extraordinary gifts and his magnificent audacity, and there's no question that his approach often worked wonders for him, but I would not recommend that a lesser actor try to follow a way of working that is so single-mindedly external.

Actually if I had to pick one actor to hold up as a model of everything I have been advocating in this book, it would be Leslie Howard. In some ways he was not as generously endowed as some of his contemporaries: he was never as versatile as Guiness, nor did he have quite the fire of Olivier; he may have lacked Gielgud's majesty or Richardson's madness or Brando's sensuality. But he had his own special gifts, among them incomparable wit, charm, and sensitivity. Nobody could be more delicate or more romantic—no wonder Scarlett O'Hara preferred his Ashley Wilkes to Gable's Rhett Butler in *Gone With the Wind*. I have no idea how Howard worked, but I would point to his performances as models of two qualities that any actor would do well to emulate: grace and presence. He made it all look so effortless, so easy, he was always just *there* at the moment. We don't think of him as a character actor, but the most astonishing bit of character work I ever saw was his performance—or rather performances—in the film, *The Scarlet Pimpernel*. In effect he plays two roles: the romantic hero we are used to seeing him as, and the affected fop whom the hero impersonates in order to conceal his true identity. He is absolutely outrageous as the fop, his choices are stunning, and yet he is totally convincing, always a believable individual, never the "type" that we see so many actors present. And he appeared to be having so much *fun* playing the man.

• • •

Whether you are working on a monologue, a scene, or an entire role, the process is essentially the same. It is a process of discovery. You cannot force discoveries to take place. You can only search for what is there to be found. If you find yourself stuck, you can sometimes pry yourself loose by asking questions, the kinds of questions I have been suggesting: What am

I talking about here? What's it like? What do I really want to convey? What is it in you, my listener, that elicits my words? What am I doing, and what prompts me to do it? How might the character look at this situation? And so on. These are questions, not formulas. And you don't always have to have the answers.

What interferes with the process time and time again is putting yourself under the obligation of fulfilling demands set by others or by your own internal taskmaster. The effort to please prevents you from being present, occupying this space right now, functioning as a spontaneous, receptive human being in connection with another human being. Trying too hard to "relive the past" or "play the subtext" or "pursue an objective" may cause you to break off your connection. And nothing will disconnect you from your partner more readily than trying to demonstrate to the audience what your character is like.

Instead of trying to win the approval of the audience out there in the house or within your own head, you need to become engaged in communicating what is vital to the person or persons occupying the stage with you.

You do have a connection with the audience too, but it's a different kind of connection. I'll deal with that in Part Three.

Part Three:

PERFORMING

16

Setting Goals, Building Networks and Support Systems

When actors come to me for help with monologues, I usually begin by asking what their goals are as performers. Would they prefer, for example, to work on stage, in film, or on television? What *kind* of stage, film, or TV? Often their responses are rather vague: "I just want to act," they say, "I don't care, I'll take whatever I can get." Rather than being a sign of broadmindedness, that may well be a sign of desperation. As Jay Perry points out in his career workshops at Actors' Information Project in New York, it's a bit like saying, "I just want to get married, I don't care, I'll take anybody who will have me."

Even actors who say they want to work "on Broadway," for example, may have difficulty seeing themselves doing that in any specific way. Stepping onto a Broadway stage seems such a remote and terrifying possibility that they can entertain only a vague and fleeting impression of what they might actually do there. It could be that their fear of being "unworthy" prevents them from even fantasizing about their deepest desires. It could also be that they have no special desire to work on Broadway, they feel only that if they're any good at all they *ought* to be on Broadway.

Fear and confusion about goals may manifest themselves

in other ways. If you keep putting off such tasks as making rounds, sending out pictures and resumes, and following up with phone calls, if you keep promising yourself you're going to work on a monologue but never get around to it, you may conclude that you are simply "lazy." But the real problem may be that you have not yet developed a clear and compelling need to do a particular kind of work. You may be struggling instead to attain some vague kind of "success" that would finally bring you the recognition you have always craved. The need to compensate for a deep feeling of unworthiness can be a powerful motivating force, but if it is the *only* such force, if we have no real need to express ourselves in a particular way or make something beautiful or useful, then we may become so terrified of "failure" that we sabotage our own efforts. Or if we are "successful" for a moment, that success feels hollow, and we crave even more.

• • •

Perhaps the greatest difficulty we encounter in getting what we want in life is being clear about what that really is. Suppose that a few years from now you could have everything you ever wanted, not only in your career, but in your personal life as well. Do you know what your life would be like? Let's take an imaginary trip into that future and find out. Make yourself comfortable, lie back in a chair or on the floor, close your eyes and allow any tension to drain out of your body with each outgoing breath. Gradually let your body sink into the chair or floor. Feel that you are being supported by a kind of "magic carpet" that is capable of lifting you up and carrying you off, wherever you want to go. When you feel ready, ask to be taken about three to five years into your future. If you're not sure exactly what you want in that future, make something up. Ask your magic carpet to set you down in the place where you would most like to live. Take a little walk through your house or apartment or castle or cabin—whatever comes to mind. Greet anybody you live with—of course it will be the kind of person with whom you would most like to share your life—and any friends who may have dropped by. Enjoy some leisure time doing something you especially like, either by yourself or with others.

Now see yourself going to work. Naturally it's the kind of work that would be most satisfying to you. I will assume that it's acting, but if you happen to see yourself "performing" in some other capacity, perhaps as a teacher in a classroom or the owner of your own business, go with that fantasy and adapt my directions accordingly. Picture the place where you will be working: a specific theater or television or film studio or other space. See yourself travelling to that place by car, subway, taxi, helicopter, whatever. When you get there, greet the people you will be working with. Go to your dressing room and prepare for your performance. Allow yourself to get caught up in the familiar, comforting rituals of putting on makeup and getting into costume. Sit there quietly for a time if you like.

You are about to perform your ideal role, written for you by your favorite author, in the company of some of your favorite actors, for an audience eager to see this particular work. As you step onto the stage or set, you feel both keyed-up and at ease, full of free-flowing energy.

The performance begins. You feel keenly aware of your partners, you play back and forth together with a special abandon. Your audience is thoroughly caught up with you. The work stirs them and animates them and sweeps them along. You know they are with you every second, not only by their laughter and applause, but also by the quality of their silence.

Now imagine yourself out in the audience, watching your performance. Take in the details of your costume and makeup, notice the choices that work especially well. Stroll out during the intermission and see your name on the marquee and read your bio in the program. Or, if you're watching a film, see the credits roll by at the end, your name right up there with those of all the people you've always wanted to work with.

The performance ends, and the audience rises in acclamation. As the entire company acknowledges their warmth and appreciation, you feel that something quite special is being shared tonight. You go back to the dressing room, get out of costume and makeup, and greet the friends and family who have come back to congratulate you. Feel free to go out with them wherever you like—money is no longer a concern. Perhaps you'll wait up to read the rave reviews; perhaps you'll go home, spend some quiet time, and then to bed. After all, you have another show tomorrow .

• • •

You'll have to come back to the present at some point. But you can take this trip again any time you like. Shorter excursions are available too: if you can't get a clear picture of yourself doing a contract role on a "soap" five years from now, you may more readily see yourself doing an extra job or an "under-5" (a character with fewer than five lines) in three to six months. Each time you travel, you may see your future somewhat differently, possibly because of some experience you've had between journeys, possibly because you are getting in closer touch with what you really want. Just keep entertaining whatever scenarios come spontaneously to mind, even those you might tend to reject as either "too grandiose" or "not good enough." You may discover that you want to do something you never dreamed of before, or that you no longer want to do something you once wanted to do. You may find that one of your fantasies is so compelling that you want to focus single-mindedly on making it real. Or perhaps you'll find a way to satisfy a number of your deepest wishes simultaneously.

I used to think, for example, that I had to be either an "actor" or a "teacher," that I couldn't be both. When I first took a full-time teaching job in a college I was afraid I wouldn't be able to act much, but actually I managed to do quite a lot. And when I took an early retirement from that job after twenty years, I told myself I didn't want to teach any more, I just wanted to act. But now I find myself coaching actors privately and running occasional weekend workshops. And when I project myself five years into the future I find, somewhat to my surprise, that I am still doing that, only now I have my own studio as part of a large co-op apartment on Riverside Drive in the 70s. (I also have, in my mind's eye, a summer cabin by a lake in Vermont.) And I am delighted to discover that the teaching does not really prevent me from doing what I want as an actor. I can arrange my schedule (as I already do in fact) so that I am free on short notice to take a role in a film (my main interest) or go off for a month or two to a regional theater (I love to travel). I see myself having time, too, to spend with my family, to continue doing volunteer work in my neighborhood, and to enjoy running, going to plays and films, and watching baseball on television.

But my strongest desire is still to act. In my most vivid fantasy, I see myself being picked up by a car at my apartment quite early in the morning and being driven to a film location in Central Park, where I will play a feature role in a new film written, of course, by A. R. Gurney, Jr. (It's his first screenplay.) I'm not the star of the film, and I feel OK about that, I don't think I really want to be a star, but I do have my own Winnebago camper with my name on the door, and somehow that really matters. Naturally I am doing the ideal role I described in Part One: I have a scene today on a park bench, a reunion with a son I haven't seen in years. It's a peculiarly touching scene, funny and awkward and sad all at the same time. The weather is just right: a cool fall day, the leaves turning bright red and orange. Whenever we take time out for the crew to set up a new shot, I sit out on the grass with the other actors or go back to my camper to rest. Some of the shots are difficult to get right, and I am glad to be able to do a number of takes on each. What I particularly enjoy about film work is being able to summon up intense, highly concentrated energy for short periods of time, and then to feel, once a take really works, that it is "in the can." It's like being able to create and preserve forever a moment of perfection. (On stage you have to do the whole thing all over again, and you have to suffer through some nights that are considerably less than peak experiences.) The work moves along, slowly but enjoyably, and before dusk we are ready to wrap. I can't think of a better way to spend a day.

• • •

The clearer your vision of your future, the easier it will be for you to begin making connections with the people who can best help you realize it. Suppose, for example, you want to become part of an ensemble that creates challenging and innovative theater pieces. Don't waste your time auditioning for *Oklahoma*. Explore your local theater scene, and when you've staked out an avant-garde group that challenges you and the audience, make your desire and abilities known to them: drop by and ask to audition for them, or perhaps volunteer to do backstage work as a way of getting started. Or get together with some other actors and form your own group. If you readily see yourself performing a repertoire of classics and new plays in a regional theater, you can arrange your own tour of theaters in a certain section of the country, the New England states for example, writing ahead of time to ask for a chance to do some monologues for them, and then calling the day you arrive. If you decide to center yourself in New York or Los Angeles or some other large city, you can choose to concentrate on getting the kind of work you most want: stage, daytime television, a TV series, commercials, whatever. You can find out which agents specialize in submitting people for that kind of work, and which casting directors set up auditions for it; you can then focus on getting these particular people to see you. Or you can go directly to the people who write and produce the kind of material you want to work on.

You can walk into an audition looking for collaborators for your work, just as the auditors are looking for collaborators for theirs. In addition to the satisfaction of performing material you love for a small audience who may appreciate it as much as you do, you may meet people you would like to work with someday. Of course they may not want to work with you, but then you may not want to work with them. In any event, if you go in with the goal of doing *your* work as best you can, you can walk away feeling good about the experience, no matter how other people react.

• • •

Actors often set themselves goals in an audition quite different from their goals in other kinds of performances. That is a major cause of monologue phobia. As an antidote, try this: pick a monologue you like a lot, imagine that you are doing it as part of the whole play in a particular theater, and ask yourself how you would want the audience to be affected by this passage in the play. For example, a young actress I coach imagined she was doing a piece from Sam Shepard and Joseph Chaikin's *Savage Love* at a small off-Broadway theater, and she wanted the audience to be touched by the openness and vulnerability of the character, who is begging for the slightest sign of affection from a man she adores. An older actress saw herself on stage at the Berkshire Theater Festival in Stockbridge, Massachusetts, doing a speech from Gurney's *Children* in which the character announces, with enormous delight, that she is throwing off all responsibility for the ancestral home and her children and grandchildren and running off with her lover to enjoy what's left of her life. The actress imagined that the audience, particularly those of her generation, would share her delight and cheer her on. They might themselves long to cast off a lifetime burden of caring for others and start enjoying their own lives more. Even if they cannot quite manage that (as indeed the character in the play ultimately cannot), at least they will feel they are not alone.

The next step is to imagine that one night you hear in the dressing room (from one of those actors who just can't keep such information to themselves) that a very important person, somebody whose opinion matters a lot to you, will be in the audience that night. The young actress picked Uta Hagen. (She wanted to study with Hagen but could not bring herself to audition for her classes.) The other actress picked an influential casting director. (She was just coming back into the business after a long absence and was fearful of auditioning again.) Both actresses felt that the presence of this special person, although it might add a certain excitement, would not really prevent them from doing what they wanted in the role. Next, imagine that the house is only half full. Would that really make a difference? What if it were only a quarter full? Keep narrowing down the size of the audience in your mind until you see yourself playing before a handful of people, including of course the person whose opinion matters so much to you. Finally, perform for that one person alone. When you are finished, imagine that person coming up to you, taking you by the hand, and saying, "You know, I enjoyed the whole performance, but there was one moment in particular that really got to me . . . " The person then goes on to say that they were affected by your monologue in exactly the way you intended.

• • •

Many actors go into auditions hoping for another kind of response ("You're the greatest actor I've ever seen!") and fearing its opposite ("Get out of here, you have no right to be in the business!") In reality, however, not many people set up auditions for the sake of separating the sheep from the goats. You may run into a few people in the business who, insecure about their own worth, use their positions of power to humiliate the actors who come before them. (The best way to protect yourself against their harsh judgment is to just do the work you believe in as best you can.) Fortunately such people are rare. Most casting people do not set themselves up as judges. Their concern is to cull from the many talented people they see the ones who might best meet their particular needs. An agent, for example, may be looking for clients in a certain age range or with a certain "look." A casting director may be hoping against hope that somebody will finally walk through that door with exactly the right "quality" that the producer and director have been searching for for months. They may see a lot of people who audition quite effectively without getting excited by anybody or calling anybody back. Or they may call back somebody who happens to audition rather ineffectively but seems to have some potential for doing the job they want done. The great mass of actors who pass in and out of the room are likely to go unnoticed and unremembered. Even an actor who auditions abominably (and we all have days like that) may be quickly forgotten.

A few actors may stand out, whether they are what the auditors are looking for or not, simply by reason of the vitality they bring into the room. They may exhibit a rare spontaneity or susceptibility to feeling or originality of mind that makes everybody in the room sit up and take notice. Naturally you will hope to make that kind of impression, but you can hardly expect to make it all the time on every audience. Even if you feel that you make it rarely or not at all, that does not mean that you are not talented. It could be that you have not yet found the right material or a way of doing it that would let your special gifts shine through. I am often astonished to find that an actor who appears rather wooden and uninteresting at first sight will suddenly reveal warmth, charm, humor, and passion simply by doing different material or taking a different approach to the same piece. It could also be that your gifts are still hidden, like treasure in a locked chest, and you have yet to find the key. You may find it through your training as an actor or your growth as a human being. Or you may discover that you don't really want to unlock your treasures before strangers in public (especially under the conditions that now prevail in the entertainment business), and you may find another way to share them.

• • •

Even with the clearest of goals, peddling monologues from audition to audition can be a lonely business. Isolation seems to be a built-in condition of the actor's life today. Until recently in the history of the theater, actors belonged to permanent companies who lived in the community for which they performed. Actors in the 5th century, B.C., doing a play by Sophocles must have felt a special bond with their fellow Athenians in the audience, and the play must have had overtones for that audience that we cannot hear, just as those of Shakespeare must have had for the Elizabethans and those of Chekhov for the Russians of his day. It is still possible on occasion for a group of actors with a common background and common interests to get together to do a piece that means something rather special to them and to the particular audience they play it for. But in an age when most actors go from job to job, that sense of theater as a communal ritual is rare.

Actually, actors spend most of their time these days *between* jobs. And in their search for work they must often seek out contacts with strangers. As recently as fifty years ago an actor went directly to a producer's office and asked for work. The producer and director were likely to know the actor's work already and might cast the actor without an audition or, at most, have the actor read a scene from the script. An agent's job in those days was mainly to negotiate terms. But as the number of jobs declined and the pool of applicants grew larger, agents had to step in to screen the applicants and submit some of them to the producer for consideration. Then, as both agents and actors kept proliferating, the producer needed an assistant to cull from the submissions those actors who would get a chance to read. Hence the very recent emergence of the casting director. (Twenty years ago there were only a handful, today there are about 225 in New York City alone.) Since most actors are out of work most of the time, where are agents and casting directors supposed to discover the talent they need? The solution to that problem was the final step in the process of fragmentation, a practice that was quite rare twenty years ago but is very common today: a single actor gets up before strangers in an alien space to do a monologue out of context. No wonder the poor actor feels he is being judged!

If you want to survive in the rather peculiar circumstances of show business today, I suggest you make it one of your goals as an actor to rebuild a sense of community. An obvious way to do that is to join a resident theater, but it's not the only way. Wherever you choose to work, you can seek out opportunities to do material that means something special to you and to the people you most want to reach, whether they be gathered in your hometown in a community theater or scattered throughout the nation in front of their television sets.

You can even use the audition process, awkward as it may be, as a way of building a small community of sorts. Let's say, for example, that at this point in your career doing television commercials is either your primary goal or a secondary goal that will support your "habit" of acting on stage. If you audition often enough for the agents who specialize in submitting people for commercials and for the various casting directors who work for the advertising agencies, for the production houses, or independently, you will eventually get to know a number of these people and they will get to know you. They will see you on good days and bad days, doing various kinds of copy, and they will come to appreciate what is special about you, what you really do best. You will also get to know them personally and become more comfortable auditioning for them. Some of them may become your friends. Most of them will become part of a network who know you, have you in mind already when they get a call for a particular kind of person, and recommend you to other people. When you begin to get some commercial bookings, even extra jobs, you will get a chance to work with directors, art directors, assistant directors, crew members, and other actors who work regularly on commercials. They may become part of your network too. You will tend to run into the same people again and again, at auditions, on the set, and at social occasions, and any one of them may give you a bit of information or make a connection for you that will get you work. You will feel that you belong to the small community of people who make television commercials.

With a different goal you would have to build a somewhat different network. If your main interest is regional theater, for example, you would probably not work with the same agents who submit you for commercials, and you would almost certainly work with different casting directors and artistic directors. Your various networks may overlap somewhat: at a commercial audition, for example, you are likely to run into actors you have worked with in regional theater. Your networks can keep growing and, to some extent coalescing, like separate circles that keep expanding until they overlap and share some common areas.

Perhaps you feel some reluctance to seek out friendships for the sake of advancing your career. I know there was a time when I was so afraid of appearing sycophantic or even "insincere" that I was hesitant to make friendly overtures to anybody who might think I was just trying to get a job out of them. I realized that I must have been coming across as cold and withdrawn, possibly even hostile! I found a simple solution: I now try to extend to the casting people I meet and audition for at least the same degree of warmth and openness that I extend to actors who inquire about my workshops or private coaching. In both cases I simply feel that I have something of value to offer. I don't feel that I am "selling myself" (an expression I happen to loathe), I am simply assuming that I may be working together with somebody in a way that might be beneficial to both of us and might turn out to be a lot of fun too.

• • •

Some of the people in your network will do more than give you information or make connections for you. They may provide you with some emotional support as well. The feeling that a group of people care about you, appreciate your work, and want you to succeed in it is pretty important to everybody, but especially to actors. Some actors may feel that they are so "strong" or "self-sufficient" that they can go it alone. I don't know about that. It may be possible for an artist or a writer to sustain a creative effort over a long time without support, but I doubt that it is for an actor.

Probably your first "support group" consisted of your parents. If you were fortunate they fussed over you and applauded your every performance, from your first efforts on the toilet seat to your struggles to master your first two-wheeler. Eventually this small "fan-club" may have grown to include other family members, friends in school and college, and colleagues at work. If you chose acting as your work, however, your chances of getting steady support from an ongoing group may have been considerably reduced. Your parents, for example, may be so anxious about your future in an uncertain profession that, rather than supporting your efforts, they may actively try to discourage you, giving you the message that you "don't have what it takes"—at least not in *that* business—and thus strengthening your determination to prove that by God you *are* worthy. In an age of two-income households, your lover or spouse may be so absorbed in their own career or so resentful of having to bring in enough money for the two of you (your contribution to the family finances being rather meager at present) that they are unable to give you the emotional support you need. You may feel resentful in turn and try still harder to compensate for what seems to you a lack of love by being "successful" in spite of them all!

The absence of support acts like a powerful vacuum, and actors have found many ways to fill it. Almost every time they have a chance to work with other actors they quickly form new friendships and cement old ones, offering each other information, assistance, and encouragement not only about the work at hand but also about career matters, even personal problems that might arise. I have seen this happen again and again, even among a busload of actors who have been hired to work as extras on a movie for one day only. With longer engagements an *esprit de corps* can develop comparable to what one finds among a group of soldiers in battle—and for similar reasons. (Sometimes, also for similar reasons, morale deteriorates and jealousy and infighting begin.) When the group disbands, friendships may end abruptly. How often, for example, have you run into an actor you felt rather close to only a year or two ago when you worked together, and now you can't even remember her name!

It's not surprising that actors should support each other wholeheartedly when they work together. What is astonishing is that they often do so when they are competing for the same jobs. Notice what happens when a group of actors are waiting to go in to an audition: the atmosphere is likely to be as convivial as you would find in a green room before a performance. They tell jokes, gossip, talk politics, or commiserate with each other about how "slow" things are: "How's it going for you?" . . . "Slow, very slow. How about you?" . . . "Same thing. Can't figure out why it's so slow lately, must be the stock market." (Or the election or the weather. If in fact you feel that things are going well, it's considered bad form to say so. What you say instead is, "Not too bad. Just finished six weeks on the new Woody Allen film, booked a national commercial yesterday, and next week I fly out to the Guthrie to play Hamlet, but other than that it's been pretty slow.") An actor coming out of the audition room may share some helpful information about what is going on inside. One actor may say to a friend, "I hope I get it, but if I don't, I hope you do." Or if more than one part is being cast, "Wouldn't it be great if we could work together on this!" or "You should ask to read for the mother, you'd be perfect for it!"

One reason for the camaraderie is that actors tend to know each other, either from having worked together or having auditioned so many times for the same kind of role. I sometimes feel, for example, that I know every "warm, lovable grandpa" type in New York, and whenever we get together for yet another commercial audition it's like old home week. A second reason is that, having no illusions about the odds they face, actors are aware that luck must play some part in the selection process. When you're standing outside the Equity building in a line with several hundred other actors, some of whom have been there since 5:00 a.m., just for the chance to sign up to do a monologue for a summer stock company which may already have cast most of its season anyway, it's a bit like waiting in line to buy a lottery ticket for a multi-million-dollar jackpot. Yet another reason for the cooperative spirit is that actors who audition frequently are likely to have already gotten over any hangups about their relative worth. They know very well they are talented, and they know that the actors they are going up against are also talented, but in different ways and perhaps at different stages of development. Once you come to accept that everybody is talented, you no longer have to prove that *you* are. You may still benefit from the kind of healthy competitive spirit that often makes Olympic athletes perform at their very best in their final chance to win the gold medal, but that's quite different from a need to prove your worth.

• • •

What if you're just starting out, have no friends in the business, are totally unknown to agents and casting directors, and seldom get a chance to audition for anything? How can you find support? One way is to take classes. In a good acting class you can not only improve your skills, you can also get encouragement, information, and advice about the business both from the teacher and your fellow students. The same can be true of a dance or voice class. In some cities you can also find classes in audition techniques that are designed specifically to help you in your search for work.

The various actors' unions and some private organizations also set up "seminars" or "workshops" that give you a chance to meet agents and casting directors and in some cases audition for them. One such organization in New York, Actors' Information Project, also provides career counselling and workshops in which the members meet weekly to set goals and support each other in reaching them. You could easily set up such a group yourself: just get together regularly with a few other actors and be accountable to each other for actually doing the particular things you said you were going to do to move towards your goals.

You could also form a support group specifically for the purpose of working on monologues. When you know that you are expected to do a monologue at the next meeting, that can be an incentive to get you working. It's also very helpful to be able to try out your monologue in front of a supportive audience before taking it in to an audition. You can give each other useful feedback too, but nobody in the group should assume the role of "critic." Rather than telling somebody what they did wrong or offering helpful "suggestions," just say honestly how you were affected as an audience, what moved you or amused you or what seemed to puzzle or distract you. After you've done your own monologue, try to ask questions that will help you sharpen your performance: "Was this clear?" for example, or "Did I come across as too strident here?" or "Did it seem that I was really talking to somebody I loved?"

• • •

Setting specific goals and building networks and support systems to help you reach them can do a lot more for you than make you more comfortable auditioning with a monologue. It can relieve you of the misery that afflicts so many actors who get caught up in an endless struggle to prove their worth against overwhelming odds. It has been estimated that there are about 100,000 actors seeking work in New York City alone, of whom only two percent are working at any one time, and only one tenth of one percent (that's right, that's .001!) earn their living solely by acting. If you feel you must defer any satisfaction in your life until you join that minuscule percentile, you may have to wait quite a while.

Even actors who work all the time are often frustrated and unhappy: they feel they ought to do bigger parts or become better known. Those who are rich and famous may crave more riches and more fame. Some famous actors, it is true, give interviews in which they talk about how content they are. You might think they are content because they are successful, but it could be that they are successful because they are content. Secure in their own worth, they are driven not so much by a need for approval as by the pure pleasure of doing things well.

Even when you have a distant goal in mind, you can still find satisfaction in what you are doing here and now. If you have to hold down a part-time job waiting tables or doing word processing, you may regret that you cannot devote yourself full-time to acting, but so long as you are doing these other things anyway, try to think of them as a *form* of acting: you may find a way to express something of yourself in this work or connect with others in a way that improves their lives, or at least have the satisfaction of mastering a difficult task. Even what may seem to you the dreary duties of sending out yet more pictures and resumes and making still more phone calls can be a way not only of searching for acting but also exercising your skills as an actor. In a sense you can act *all the time.*

If you decide that you don't really want to pursue a career in show business, it doesn't have to be because you're not "good enough," it can be because you choose to use your talents in another arena. If you stay in the business for a lifetime and never achieve any notable fame or fortune, you don't have to feel that you have wasted your life. I know actors in their sixties who still drive cabs or collect unemployment benefits, and many of them are happy, productive people. They may not work as much as they would like, but they do work some, and they enjoy all of it, even extra work. Moreover, they are leading the life they chose for themselves. There's a lot to be said for the life of an actor, even one who is for the most part unemployed. There's something almost licentious about it, and I don't mean that we can have a lot of affairs (you can do that in any line of work if that's what you want), I mean that we are free to travel about and meet different people and assume different roles. When we are in rehearsal or performance, we are free to shut out all other cares and responsibilities for a time and immerse ourselves totally in the world of the play, like inhabitants of a submarine suspended in silence in deep waters, the interior aglow with warmth and light and a rather pleasant sense of bustle, and when we surface the world seems new again. When we are "between engagements" or "at liberty" as they say, we are free to savor that delicious sense of not knowing for sure what we will be doing next Tuesday or Wednesday. Not knowing can be rather unnerving, especially if the rent is due on Thursday, and there are limits to anybody's tolerance for uncertainty, but some degree of it is preferable to complete certainty, for then we can still entertain the delightful possibility that Wednesday will bring an unexpected joy. Meanwhile there is still Monday to be lived, and an actor who has learned to play all the time will manage to make it not too bad a day.

17

The Performance Experience

I want to invite you to take one last imaginary trip with me. This time we'll be traveling to a studio where you will be performing a monologue for an audition. Along the way I'll try to anticipate some questions you might have about such practical matters as what to wear, whether to sit or stand, whether to look the auditors in the eye, that kind of thing. I'll also point out how this same kind of "mental rehearsal" can be useful to you when you are auditioning with a cold reading rather than a prepared monologue and when you are performing in class or in public.

● ● ●

Again take a few minutes to prepare for your journey by getting comfortable, giving up control of your body, and allowing your mind to quiet down a bit. When you feel deeply relaxed, begin to picture yourself getting dressed for the audition. If you're auditioning for a specific role you might want to wear something that would at least suggest the character without looking conspicuous on the street. Otherwise choose something that projects an image of yourself at your most interesting or attractive: in other words, dress for your ideal role. If you're doing two contrasting monologues, you might find a way to make a simple adjustment in your hair or costume between pieces to suggest a different image. Whatever you wear, the important thing is to feel *good* in these clothes, the way you feel in a dressing room before a performance when every detail of your costume, hair, and makeup seems just right. See yourself in a mirror, looking that way.

Imagine yourself walking down the street in that outfit with a sense of ease and power. You probably have that feeling spontaneously at times, both in life and on stage, and each time it comes try to get a sense of how you move, so that you can recapture it at will. Find your own name for that feeling, such as "moving easy" or "feeling good" or "filled with grace." You could even see yourself maintaining that feeling in the subway or on a bus, in spite of the crowds and the noise—after all, you are going somewhere!

If the place you're headed is a familiar one, such as the Equity lounge in New York, you can go over in your mind the whole process of standing in line outside the building in the early morning hours, getting your number, waiting in the lounge and then in line again when your name is called (finally!). If the place is an unfamiliar one, try to visualize it anyway, using components of places you already know. You might see yourself riding up in a carpeted elevator to the sound of Muzak in a high-rise office building, or perhaps climbing a dingy metal staircase with peeling walls and a cast-iron ceiling in an old loft building—whatever you anticipate for this particular audition. You walk in, greet the person at the desk and any friends who might be there, sign in if necessary, and take a seat. No matter how you visualize the place, imagine yourself feeling comfortable there, really *belonging* in the space.

While you are waiting, do whatever you normally do to get yourself ready for a performance. I just like to sit quietly, perhaps read or chat with friends if I have a lot of time, but then go back to sitting or maybe pacing slowly as my time grows near. I don't like to think of anything in particular, and I certainly don't like to give myself last-minute instructions or reminders—I already *know* what I want to do, I can only trust myself to do it and hope that this will be one of those occasions when an angel of the Lord sits on my shoulder and prompts me.

• • •

However you spend the time while you're waiting, see yourself taking charge of the situation. If you need a drink of water or want to go to the bathroom or find a mirror to check your hair and makeup, ask for what you want. If it helps you to go out in the hall and do a few stretching exercises, do that. Decide ahead of time what you're going to do with your coat and other belongings, whether you plan to take your valuables into the audition room with you or ask somebody to look after them. Have your picture and resume handy if one is required. Then, when your name is called, you can just get up and walk calmly into the room without a lot of last-minute bustling about.

You can never be sure exactly what will happen when you enter the room. There may be one person there or half a dozen. Somebody may take you in and introduce you, or the auditors may introduce themselves. You may hand them a picture and resume, or they may have one already. They may or may not offer to shake hands. (I find it's better to let them take the initiative in this matter, as some casting people are uncomfortable shaking hands all day long.) They may sit you down and initiate a conversation, or they may simply glance at your picture and resume and look up as if to say, "Okay, go ahead." Whatever happens, see yourself remaining flexible and open, responsive to the actual human beings in front of you, rather than to the gods or villains who may exist in your mind.

If you do have a chance to chat before the audition, assume that it will be the kind of conversation you would strike up with somebody you meet at a party and would like to get to know better. Look for an opening to talk about something other than "what you've done lately": talk about where you're from or what you did before you became an actor or how you spend your free time. Look for a chance also to ask the auditors anything you might be curious about. Try to get to know them, if you can, as individuals. In a sense *you* can interview *them*. After all, this may be the beginning of a working relationship.

• • •

When it's clear that chat time (if any) is over, see yourself taking the time you need to set yourself up in the space. This is your space now, take over. I'm not suggesting that you lug in a suitcase full of props and spend most of your three minutes setting them up. That's fine for an acting class, but for an audition a single hand prop (if you need even that) should suffice. For a monologue on the telephone you may feel more comfortable bringing in a real phone. Usually it's best not to try to pantomime a lot of action.

The management can almost invariably be counted upon to provide one prop: a metal folding chair. The question then becomes, should you use it or not? There are varying views about that. I once heard a casting director say to an actor, "Why are you sitting down? Don't you know that you can't possibly show yourself to advantage unless you stand up?" And I've heard other casting people say, after an actor has done a monologue standing, "Pull up a chair, sit down, and just talk the monologue to me." Rather than trying to anticipate what others expect of you, do whatever is comfortable for you. The late Mabel Mercer, who introduced a whole new way of singing popular ballads that influenced Tony Bennett, Frank Sinatra, Ella Fitzgerald, and just about every other pop singer, shocked her friends and advisors when she first insisted on sitting in a big armchair on stage and just talking the songs to the audience. "You can't do that, Mabel," they all told her, "nobody will listen." I have had the good fortune to hear her, and believe me, when Mercer performed, people listened!

You do what feels right for you—and for the material. Some monologues, such as a political speech or a dramatic confrontation, seem to call for you to stand up and speak out. Others, such as an intimate revelation, ring false the minute you get on your feet. Of course it often happens that you begin rehearsing a monologue seated, and after you've mastered it, you feel just as comfortable with it standing. You could also sit for a time and stand for a time. I would not try to introduce a lot of elaborate staging, however. With some monologues it may help you to start upstage and then cross down as if you are making an entrance. Usually it's enough to stay in one place, or at most make one or two moves.

Take a moment to set the chair where you want it or find the spot where you want to stand—probably center stage in good light, not too far back, but not so close as to make your auditors uncomfortable. Find a way to sit or stand comfortably, not the way you're "supposed" to, but the way you do in life. If you're not sure what to do with your hands when you are standing, notice what you do next time you find yourself talking to somebody while standing in a real situation: I don't think you will stand rigidly in a military posture, arms stiffly at sides. Nor will you shuffle about, moving a few feet here and a few feet there, as actors tend to do when they are self-conscious. Very often, if you feel awkward or physically uncomfortable on stage, the simplest solution is to connect more strongly with your listener.

● ● ●

And now we come to the classic question, the dilemma for which no actor has ever found a simple, satisfactory solution: should I address my monologue to the auditors or not? Again, first decide which you would feel more comfortable doing. If you'd rather address an imaginary person, there's no problem, just do it. If you want to use one of your auditors, that may be appropriate in an informal situation, for example, if you are in an agent's office and have already had a chance to talk a bit. (Sometimes addressing an imaginary person when a real one is sitting right across a desk from you in a small office feels a bit odd.) In that case you might ask, "Do you mind if I address this piece to you?" Some people prefer that and some are put off by it. It's a bit like dancing: you have to feel out the person ahead of time, and you can't just go up and grab them, you do have to ask. In a more formal situation—for example, if you walk into a studio with three strangers seated behind a desk and have to launch right into your monologue—I would not even consider addressing them. In such circumstances most auditors are more comfortable being able to sit back and observe you as an audience rather than get involved with you as actors. You can then, as I've suggested, talk to an imaginary person or a real object on the back wall, but only slightly to the right or left of the auditors, or perhaps over their heads, so that you can be seen full face. You can talk to an imaginary person sitting by your side, in which case you need only glance once or twice in that direction to establish their presence. Or you can talk to an imaginary group of people sitting between and around the actual auditors.

• • •

So. You've set up the space, you've taken your place, seated or standing, and you've decided where to focus. Can you begin at last? Not quite. You need to glance for a second at your auditors and make sure *they* are ready for you to begin. If one of them is still reading your resume, wait till they look up at you. You don't want to perform without their full attention. Some auditors, however, will make it very hard on you: they will look up, indicating that you can start, then once you've started, they will look back down and keep reading your resume during your entire monologue. No matter how good your concentration is, you can't help noticing that out of the corner of your eye. You may even find—although this is rare—that auditors will be rude enough to carry on a conversation during the audition. You don't mind, of course, if they take a few notes or whisper an occasional comment to each other, but you can tell when you are being totally ignored, and there's no reason why you should have to perform under these circumstances. One way to cope is simply to stop. That's all, stop without saying a word. The offender will look up, puzzled. You then say, quite calmly and with no trace of sarcasm, "I didn't realize you hadn't finished reading my resume, go ahead and finish, I have plenty of time," or "Finish your conversation, I can wait." If the auditors object that they can listen to you at the same time that they read or carry on a conversation, you say, "I'm sure you can, but I prefer not to perform while you do."

When you have the auditors' attention, it's customary to announce the title and author of the piece, no more than that, unless there's some special circumstance that would seem peculiar without an explanation, for example if you are playing somebody who is blind and there is no indication of that in the text.

• • •

And now, at last, you begin. This is the point at which your mental rehearsal will be most helpful to you. When you are lying at home in a state of deep relaxation, you may be able to tap the wellsprings of your monologue more fully than at any other time. You may feel more closely connected with your listener or more completely possessed by the thoughts and feelings you want to convey to that person. Visualize yourself in the audition room, taking a moment to feel connected and possessed. If you simply focus on an object or person, as I've suggested, and perhaps listen to an imaginary cue or say something silently, you may feel in that moment, even before you speak, that you are drawn so powerfully into your fictional world that others in the room are pulled in with you. Let go now of all the work you did in rehearsal, all the finding what's it like and making choices and staying alive in the pauses—you've done all that already, and now all you have to do is focus on your listener and make it your task to convey what you feel. Your listener looms large in the foreground of your awareness, like the catcher's mitt in the mind of a pitcher who has learned not to "think" on the mound but just to deliver the ball into the mitt. Your auditors are still there, but they are in the background, and you can assume that they are reacting in the way you would want an audience in the theater to react. Above all, enjoy doing this monologue, relish everything about it that attracted you to it in the first place.

As you go through your monologue at home in your mind's eye, line by line, the content may become so vivid and real to you that you experience an almost irresistible urge to get up and speak the words. Get a sense of what it would feel like, physically and vocally, to speak with that kind of commitment at the audition: don't just "see" yourself doing it, "feel" it in your body. You may feel, for example, that your voice is coming from deep within you and is flowing freely and effortlessly.

When you get to the last line of your monologue, keep doing whatever you are doing for a few seconds beyond the words, then drop out, look at your auditors and nod or say "Thank you." (Some actors are told in their classes to say "monologue" or "scene" to indicate that they are finished, but I don't think that's necessary in an audition.) At that point leave yourself open to whatever happens. You may be dismissed, or you may be asked to stay and talk some more or perhaps do another piece. Your auditors may even be thinking about scheduling a callback on the spot, but if you're already half way out the door, they may change their minds.

• • •

If you are auditioning with a cold reading rather than a prepared monologue, you may be able to do only a brief mental rehearsal in the waiting area after you have picked up your "sides." (Originally sides were an abbreviated text of your role, with only your own lines and the last five words of the preceding line to give you your cue, but nowadays the same word is used to refer to a xeroxed copy of a few pages from a script to be used in casting sessions. For television auditions, the text is often called "copy" rather than "sides.") Sometimes you will be able to pick up the sides a day or two ahead of time, or if the script is published you may be told which pages to study, but often you won't know what you will be reading till you get there, in which case it's a good idea to arrive at least half an hour before your appointment.

You may be asked to read a monologue, a dialogue, or some combination of the two, and your sides are likely to run from one to five pages. For a commercial audition the copy will consist of a very brief monologue or dialogue. Since many commercials are silent or improvised, there may be no copy at all, or at most a "storyboard," a kind of cartoon strip of the action, posted on the wall.

In any event, begin by reading the text silently and letting the words suggest pictures and images, just as you did in your first monologue rehearsal. The technique is easily adapted to dialogues: just break the scene down into manageable chunks, finding the places where there is a transition from one subject to another or a change of tack by one of the characters. Normally a two-page scene can best be broken down into three to five units—if the units are too large they may be difficult for you to grasp, and if you have too many small units, the scene may become too complicated. Read a unit at a time silently, both your lines and those of your partner, getting a clear sense of the content, put the sides down and paraphrase that bit of dialogue in your head. Repeat each unit till you have a fair command of the thoughts that are being expressed, then go on to the next. Finally, "play" the whole scene in your head. While you are trying to grasp the content you may at the same time be finding what the situation is like for you, discovering how you feel towards your partner, exploring possible choices—the same kinds of discoveries you made in your monologue rehearsals.

Try not to get particular line readings fixed in your mind—it's all too easy, under the pressure of the audition, to repeat them mechanically. Don't try to memorize the text either; all you want is to become familiar enough with it to glance down at the page, pick up the words easily, and deliver them to the person you'll be reading with. If you will be reading with another actor who is also waiting, ask if your partner wants to read the scene with you a couple of times before going in.

If you're called into the audition room before you've had enough time to study the sides to your satisfaction, don't hesitate to say, "I'd like to have a little more time with this," and it will usually be given to you. (That's very important if, like many actors I've worked with, you have special difficulty with cold readings.) On the other hand, you may prefer to glance through the sides one time only to make sure you understand everything. I know that if I study a script *too* much, especially if I've had it a couple of days in advance, I tend to get caught somewhere in that no-man's land between a first reading, which often goes surprisingly well, and a finished performance, which may also go well. (In between it's not always so good.) You'll need to learn from experience how much preparation is enough for you. For a really important audition you might decide to go all the way if you have time, memorizing the material and rehearsing it thoroughly, just as you do with a monologue of your own choice.

When you are called into the room, you may find that you will be reading with another actor who has been hired for the day to read with everybody, and it may be somebody of the opposite sex from the person you're supposedly addressing. You might also be reading with the casting director, a stage manager, even a member of the crew. The reader usually sits facing you, a bit to the right or left of the auditors, leaving you free to use the playing space however you like. Some readers, however, will come up and share the space with you. If you are reading with another actor who is also auditioning, you will of course share the space. (Be careful, by the way, not to upstage yourself: if you find that you have to turn your back to the auditors to look at your partner, move upstage.) For a commercial audition you will often be talking directly into the camera and reading from a large cue card placed below the camera, so that you do not have to hold copy in your hands. In that case it's helpful to address the camera lens as you would a particular person, usually a close friend.

The reader may be very responsive to you and may give you a lot to work off, or they may keep their eyes glued to the page and read the words in a monotone. No matter how much or how little you get from them, you still have to create the illusion that you are talking to them and mean every word you say. There's a simple rule of thumb that will help you do this whenever you read from a script, whether it's at an audition or in the early stages of rehearsal: *Never read and talk at the same time*. It's a two-step process: first look down at the page, read one or two sentences silently, and grasp the thought or feeling; *then* look up and speak those words to your partner. You don't always have to focus directly on the partner, but never talk to the page. If you are reading a monologue, you will need to pick up a bit at a time, deliver that much, then glance down and pick up some more. Keep the script at about chest level, so that you're not constantly lifting it up and putting it down, and if necessary keep one finger on the page to avoid losing your place.

When you finish you speech, don't dive right back into the script. Stay up, so that you really hear *and see* what your partner does. You may find that what you receive from your partner propels your next line with peculiar force, or that something quite interesting happens *between* the lines. Then look down, find your next line, look up and say it, notice what your partner does again, and so on. If your partner has a monologue, look ahead to the last five words of it, keep them in mind as your cue, then look back up and listen to the rest of the speech; when you hear your cue, go back down again. Let yourself remain open to whatever you feel is coming from your reader. Even if you get nothing, listen at least to the words and let them affect you. That doesn't mean, however, that you let the person you're reading with dictate your choices. Suppose, for example, you feel the scene is about two people who love each other very much and are desperately trying to come to an understanding, and your partner is giving you nothing but petty resentment. You can be aware of what you are getting and still choose not to respond in anger. If you have made compelling choices, your partner may get caught up in playing the scene as you see it. If that doesn't happen, it's too bad you're out of synch, but I prefer a scene that is half right to one that is all wrong. Also, I don't think it's a good idea to ask for direction from the auditors. They may volunteer some, or you may need to ask a factual question about the situation or relationships, but usually it's best to make your own choices and go with them. Then, if the auditors want you to try it another way, they'll tell you.

If you can get together with some other actors and practice cold readings regularly, you will soon become fluent with them. You may not feel as sure of yourself as when you do a prepared monologue, and you'll have to trust even more to your instincts. On the other hand, you may imagine that less is expected of you, and so you demand less of yourself and are more at ease.

• • •

The basic problem in any performance, for an audition, for a class, or for the public, is repetition. Any actor can be brilliant at times, just as any ballplayer can occasionally hit a home run. The difficulty is to play for a high average over a period of time. Paradoxically in order to do that you have to let go any determination you might feel to be brilliant *all* the time. Nobody can be at their best at all times, that's a contradiction in terms: if you are always at your "best," there *isn't* any best. You have to accept that you're going to strike out sometimes; if you try to hit a home run with every swing of the bat, you'll strike out a *lot*.

There are only two things you can do to enhance the possibility that you will perform at a reasonably high level most of the time. One is to follow the advice of the lady in the old joke who is asked how to get to Carnegie Hall: "Practice, practice, practice!" Like a hitter in the batting cage, you can rehearse each moment of your performance over and over again, correcting a problem here, making an adjustment there, getting a feel for the smooth swing, the solid crack of the bat against the ball. The clearer and more precise the choices you find in rehearsal, the easier it will be for you to perform with consistency under pressure. You will find that you are not really at the mercy of your moods: if you don't know what you are doing, being in a good mood won't help much, and if you do know, even a bad mood is likely to improve remarkably the moment you start doing it.

The second thing you can do to raise the level of your performance is to cultivate positive attitudes. Again it's like baseball: in the immortal words of Yogi Berra, "Ninety percent of this game is half mental." The mental rehearsal, which can be used for any kind of performance (in fact I borrowed the idea from sports psychologists), is simply a way of anticipating that we will perform with ease and confidence. It is the exact opposite of the process that we call "worry." When we worry, we not only anticipate bad things happening, we feel that we could not possibly cope with them. You might try sometime doing a "worry rehearsal": that is, deliberately imagine terrible things happening, and then see yourself finding a way to either forestall them or cope with them. For example, picture yourself stalled in a subway tunnel for half an hour on your way to an audition. Then see yourself leaving home somewhat earlier to prevent that from making you late; or see yourself making a phone call as soon as you can get off the train and scheduling another appointment. Or you might picture yourself getting off to a very bad start in the audition, perhaps even going up in your lines. See yourself taking enough time before you begin so that is unlikely to happen. If it does happen, see yourself stopping, saying "I'd like to start over again" (nothing wrong with that), taking a moment to collect yourself, and beginning again.

• • •

There is an enormous difference, however, between *anticipating* that good things will happen and trying to *make* them happen. It's one thing to relax at home and envisage yourself feeling confident and at ease. It's something else entirely to try to wrench yourself out of one mood and into another while you are actually in the situation. Suppose, for example, that in spite of your mental rehearsal you find yourself sitting outside an audition room with trembling hands and racing heart. Some actors are taught that they must try very hard at such times to "relax" and "concentrate." I find that counterproductive. In fact, I recommend the opposite: accept your anxiety, let yourself experience it fully, allow your heart to race and your hands to tremble as much as they want. Notice your breathing, too, and let the breath flow in and out in its own rhythm. As you become more aware of your breath and go with it, it may slow down and become a bit deeper. Carry that feeling of being present, experiencing whatever you're experiencing, right into the audition room; allow yourself to breathe freely three or four times before you start to perform. Be aware of whatever you actually see or hear in the room, even while you perform. Don't shut anything out.

Don't try to control your thoughts either. Stand aside and become a kind of objective "witness" to whatever enters your mind. If you find yourself thinking that this is a very influential casting director and your whole career may hinge on what you do at this one audition, don't try to argue with yourself, accept that that may indeed be true. Exaggerate your fears even, picture the casting director turning away from you, grabbing a wastebasket, and vomiting into it. Imagine that person calling every agent in the business and telling them never to submit you again. If you find yourself thinking that you shouldn't be thinking such thoughts because they will interfere with your performance, say to yourself, "That's right, I can't possibly be any good in there if I'm this anxious, I'm going to be awful, absolutely awful." Accept that, I mean really accept it. Even more, be grateful for it. That may seem like a strange thing to say, but a wise man once told me, "Be grateful for everything." For a long time I thought he meant that there was a good side to everything, or that we can learn from bad experiences, or that there's always somebody else who is worse off; but I know now that he didn't mean any of these things. He meant, just be grateful.

I can't explain it any better, and I can't promise that by embracing your fears you will dissolve them. I can tell you that the harder you try to shut them out the worse they will get. It's like lying awake in the middle of the night: the worst thing you can do is try to get back to sleep. If you decide to read or watch television or just lie there, accepting the inevitability of your remaining wide awake until the alarm goes off, you may actually fall asleep. That's the only thing that works, but of course if you think it's going to work, it won't.

Giving up control is not easy. We have no idea, as we approach the moment of performance, how it will go, and not knowing is hard. We desperately want to do well, we are terrified of doing badly, and we feel there has to be *something* we can do to make sure things go the way we want. There isn't really. We certainly can't control the reactions of the audience. And it's too late now to do anything to influence our own thoughts and feelings. We may have found certain channels for them in rehearsal, but if we try to force them into those channels now, they will dry up on us. Acting is a risky business. All we can do now is take our chances and give ourselves over to forces that are not in our control.

William James said it best:

Give up the feeling of responsibility, let go your hold, resign the care of destiny to higher powers, be genuinely indifferent as to what becomes of it all, and you will find that you gain . . . the particular goods you sincerely thought you were renouncing.

You may or may not believe in a personal God. But anybody who has ever felt the rush of inspiration will find it hard not to believe at least in "higher powers" within us, creative forces that have a will of their own. When we submit to that will and allow ourselves to be swept away wherever these forces want to take us, we may find ourselves possessed by thoughts and feelings that astonish us. We have no idea where they came from. We hardly want to take credit for them, since all we are is an open channel through which they flow. The composer of the hauntingly beautiful Shaker hymn, "Simple Gifts," wrote on the title page not that the hymn was "composed" by her, but that it was "received."

• • •

After the performance—and again it doesn't matter whether it's for an audition, for a class, or for the public—it's helpful to go over the experience in your mind. If some things went especially well for you, was there anything you did that allowed that to happen? If some things went not so well, is there anything you could do next time to make them go better? You might also want to check your impressions with those of other actors, with the director if he's still around, and with any friends who saw the show. If you've just done an audition for which you were submitted by an agent, you might call the agent and see if she can get any feedback from the casting director.

There comes a time, however, when you have to forget about the last performance and start getting ready for the next one. That is especially important after an audition for a role that you want badly. Don't anticipate that you are going to get the part and don't anticipate that you are not going to get the part. You just don't know, and usually you don't know *when* you'll know: you may wait for days for a call that never comes. You might as well use this time productively instead of kicking yourself for "blowing it" or indulging in dreams of run-of-the-play contracts and rave reviews.

Above all, do not try to read the minds of your auditors. If they seemed cold and aloof, perhaps it was the end of the day and they were tired and the part was cast already anyway. Or maybe what you were doing was not their cup of tea, in which case it's likely that what they are doing will not be *your* cup of tea.

Surely you've played to an audience before that was

somewhat less than appreciative and you managed not to be torn to pieces. Why should you feel any differently about the reactions of auditors at an audition? If anything, you should expect *less* of them. Remember how awkward and artificial the audition situation is for you, how difficult it is for you to approach it as just another performance. Well, it's just as awkward and artificial for the people on the other side of the room. If they were sitting anonymously in a crowd in a darkened auditorium they would know how to behave. In these peculiar circumstances, some of them know how to be a good audience and some of them don't.

But what if they beam at you approvingly throughout the entire audition, laugh uproariously at all the right places, and then say, grasping your hand warmly, "That was wonderful! Absolutely wonderful!"? Now you *really* have to watch out! Do not start scouting restaurants in the neighborhood where you can hang out with the cast. Do not plan how you will spend your first paycheck. Do not sit by the phone all day or check your answering service every ten minutes.

Nothing in this business is more disheartening than not to get a role that you were certain in your mind was yours. It's like getting fired. Worse even, because in actuality it's pretty hard to get yourself fired more than once or twice in your whole career (there just aren't that many jobs to get fired *from*), but with enough good auditions and a little imagination you can manage to hire and fire yourself twenty times a season. And you never have the opportunity to investigate the situation objectively and find out *why* you got fired, which may have been for reasons having nothing to do with your abilities. Instead you find yourself indulging in endless recriminations on the theme, "Why do I always come so close and no closer? What's missing? What am I doing wrong?"

Probably you're not doing anything wrong. The only thing you did wrong was you picked an impossible business in the first place. Didn't your parents warn you about that?

Perhaps, like many of us, you can't help sticking with it despite your knowledge of the odds. Some of us, I suspect, persist in our assault on this insurmountable challenge simply because, like Everest, "it's there." And the number of those who make it to the top is very small indeed by comparison with those who are forced to turn back or, worse, perish on the slopes. Smaller still by comparison with those who stay at home and only dream of climbing.

You may never reach the summit of your own particular ambition. If you've ever climbed in the White Mountains of New Hampshire, you will realize how deceptive summits can be. After hours of laborious climbing you see, finally, a rocky knoll ahead that is clearly the top, and you clamber eagerly towards it, gasping for air, only to see, when you get there, *another* rocky knoll a quarter of a mile away and considerably higher. You struggle on towards that one with the same determination, and you find a third beyond that. If you ever do reach the true summit, you may find some temporary satisfaction, but a few days later you're likely to see in your guide book that there is another mountain in the area even higher.

Fortunately there are considerable satisfactions to be found in the climb itself. I leave you now at this point on the trail, and I wish you good hiking, breathtaking views, and pleasant company along the way.

APPENDIX

Useful Lists

Permissions

List A
"THE STANDARD REPERTOIRE"

I have listed below those playwrights whose work I feel is most likely to be produced in the United States today, and I have given one or two titles by each. I cannot guarantee that you will find monologues you like in all the plays listed, but I hope you will find a few writers whose work you want to explore further. In any event, reading the plays on this list is a good way of becoming familiar with the kind of material you are likely to be auditioning for, especially in regional theater.

The list is arranged in reverse chronological order. I have decided, somewhat arbitrarily, that "Contemporary" playwrights should include those who have produced major work since 1960, "Modern Classics" those who produced their major work between 1870 and 1960, and "Classical" writers those who wrote before 1870. Naturally there is some overlapping: I have included Arthur Miller, for example, among "Modern Classics," although he continues to write today. I have also subdivided the list by country of origin, giving more weight to American writers.

CONTEMPORARY (since 1960)
American
Edward Albee: *Who's Afraid of Virginia Woolf?; The Zoo Story*
Amiri Baraka (LeRoi Jones): *Dutchman*
Eric Bogosian: *Drinking in America; Talk Radio*
Michael Cristofer: *The Shadow Box*
Christopher Durang: *The Marriage of Bette and Boo; Laughing Wild*
Jules Feiffer: *Feiffer's People; Grown Ups*
Harvey Fierstein: *Torch Song Trilogy*
Horton Foote: *Lily Dale; Valentine's Day*
Herb Gardner: *A Thousand Clowns; I'm Not Rappaport*
Spalding Gray: *Sex and Death to the Age 14; Swimming to Cambodia*
Richard Greenberg: *Eastern Standard*

John Guare: *The House of Blue Leaves; Landscape of the Body*
A.R. Gurney, Jr.: *The Dining Room; The Cocktail Hour*
Lorraine Hansberry: *A Raisin in the Sun*
Cynthia Heimel: *A Girl's Guide to Chaos*
Beth Henley: *Crimes of the Heart*
Israel Horowitz: *The Indian Wants the Bronx*
Tina Howe: *Coastal Disturbances; Painting Churches*
Harry Kondoleon: *Zero Positive*
Arthur Kopit: *Oh Dad, Poor Dad, Mama's Hung you in the Closet and I'm Feeling So Sad*
David Mamet: *Glengarry Glen Ross; Reunion*
Leonard Melfi: *Birdbath*
Terence McNally: *Bad Habits; It's Only a Play*
Marsha Norman: *Getting Out; 'night Mother*
David Rabe: *Hurlyburly; Sticks and Bones*
Ntozake Shange: *for colored girls who have considered sucide when the rainbow is enuf*
John Patrick Shanley: *Italian-American Reconcilation; Women of Manhattan*
Murray Schisgal: *Luv*
Sam Shepard: *Buried Child; A Lie of the Mind*
Neil Simon: *Barefoot in the Park; Brighton Beach Memoirs*
Jane Wagner: *The Search for Signs of Intelligent Life in the Universe*
Wendy Wasserstein: *Uncommon Women; The Heidi Chronicles*
Michael Weller: *Moonchildren; Loose Ends*
August Wilson: *Fences; Joe Turner's Come and Gone*
Lanford Wilson: *Serenading Louis; Talley's Folly*
Paul Zindel: *The Effect of Gamma Rays on Man-in-the-Moon Marigolds*

British

John Arden: *Serjeant Musgrave's Dance*
Alan Ayckbourn: *The Norman Conquests*
Caryl Churchill: *Cloud 9; Top Girls*
Michael Frayn: *Benefactors*
Christopher Fry: *The Lady's Not for Burning*

Simon Gray: *Quartermaine's Terms; The Common Pursuit*
Christopher Hampton: *Les Liaisons Dangereuses* (from the 18th century novel by Choderlos De Laclos)
David Hare: *Plenty*
Peter Nichols: *Joe Egg*
Joe Orton: *Loot; Entertaining Mr. Sloane*
John Osborne: *Look Back in Anger; The Entertainer*
Harold Pinter: *The Collection; Betrayal*
Peter Shaffer: *Five Finger Exercise; Equus*
Tom Stoppard: *Rosencrantz and Guildenstern Are Dead; The Real Thing*

Irish
Samuel Beckett: *Waiting for Godot; Endgame*
Brian Friel: *Lovers*
Hugh Leonard: *"Da"*

South African
Athol Fugard: *Master Harold and the Boys; The Road to Mecca*

MODERN CLASSICS (1870-1960)
American
Maxwell Anderson: *Elizabeth the Queen*
Philip Barry: *Holiday; Philadelphia Story*
S.N. Behrman: *No Time for Comedy*
Lillian Hellman: *The Children's Hour; The Little Foxes*
William Inge: *Picnic; The Dark at the Top of the Stairs*
George S. Kaufman and Moss Hart: *The Man Who Came to Dinner; You Can't Take It with You*
George S. Kaufman and Edna Ferber: *Dinner at Eight; Stage Door*
George Kelly: *The Show Off*
Sidney Kingsley: *Dead End*
Sidney Howard: *They Knew What They Wanted*
Howard Lindsay and Russell Crouse: *Life with Father*

Arthur Miller: *A View from the Bridge; Death of a Salesman*
Clifford Odets: *Waiting for Lefty; Awake and Sing*
Eugene O'Neill: *A Moon for the Misbegotten; Long Day's Journey into Night*
Elmer Rice: *Street Scene*
William Saroyan: *The Time of Your Life*
Robert E. Sherwood: *The Petrified Forest*
Sam and Bella Spewak: *Boy Meets Girl*
John Steinbeck: *Of Mice and Men*
John Van Druten: *The Voice of the Turtle; I Am a Camera*
Thornton Wilder: *Our Town; The Skin of Our Teeth*
Tennessee Williams: *The Glass Menagerie; A Streetcar Named Desire*

British

J.M. Barrie: *Peter Pan*
Noel Coward: *Private Lives; Blithe Spirit*
Terence Rattigan: *The Winslow Boy*
Bernard Shaw: *Pygmalion; St. Joan*
Oscar Wilde: *The Importance of Being Earnest; Lady Windermere's Fan*
Emlyn Williams: *The Corn Is Green*

Irish

Sean O'Casey: *Juno and the Paycock; The Plough and the Stars*
John Millington Synge: *The Playboy of the Western World*

German

Bertolt Brecht: *The Caucasian Chalk Circle; The Good Woman of Setzuan*

Russian

Anton Chekhov: *The Sea Gull; Uncle Vanya*
Nikolai Gogol: *The Inspector General*
Maxim Gorky: *The Lower Depths*

Scandinavian
Henrik Ibsen: *A Doll's House; Ghosts*
August Strindberg: *Miss Julie; The Father*

Italian
Luigi Pirandello: *Six Characters in Search of an Author*

French
Jean Anouilh: *Antigone; Ring Round the Moon*
Jean Giraudoux: *Ondine; The Madwoman of Chaillot*
Edmond Rostand: *Cyrano de Bergerac*

Spanish
Federico Garcia Lorca: *The House of Bernada Alba*

Rumanian-French
Eugene Ionesco: *The Bald Soprano; The Lesson*

CLASSICAL (before 1870)
British, 1660-1870
William Congreve: *The Way of the World*
Sir George Etherege: *The Man of Mode*
George Farquhar: *The Beaux' Stratagem*
Oliver Goldsmith: *She Stoops to Conquer*
Richard Brinsley Sheridan: *The Rivals; The School for Scandal*
William Wycherley: *The Country Wife*

British, 1570-1660
Ben Jonson: *Volpone*
Christopher Marlowe: *The Tragical History of Dr. Faustus*
William Shakespeare: *Twelfth Night; Hamlet*
John Webster: *The White Devil; The Duchess of Malfi*

French
Pierre Beaumarchais: *The Marriage of Figaro*
Molière: *The Misanthrope; Tartuffe*

Italian
Carlo Goldoni: *The Servant of Two Masters*

Greek
Aeschylus: *Agamemnon; Choephoroe (Orestes)*
Aristophanes: *The Birds; Lysistrata*
Euripides: *Medea; The Trojan Women*
Sophocles: *Oedipus the King; Antigone*

List B
THEATER BOOKSTORES
THROUGHOUT THE COUNTRY

Compiled by Jill Charles in her
Regional Theater Directory 1989-90

California
Drama Books, 134 Ninth St., San Francisco, CA 94103;
(415) 255-0604
Limelight Bookstore, 1803 Market St., San Francisco, CA
94103; (415) 864-2265
Front Row Center, 8127 West 3rd St., West Hollywood, CA
90048; (213) 852-0149
Larry Edmund's Bookstore, 6658 Hollywood Blvd., Holly-
wood, CA 90028; (213) 463-3273
Samuel French's Theater and Film Bookshop, 7623 Sunset
Blvd. Hollywood, CA 90046; (213) 876-0623
Samuel French's Theater and Film Bookshop, 11963 Ven-
tura Blvd., Studio City, CA 91604; (818) 762-0535

District of Columbia
Backstage, Inc., 2101 P St., NW, Washington, DC 20037;
(202) 775-1488

Illinois
Act I Bookstore, 2632 North Lincoln, Chicago, IL 60614;
(312) 348-6757

Massachusetts
Baker's Plays, 100 Chauncy St., Boston, MA 02111; (617)
482-1200

New York
Actors' Heritage, 262 W. 44 St., New York, NY 10036;
(212) 944-7490
Applause Theatre and Cinema Books, 211 W. 71 St., New
York, NY 10023; (212) 496-7511

Drama Book Shop, 723 Seventh Ave., New York, NY 10019; (212) 944-0595

Samuel French, Inc. (East Coast), 45 W. 25 St., New York, NY 10010; (212) 206-8990

Theater Arts Bookstore, 405 W. 42 St., New York, NY 10036; (212) 564-0402

Theaterbooks, Inc., 1600 Broadway, Room 1009, New York, NY 10019; (212) 757-2834

Pennsylvania

Intermission: The Shop for Performing Arts, 8123 Germantown Ave., Philadelphia, PA 19118; (215) 242-8515

Washington

Cinema Books, 4752 Roosevelt Way N.E., Seattle, WA 98105; (206) 547-7667

List C
THEATERS THAT DO NEW WORKS
(Exclusively or nearly so)

Compiled by Jill Charles in her
Regional Theater Directory 1989-90

California
Ensemble Theater Project, Box 2307, Santa Barbara, CA 93120

Antenna Theater, P.O. Box 176, Sausalito, CA 94966

Illustrated Stage Company, 25 Van Ness Ave., San Francisco, CA 94102

Back Alley Theater, 15231 Burbank Blvd., Van Nuys, CA 91411

Cast Theater, 804 El Centro, Hollywood, CA 90038

L.A. Theater Works, 681 Venice Blvd., Venice, CA 90291

Victory Theater, 3326-24 West Victory, Burbank, CA 91505

Zephyr Theater, 7458 Melrose Ave., Los Angeles, CA 90046

District of Columbia
American Playwrights, 1742 Church St., NW, Washington, DC 20036

Living Stage Theater Co., 6th St. & Maine Ave., S.W., Washington, DC 20024

Smallbeer Theater Company, 409 6th St., SE, Washington, DC 20003-2704

Illinois
Organic Theater, 3319 North Clark St., Chicago, IL 60657

Theater Building/New Tuners Theater, 1225 W. Belmont, Chicago, IL 60657

Massachusetts
Gloucester Stage Company, 267 E. Main St., Gloucester, MA 01930

New Voices, Boston Center for the Arts, 551 Tremont St., Boston, MA 02116

Minnesota

Brass Tacks Theater, 200 N. 3rd Ave., Minneapolis, MN 55401

Cricket Theater, 9 W. 14 St., Minneapolis, MN 55403

Illusion Theater, 528 Hennepin Ave., Suite 704, Minneapolis, MN 55403

Playwrights Center, 2301 Franklin Ave. East, Minneapolis, MN 55406

Nebraska

Omaha Magic Theater, 1417 Farnam, Omaha, NE 68102

New York

East Coast Arts, Inc., 44 Wildcliff Road, New Rochelle, NY 10805

First Street Theater, 423 1st St., Ithaca, NY 14850

Arts Club Theater, 80 E. 3rd St., #10, New York, NY 10003

The Ensemble Studio Theater, 549 West 52 St., New York, NY 10019

Hudson Guild Theater, 441 W. 26 St., New York, NY 10001

Irondale Ensemble Project, 782 West End Ave., New York, NY 10025

Manhattan Theater Club, 453 W. 16 St., New York, NY 10019

National Improvisation Theater, 223 8th Ave., New York, NY 10011

New Dramatists, 424 W. 44 St., New York, NY 10036

The New Stagecraft Company, Inc., 553 W. 51 St., New York, NY 10019

The New Theater of Brooklyn, 465 Dean St., Brooklyn, NY 11217

New York Theater Workshop, 220 W. 42 St., New York, NY 10036

The Open Eye: New Stagings, Henry Lindenbaum Community Center, 270 W. 89 St., New York, NY 10024

Playwrights Horizons, 416 W. 42 St., New York, NY 10036

Playwrights Theater Workshop, Inc., 290 Southwood Circle, Syosset, NY 11791

Primary Stages, 584 Ninth Ave., New York, NY 10036

Ryan Repertory Company, 2445 Bath Ave., Brooklyn, NY 11214

Theater for the New City, 155-157 First Ave., New York, NY 10003

13th Street Repertory Co., 50 W. 13 St., New York, NY 10011

Westbeth Theater Center, 151 Bank St., New York, NY 10014

Wings Theater Company, 521 City Island Ave., Bronx, NY 10464

The Wooster Group, Box 654, Canal St. Station, New York, NY 10013

WPA Theater, 519 W. 23 St., New York, NY 10011

The Writers Theater, 145 W. 46 St., New York, NY 10036

Ohio
Mad River Theater Works, Box 248, West Liberty, OH 43357

Pennsylvania
The Independent Eye, 208 E. King St., Lancaster, PA 17602

Philadelphia Festival Theater for New Plays, 3900 Chestnut St., Philadelphia, PA 19104

The Philadelphia Theater Company, 21 South 5th St., Suite 735, Philadelphia, PA 19106

South Dakota
Dakota Theater Caravan, Box 1014, Spearfish, SD 57783

Tennessee
The Road Company, Box 5278 EKS, Johnson City, TN 37603

Washington
Empty Space, P.O. Box 1748, Seattle, WA 98111-1748

List D
AUDITION PIECES CURRENTLY OVERDONE

Compiled by Jill Charles in her
Summer Theater Directory, 1989

(Note: Jill Charles compiles this list every year from producers who attend various combined auditions for summer theater. "There are producers," she notes, "who disagree with the idea of this list, and I can see their point. As one producer wrote me this year: 'In my opinion it is inappropriate to exclude any material. If the material is done well, then it works for the actor. I don't tune out any actor who knows what he is doing.' And another: 'A *good* performance negates any feeling of déja vu one may have. Only *bad* performances make you feel a song or monologue is done.'")

Monologues, Contemporary

A . . . My Name is Alice: Jock strap speech
Beyond Therapy
Butterflies Are Free: Jill Tanner's speeches
Chapter Two: Jenny's "I'm worth it" speech
Crimes of the Heart: They're all overdone, especially Babe's monologue.
'dentity Crisis: Peter Pan speech
Division Street: Earthenware mugs and Boat People speech
Fantasticks: Luisa's speech into song, "Much More"
Feiffer's People: !!!
Hold Me: !!!
House of Blue Leaves: Most of the monologues are done a lot.
It's Called the Sugar Plum: The infamous "Strudel Dee—Strudel Dough"
Knock, Knock: St. Joan's walking on water speech
Lakeboat (Mamet): The jock who always wanted to dance
Last of the Red Hot Lovers: "Humping Charlotte Korman"
Lone Star: The Grand Canyon speech
Matchmaker: Cornelius' monologue
Mass Appeal: Dead goldfish speech
Nourish the Beast: Orphan speech
Nuts: "I love you and you love me . . ."
P.S., Your Cat Is Dead: Auditioning for the commercial

Painting Churches: Both melting the crayons and Mags' first art
show
Quilters: "Sunbonnet Sue"
Say Goodnight, Gracie: Chunky turkey soup
Slow Dance on the Killing Ground: Rosie's virginity
Split: "Stevie Wonder's blind . . ."
Star Spangled Girl: Sophie's "Mr. Cornell" speech
Talking With: Anything

Monologues, Shakespeare
King Lear: Edmund, "Thou, Nature, art my goddess . . ."
Macbeth: "Out, damned spot" and "unsex me"
Merchant of Venice: Lancelot Gobbo
A Misummer Night's Dream: Puck
Romeo and Juliet: Juliet's candle speech, Romeo's balcony
speech
Two Gentlemen of Verona: Julia's "hateful hands"
Richard II: Death of Kings
Henry VI: Joan
Julius Caesar: Tiber speech

List E
COLLECTIONS OF MONOLOGUES

(Note: This list includes both monologue collections and scenebooks that include some monologues. It does not include any of the collections of "original" monologues written especially for actors to use at auditions; with a few exceptions, I find that the writing in these books is not as interesting as you will find in anthologies of material that has already been produced.)

The Actor's Book of Classical Monologues, collected and introduced by Stefan Rudnicki; Penguin Books, 1988

The Actor's Book of Movie Monologues, edited by Marisa Smith and Amy Schewel; Penguin Books, 1986

The Actor's Scenebook: Scenes and Monologues from Contemporary Plays, edited by Michael Shulman and Eva Mekler; Volume I, 1984; Volume II, 1987; Bantam Books

Film Scenes for Actors, edited by Joshua Karton, Volume I, 1983; Volume II, 1987; Bantam Books

Great Scenes from the World Theater, edited by James L. Steffensen, Jr., Volume I, 1965; Volume II, 1972; Avon Books

Modern American Scenes for Student Actors, edited by Wynn Handman; Bantam Books, 1978

Monologues: Men: 50 Speeches from Contemporary Theater, edited by Robert Emerson and Jane Grumbach; Volume 1, 1976; Volume 2, 1983; Volume 3, 1989; Drama Book Publishers

Monologues: Women: 50 Speeches from Contemporary Theater, edited by Robert Emerson and Jane Grumbach; Volume 1, 1976; Volume 2, 1982; Volume 3, 1989; Drama Book Publishers

Monologues from Chekhov, translated by Mason W. Cartwright; Dramaline Publications, 1987

Monologues from Restoration Plays, edited by Edith B. Maag; Dramaline Publications, 1988

Monologues from George Bernard Shaw, edited by Ian Michaels; Dramaline Publications, 1988

Monologues from Oscar Wilde, edited by Ian Michaels; Dramaline Publications, 1988

New Drama—Men: A Selection of Fifty Speeches for Actors, edited by Barbara Bolton and John Richmond; Samuel French, 1966

New Drama—Women: A Selection of Fifty Speeches for Actresses, edited by Barbara Bolton and John Richmond; Samuel French, 1966

100 Monologues: An Audition Sourcebook from New Dramatists, edited by Laura Harrington; New American Library, 1989

Scenes and Monologues from the New American Theater, edited by Frank Pike and Thomas G. Dunn; New American Library, 1988

Scenes for Young Actors, edited by Lorraine Cohen; Avon Books, 1973

Soliloquy!: The Shakespeare Monologues (Men), edited by Michael Earley and Philippa Keil; Applause Theatre Books, 1988

Soliloquy!: The Shakespeare Monologues (Women), edited by Michael Earley and Philippa Keil; Applause Theatre Books, 1988

Solo: The Best Monologues of the 80s (Men), edited by Michael Earley and Philippa Keil; Applause Theatre Books, 1987

Solo: The Best Monologues of the 80s (Women), edited by Michael Earley and Philippa Keil; Applause Theatre Books, 1987

The Young Actors' Workbook: A Collection of Specially Chosen Scenes and Monologues with Directions for the Actor, by Judith Roberts Seto; Grove Press, 1979

PERMISSIONS

Jack Poggi has pursued parallel careers as an actor, teacher, and writer. Since making his debut in F. Scott Fitzgerald's *This Side of Paradise* at the Sheridan Square Playhouse in New York in 1962, he has played some seventy roles in New York, in resident theaters throughout the country, and on national television.

From 1963 to 1983 he taught acting at C.W. Post Center of Long Island University, where he founded and headed the BFA Acting Program. He is the author of *Theater in America*, several articles on actor training in *The Drama Review* and other periodicals, and translations of several plays by Chekhov.

Poggi currently works as an actor in New York, coaches actors privately, and leads Weekend Workshops in Monologues.

SOLO!
The Best Monologues of the 80's
Edited by Michael Earley and Philippa Keil

Over 150 speeches in two volumes (MEN and WOMEN) from the best American and British plays of the 1980's have been selected with the actor's needs in mind. Each volume boasts work from such top dramatists as Sam Shepard, David Mamet, Beth Henley, Marsha Norman, Lanford Wilson, Emily Mann, Christopher Durang, Harold Pinter, Caryl Churchill, David Hare, and Simon Gray. With notes on character, context and approach accompanying each piece, SOLO! takes the mystery out of the audition process and replaces it with confidence and poise.

An invaluable resource entitled *Your 60 Seconds of Fame* guides the actor through the art, business and science of monologue performance. After grasping the demands of the monologue form, the actor is ready to meet the casting director and his or her demands before . . . the dreaded "Next!" *Your 60 Seconds of Fame* covers the terrain from monologue selection through performance.

paper • MEN: ISBN 0-936839-65-1 • WOMEN: ISBN 0-936839-66-X

SOLILOQUY!
The Shakespeare Monologues
Edited by Michael Earley and Philippa Keil

At last, over 175 of Shakespeare's finest and most performable monologues taken from all 37 plays are here in two easy-to-use volumes (MEN and WOMEN). Selections travel the entire spectrum of the great dramatist's vision, from comedies and romances to tragedies, pathos and histories.

"SOLILOQUY is an excellent and comprehensive collection of Shakespeare's speeches. Not only are the monologues wide-ranging and varied, but they are superbly annotated. Each volume is prefaced by an informative and reassuring introduction, which explains the signals and signposts by which Shakespeare helps the actor on his journey through the text. It includes a very good explanation of blank verse, with excellent examples of irregularities which are specifically related to character and acting intentions. These two books are a must for any actor in search of a 'classical' audition piece."

ELIZABETH SMITH
Head of Voice & Speech
The Juilliard School

paper • MEN: ISBN 0-936839-78-3 • WOMEN: ISBN 0-936839-79-1

DUO!
The Best Scenes for the 90's
Edited by John Horvath & Lavonne Mueller

DUO! delivers a collection of scenes for two so hot they sizzle. Each scene has been selected as a freestanding dramatic unit offering two actors a wide range of theatrical challenge and opportunity.

Every scene is set up with a synopsis of the play, character descriptions, and notes. DUO! offers a full spectrum of age range, region, genre, character, level of difficulty, and non-traditional casting potential. Among the selections:

**EMERALD CITY · BURN THIS · BROADWAY BOUND
EASTERN STANDARD · THE HEIDI CHRONICLES
JOE TURNER'S COME AND GONE
RECKLESS · PSYCHO BEACH PARTY
FRANKIE & JOHNNY IN THE CLAIR DE LUNE
COASTAL DISTURBANCES · THE SPEED OF DARKNESS
LES LIAISONS DANGEREUSES · LETTICE AND LOVAGE
THE COCKTAIL HOUR · BEIRUT
M. BUTTERFLY · DRIVING MISS DAISY · MRS KLEIN
A GIRL'S GUIDE TO CHAOS · A WALK IN THE WOODS
THE ROAD TO MECCA · BOY'S LIFE · SAFE SEX
LEND ME A TENOR · A SHAYNA MAIDEL · ICE CREAM
SPEED-THE-PLOW · OTHER PEOPLE'S MONEY
CUBA AND HIS TEDDY BEAR**

paper · ISBN: 1-55783-030-4

SHAKESCENES
SHAKESPEARE FOR TWO
Edited with an Introduction
by John Russell Brown

Shakespeare's plays are not the preserve of "Shakespearean Actors" who specialize in a remote species of dramatic life. John Russell Brown offers guidance for those who have little or no experience with the formidable Bard in both the Introduction and Advice to Actors, and in the notes to each of the thirty-five scenes.

The scenes are presented in newly-edited texts, with notes which clarify meanings, topical references, puns, ambiguities, etc. Each scene has been chosen for its independent life requiring only the simplest of stage properties and the barest of spaces. A brief description of characters and situation prefaces each scene, and is followed by a commentary which discusses its major acting challenges and opportunities.

Shakescenes are for small classes and large workshops, and for individual study whenever two actors have the opportunity to work together.

From the Introduction:

"Of course, a way of speaking a character's lines meaningfully and clearly must be found, but that alone will not bring any play to life. Shakespeare did not write for talking heads ... Actors need to be acutely present all the time; ... they are like boxers in a ring, who dare not lose concentration or the ability to perform at full power for fear of losing consciousness altogether."

paper • ISBN: 1-55783-049-5

ON SINGING ONSTAGE
New, Completely Revised Edition
by David Craig

"*David Craig knows more about singing in the musical theatre than anyone in this country — which probably means in the world. Time and time again his advice and training have resulted in actors moving from non-musical theatre into musicals with ease and expertise. Short of taking his classes, this book is a must.*" HAROLD PRINCE

In the New and Revised *On Singing Onstage* David Craig presents the same technique he has given to America's leading actors, actresses and dancers over the past thirty years. By listing the do's and don'ts of all aspects of singing onstage, you will be brought closer to the discovery of your own personal "style." That achievement plus information on how to get the most mileage out of an audition (what to sing and how to choose it) makes this book an indispensably practical self-teaching tool.

For anyone who has to (or wants to) sing anywhere, from amateur productions to the Broadway stage, *On Singing Onstage* is an essential guide for making the most of your talent.

AMONG DAVID CRAIG'S STUDENTS:

Carol Burnett, Cyd Charisse, James Coco, Sally Field, Lee Grant, Valerie Harper, Barbara Harris, Rock Hudson, Sally Kellerman, Jack Klugman, Cloris Leachman, Roddy McDowell, Marsha Mason, Anthony Perkins, Lee Remick, Eva Marie Saint, Marlo Thomas, Cicely Tyson, Nancy Walker . . . and many more.

paper • ISBN: 1-55783-043-6

SPEAK WITH DISTINCTION
by Edith Skinner
Revised with New Material by
Timothy Monich and Lilene Mansell

"Edith Skinner's book is the BEST BOOK ON SPEECH THAT I HAVE EVER ENCOUNTERED. It was my primer in school and is my reference book now. To the classical actor, or for that matter any actor who wishes to be understood, this method is a sure guide."
KEVIN KLINE

At last, the "Bible" is back. New chapters and expanded verses join the classic Skinner text to create the authoritative work on American speech for the stage. The long-awaited revised edition of *Speak With Distinction* makes the Skinner Method accessible to all speakers who want to improve their diction. The details of spoken English are examined in a workbook environment, fostering useful voice habits and promoting speech which is efficient, clearly and effortlessly free of regionalisms, appropriate to the dramatic situation, easily articulated, heard and immediately understood in the back rows of a theater.

An optional 90-minute practice tape demonstrates the highlights of the Skinner method and is accompanied by a 36-page guide to Good Speech.

"Edith Skinner CHANGED THE SOUND OF THE AMERICAN THEATRE and as a director in the classical repertory, I am deeply grateful to her." MICHAEL KAHN, Artistic director
The Shakespeare Theatre at the Folger

paper • ISBN: 1-55783-047-9

THE STANISLAVSKY TECHNIQUE: RUSSIA

A Workbook for Actors
by Mel Gordon

"Without exaggeration, the Stanislavsky system has needed Mel Gordon's book for over fifty years . . . the most original and useful research by an American on our theatre's richest artistic heritage."

ROBERT ELLERMAN
Performink

Stop reading about Stanislavsky and wondering what it's all supposed to mean. Meet the master and his disciples as they evolve new techniques and exercises in a workshop atmosphere during a quarter of a century.

This volume covers:

THE STANISLAVSKY SYSTEM
First Studio Exercises 1912-1916

VAKHTANGOV AS REBEL AND THEORETICIAN
Exercises 1919-1921

MICHAEL CHEKHOV
Exercises 1919-1952

STANISLAVSKY'S FOURTH PERIOD
Theory of Physical Actions: 1934-1938

paper • ISBN: 0-936839-08-2

ACTING IN FILM
An Actor's Take on Moviemaking
by Michael Caine

"Witty, articulate, and always entertaining, Michael Caine takes the nuts and bolts of film acting to pieces and gives away more trade secrets in the process than you thought existed."
—THE LONDON SUNDAY TIMES

"You must always steal," writes Michael Caine, "but only from the best people. Steal any trick that looks worthwhile. If you see Vivien Leigh or Robert DeNiro or Meryl Streep do something stunningly effective, and you can analyze how he or she did it, then pinch it. Because," Caine explains, "you can be sure that they stole it in the first place."

In *Acting in Film*, Caine gives the reader a once-in-a-lifetime chance to rob him blind. The man who's hypnotized the camera lenses for a quarter of a century exhibits the most closely guarded secrets to the art and science of spontaneity on screen, and then invites the reader to make them his own. Michael Caine dispels the mystical rites which surround film acting, and offers instead a practical philosophy of this minimalist art, told with straightforward clarity, wit and humor: "Don't sit as if you have nothing to say. You should be bursting with things to say. You just choose, at this particular place and time, not to say them."

"Don't think of this as too esoteric or for actors only. You'll be laughing, absorbed and enchanted."
—LONDON DAILY MAIL

paper • Over 30 stills • ISBN: 0-936839-86-4